LANGUAGE, THOUGHT, AND LOGIC

Rethinking Theory

LANGUAGE, THOUGHT, AND LOGIC

John M. Ellis

Northwestern University Press
Evanston, Illinois

Northwestern University Press
Evanston, Illinois 60208-4210

Library of Congress Cataloging-in-Publication Data

Ellis, John M. (John Martin), 1936–
    Language, thought, and logic / John M. Ellis.
        p.   cm. — (Rethinking theory)
    Includes bibliographical references (p.).
    ISBN 0-8101-1095-4 (cloth : alk. paper)
    1. Language and languages—Philosophy.   2. Thought and thinking.
    3. Language and logic.   I. Title.   II. Series.
    P106.E445   1993
    401—dc20   93-1922
                                                                          CIP

The paper used in this publication meets the minimum requirements of the American National
Standard for Information Sciences—Permanence of Paper for Library Materials, ANSI Z39.48-
1984.

...it is often easier to discover a truth than to assign to it its proper place.

—FERDINAND DE SAUSSURE

Contents

Preface

Anyone who writes a book about the theory of language is likely to be asked immediately whether it is philosophy or linguistics. In answer to this I can only say that this book is, among other things, about the impasse and confusion in theory of language of which the question is symptomatic. Another initial question will likely be: does the book attempt to offer a new view of linguistic theory? To which the answer is: certainly, though some explanation of just what this means will also be necessary. Theory of language is a field that seems to tempt everyone to begin again conceptually at the beginning, and this is one of its great weaknesses; a widespread sense that no known theory of language works very well, and that somewhere there lurks a key factor that will explain this mystery, leads one scholar after another to bypass all prior thought in order to go back to the basic elements of the linguistic situation—speakers, listeners, sounds, things, and so on—to rebuild conceptually from the ground up. The reasons for this odd behavior are considered in chapter 1, but for the moment it is enough to say that this habit results in a kind of unfinished and incomplete jigsaw puzzle. The pieces are strewn all over the table precisely because despair of getting the picture right seems to impel everyone to begin his or her own anew rather than to see what coherence might emerge from the neglected pile of fragments, each of which seems inadequate when taken only by itself. In terms of this analogy, my own contribution will be to pick up the pieces, show how some of them fit together in ways that have not been seen before, and add a few of my own in order to present at the end a picture that I believe is both coherent and new, while containing some significant parts that were already on the table.

Some initial assumptions made almost universally by people who talk and theorize about language are, if I am correct, logical mistakes that are virtually impossible to recover from once made; my second chapter is devoted to an exorcism of these missteps. Chapter 3 builds on the crucial reorientations of the previous chapter to argue that categorization (not syntax) is the most fundamental aspect and process of language, and that neither anything else in language nor indeed its purpose can be properly understood until the nature of categorization has been grasped. The fourth chapter analyzes the notion of grammar in the same spirit, and the fifth the place of language in human thought. The next two chapters look at some traditional problems of philosophy and attempt to show both how those problems result from an inadequate theory of language, and how the view of language developed here leads to a solution of the problems and thus to a redirection of inquiry in the field. The eighth chapter looks at the state of the discipline of linguistics, here too suggesting that effort has been fundamentally misdirected because of the logical errors I have discussed in the course of this book. In the conclusion I summarize the main outline of the linguistic theory that has emerged during the course of the preceding chapters.

I am aware that this book covers a great deal of ground, and that many much longer books have been devoted to material and ideas that here take up just a part of a single chapter; there will certainly be more to be said about all of these topics. But since my aim here has been to establish a new general picture of linguistic theory and to suggest the major implications of that picture, it seemed to me important to concentrate on setting out its larger contours in a single argument.

Several people read the entire manuscript of this book and gave me many helpful suggestions for its improvement: Barbara Ellis, Saul Morson, Thomas Pavel, Siegfried Puknat, Austin Quigley, and Avrum Stroll. It is impossible to list the names of all those colleagues and students with whom I have discussed these issues over many decades; they all helped immeasurably.

ONE

The Scope of the Issues in Theory of Language

There is much that is unique about theory of language as a field of inquiry. Perhaps no other area of thought has its basic ideas so ever present in our ordinary, everyday speech: we mention words, meanings, reference, grammar, ideas, and concepts all the time and in all kinds of contexts. Not surprising in view of this, linguistic theory is centrally involved in many branches of knowledge. Linguistics, philosophy, computer science, psychology, language teaching, anthropology, and biology (to name only these) all have a vital interest in language and hence in the conceptual basis of our understanding of it, that is, in the theory of language. That work in one field is relevant to another is not unusual, but two special factors need to be noted here. First, to say that one field influences another does not do justice to this situation, for even the central territory of linguistic theory is claimed not by one but by two fields—philosophy and linguistics. Second, new ideas in the theory of language do not simply have an impact on other fields; they can revolutionize them. To take just one example: in 1936 A. J. Ayer published his *Language, Truth and Logic*, which is now remembered as a classic statement of the philosophical position known as logical positivism.[1] In it Ayer expounded a solution to most of the traditional issues in philosophy: epistemology, metaphysics, ethics, aesthetics, and others. For some time this position was a highly influential one in the philosophical world, but the basic assumption from which everything in logical positivism derives is a view of meaning—a particular viewpoint within the theory of language. Ayer's work is a ruthlessly consistent working out of the philosophical consequences of that view, but ultimately it stands or falls on the adequacy of its initial assumption, an assumption about language. If Ayer's view of meaning is flawed, the philosophical position he develops from it fails at the outset. And indeed the precipitous decline of logical positivism's standing as a philosophical position happened not through a direct attack on its philosophical conclusions but because of the

1

undermining of its linguistic-theoretical premises by some remarkable new ideas about language developed by Wittgenstein.[2] I shall have more to say on the philosophical and linguistic issues inherent in these events in the course of this book, but for the moment my point is simply that in this case a particular view of how language worked had the most profound consequences for an entire field of inquiry; philosophy in the English-speaking world changed radically.

Many other fields have undergone similarly far-reaching changes when a new view of some aspect of language has affected them, the most notable recent example being the impact of structuralism on some areas of the social sciences and humanities. Nor is this in any way surprising. Concepts in the theory of language are among the basic tools of thought in all intellectual inquiry. Part of the uniqueness of linguistic theory, then, is that no other field is likely to have so great an impact on so many other fields when new thought arises in it. The stakes involved in theorizing about language are therefore always likely to be relatively high. But the converse is also true: because so many fields use and are dependent on linguistic theory, new thought can come from many quarters—in fact from any of those fields where progress might significantly depend on change in or refinement of the prevailing linguistic theory. Philosophy is again the outstanding example, but anthropological concerns gave us the so-called Whorf hypothesis concerning the relation between the structure of a language and the thought and behavior of its speakers,[3] and computer scientists are currently trying to solve the recalcitrant theoretical problems of semantics, not simply because they want to help out linguists, but because they need to for their own reasons. Charles Sanders Peirce, working his way into theory of language from the direction of logic and scientific method, is perhaps the most remarkable case of all, for Peirce had already in the nineteenth century seen much that would later be set out in a different form by such thinkers as Saussure, Wittgenstein, or Whorf.[4] Like Saussure, Peirce thought the sign triadic in struc-ture, like Whorf he thought there was no thinking without signs, and like Wittgenstein he rejected the positivist notion that there were "simples"—conceptions that were ultimate, irreducible, and unitary.[5] Needless to say, all of these later thinkers got no help from Peirce, because it did not occur to them to scour the literature on the philosophy of science before making their own way into theory of language.[6]

Oddly enough, it seems that the field that should in principle be central to the development of linguistic theory—linguistics and philology—has often been the most somnolent area of general thought about language. During the thirties and forties, for example, this field seemed largely content with the commonsense theory embodied in our everyday language itself, while much progress was being made in other quarters where that theory was being ques-tioned. Its concerns at this time were certainly not unimportant—for example, producing grammars and dictionaries of disappearing languages, extending the philological approach that had served so well in reconstructing the history of Indo-European languages to "exotic" languages, working out the controversy over the relative importance of synchronic and diachronic approaches, refining the theory of the phoneme—but the pursuit of these matters did not seem to require linguists to rethink their basic theory in the way that philosophers were then having to do.

It was probably a sense that linguistics had not been an intellectually ambitious field during this period that led to the enthusiastic response on the part of the younger generation of linguists to Noam Chomsky's *Syntactic Structures*, published in 1957; Chomsky's generative grammar gave the appearance of being theory at a high level of sophistication, and thus it offered an aura of intellectual ambition that had seemed lacking.[7] As if to yield pride of place to this new thrust in linguistics, the radical rethinking in theory of language that had been taking place in philosophy began to bog down. It did not take long for generative grammar to run into trouble in its turn, as more and more of its adherents began to suggest revisions of its basic theory so radical that they called into question virtually its entire conceptual framework. But as this new thrust in linguistics became blunted by internal doctrinal squabbling, yet another area of the academy took up the slack and made a bid for center stage in theory of language: by the late sixties the most visible new aspect of the scene was the rediscovery of Saussure by the French anthropologist Claude Lévi-Strauss and by the structuralist school that followed his lead and pursued it into a number of areas of humanistic scholarship.[8] Whether and to what extent any of these developments made real and permanent contributions to theory of language are questions that will arise many times during the course of this book; what is clear from just these examples is that many fields can influence or be influenced by linguistic theory in decisive fashion.

It would be natural to assume that this widespread interest and activity must be conducive to progress, even rapid progress, in linguistic theory, but experience shows that that assumption would be mistaken. There are two competing proverbs for situations such as this: "many hands make light work" and "too many cooks spoil the broth." The factual record shows that it is the latter, not the former, that is relevant. We seem to be dealing not with a unique advantage but with a unique handicap. Why is this so? There will be many factors to consider when attempting to answer this question, but we can only begin to do so by making a distinction: to find linguistic theory useful for the solution of one's own problems is very far from having an interest in it for its own sake. Academic disciplines have their own internal priorities and political struggles, and whenever theory of language has been invoked (or even advanced) in a given discipline the particular local purposes that have led to interest in the first place have also set strict limits on the extent of that interest. The sad fact is that intellectual curiosity usually stops when the need that gave rise to it has been satisfied. As a result, the full significance of new ideas in linguistic theory is often ignored by those who use them and even on occasion by those who discover them; in practice this means that they can remain in an incomplete state once enough has been worked out to satisfy the limited purposes of a particular discipline, and even that they can then be used there in ways that do violence to them and fundamentally misconceive them.

The reception of Ferdinand de Saussure's important work is a good example here.[9] Saussure's influence on philology and linguistics in the first half of this century was certainly a strong one, but there is a sense in which this influence related more to the politics of a profession than to what was truly original in his thought. During this time the field was obsessed with the struggle between historically oriented scholars and the newer wave of more structurally oriented linguists. Saussure's distinction between synchronic and diachronic approaches was a constant source of discussion during these years because that issue was of great relevance to the parochial dispute then dominating the field, but this elementary distinction was of far less significance than Saussure's extraordinary and far more important theory of the differential character of language both in form and in content. Only after the political heat of the battle between the philologists and the linguists began to cool down was interest renewed in the real core of Saussure's theoretical work. One example will suffice to show how badly the politics of a discipline obscured the nature of Saussure's contribution. Leonard Bloomfield was one of the leading figures of the Saussurian structuralist camp in the political struggles of the profession at this time, and yet his approach to virtually every other question in linguistic theory was that of a naive realist.[10] Saussure would surely have wanted to dissociate himself completely from Bloomfield.

This narrowing of Saussure's importance in the feud between linguists and philologists probably gave outsiders the impression that his major contribution to linguistic theory was his distinction between synchrony and diachrony, and it may therefore not be surprising that philosophers, for example, showed no interest in his work at this time; but this meant that they overlooked the enormous importance of his contribution to semantic theory. Had Ayer known Saussure's work and grasped its significance, for example, the history of philosophy in this century might have been very different; his confident building of an entire philosophical system of thought on the "verification" theory of meaning would have been impossible, for this theory was essentially a subspecies of the theory that Saussure had seriously undermined, that is, the theory that words labeled things and thus denoted or referred to them. But the problem was in any case compounded by the politics of Ayer's own discipline, for here too a predominant interest in a local dispute determined how far the interest in linguistic theory would go.

Ayer's mind was focused primarily on the battle between those members of his profession who leaned to the Continental metaphysical tradition and those who, like himself, belonged to the newer, analytical movement. For the purposes of that struggle, the assumptions he normally made in a commonsense way about meaning and language seemed sufficient to deal the other side what he thought was a deadly blow; he saw no need to make his theory of language more developed or sophisticated. Nevertheless, the ensuing debate over logical positivism always seemed to return to the problems of the linguistic theory Ayer had used. And yet during all of the subsequent attempts to patch up the holes that became visible in the positivist argument, it never once occurred either to Ayer or to any of his colleagues or antagonists that since the theory was based on a particular notion of "meaningfulness" in language (as we shall see, a crude one), it might have been useful to see what the history of linguistic theory had to say on that subject.

When the logical positivist theory of meaning was finally routed by the use (among other things) of ideas that had been available for some time in the field of linguistics (though neglected there too) it was a philosopher—Ludwig Wittgenstein—who led the way by showing that the source of the trouble was the notion that words named or stood for things. But in order to do this, Wittgenstein had to rediscover on his own some of the analysis that the linguist Saussure had discovered much earlier.

The damage done by this fragmentation is not simply or even mainly a matter of the inefficiency of a needless duplication of effort. Some of the time Wittgenstein and Saussure did indeed work on much the same parts of the puzzle, but not all of the time: both also worked out aspects that the other had left blank. The result was that both produced incomplete and enigmatic edifices of thought which include much that has been recognized as valuable while also leaving unanswered some fairly obvious questions. In both cases, there are puzzling gaps that have allowed compelling objections to be made to the whole system of thought, with the result that it has been too easy for many to conclude that all of this is interesting but it does not quite work. The crucial point for the argument I shall develop in later chapters, however, is that the gaps in Wittgenstein are not the same as the gaps in Saussure, and that as a result the solutions to serious problems in the one can sometimes be found in the work of the other. This is possible only if the two are looked at side by side as different parts of the same complex of ideas in the theory of language.[11]

Wittgenstein developed a view of language as a kind of game in which the players have to agree on the rules for it to work, and in which the moves are seen as significant above all in relation to other possible moves in that game rather than to the mental states of the speakers or to ideas or independent "facts" that exist outside the structure of the game. He suggested further that many categories of things (he chose again the example of games, thus inadvertently inviting confusion between the two quite different logical points he made using games) have no one common property but instead only family resemblances in which no single feature needs to be present in all instances but only an overlapping series of traits. This is a striking alternative to the more conventional view that words get their meaning from naming things and classes of things based on specific similarities, but there is one obvious objection: if some categories are made up in the way Wittgenstein suggests, why should this be so, and why only some rather than all? To this, Wittgenstein gives no answer. In failing to deal with even the first question that would occur to a skeptic, Wittgenstein ensured that many would remain skeptical; worse, he allowed considerable uncertainty about where his thought was really pointing, and this uncertainty has given rise to many conflicting interpretations of it.

Now if we look at Saussure's thought, we can see that the notion of a game and its rules occurs there too, and in much the same spirit; both, in fact, mention the game of chess. So far it would seem that a basic thrust common to the two is a rejection of the common theory of the meaning of words as naming, denoting, or referring to things. But Saussure goes on to talk about the basic linguistic principle of differentiation and contrast, as relevant to semantics as it is to phonology, and he suggests that the function of a category of things is not to group similar things but to differentiate one group from another, with the result that linguistic categories present not real but social facts. Once again—just as in Wittgenstein's case—there is an obvious objection: what difference does it make? Do we not still end up with classes distinguished from other classes by factual criteria, and thus with classes defined just as they are by the reference theory? It was actually much less clear in this account than it was in Wittgenstein's that the conventional theory needed to be replaced rather than just supplemented. And once again there is no answer to this point in Saussure, a deficiency that, as before, has promoted skepticism about the value of his thought and misunderstanding of where it really leads.

We need only to look at these cases together, however, to see that they are mirror images of each other. Wittgenstein, because he is concerned with the positivist argument, looks mainly at the structure of categories but neglects the question of their function; Saussure looks mainly at their function but neglects their composition and structure. Each could easily have answered the question that has always been felt to be a stumbling block for the other's thought, a fact that shows how injurious it has been for progress in linguistic theory that their readerships have been largely the separate ones of their two professional disciplines. This, then, was not just duplication of effort but also halving of effect.

The two accounts should have complemented each other if they had been taken together, but that never happened; and it never happened because the two men had different audiences and different immediate aims within their own disciplines.

Wittgenstein's own interest in theory of language is evidently shaped by his intent to demolish the argument that he himself had helped to construct earlier in his career.[12] That argument had rested on the assumption that the world could be analyzed into simple facts that could not be analyzed further. Wittgenstein's intent was fulfilled once he had shown that assumption to have been false,[13] but from any more general point of view this was an arbitrary place to stop which interrupted the inquiry just as it was getting interesting.

Another example of the ill effects of the fragmentation of linguistic theory is that of Benjamin Lee Whorf, whose ideas might have been taken together with those of Saussure and Wittgenstein but for the fact that they emerged in the context of another discipline—anthropology—and immediately became embroiled in a controversy within that context, only reaching the broader world of linguistic theory in the somewhat caricatured form of the "Whorf hypothesis," which supposedly equates language and culture. Whorf's own formulations are never so extreme, and in a less prejudicial context it might have been apparent that he was simply entering and attempting to map out the area of thought that Wittgenstein had hinted at with his cryptic remark that a language was a "form of life," or that Saussure had been getting at when he said that "language is a social fact."[14] If that had happened, Whorf's analysis might have become one more piece to add to the jigsaw puzzle already worked on by these two other great thinkers, a piece that, as we shall see, is a significant addition only if the Whorf hypothesis is discarded as the misshapen result of the fragmentation of linguistic theory.

What Whorf had fallen foul of—and thus what the further advance of linguistic theory was also handicapped by—was the resentments within the field of anthropology aroused by his giving language greater importance in ethnographic research than it had previously had; this, it was felt, downgraded everything else, including all of the work done hitherto by anthropologists. Once again, as in all the other cases I have discussed, the intellectual limitations imposed by the horizons and internal politics of a particular discipline prevented the original contribution of a talented thinker from taking its place in a wider, unitary context of theoretical reflection on the nature of language, and hindered the development of a larger picture that could have resulted from the piecing together of different parts of the puzzle. Each had worked out what seemed to address his own purposes—those of his own disciplinary context—but none had produced an account of linguistic theory sufficiently complete and rounded to escape obvious objections.

To be sure, in the late 1950s a mood arose in the field of linguistics itself which at last seemed to promise a determined assault on theory of language in itself and for its own sake, but this too soon turned out to be an impulse created by immediate needs of the field and thus limited from the outset by those needs. This was the time when the achievements and prestige of the natural sciences had begun to reorder the long-standing pecking order within the academy. The humanities had traditionally ranked first in prestige in the world of scholarship, but now they were beginning to fall behind. The social sciences, doubtless responding to this shift of rankings, had begun to insist that they too were sciences. The same need was felt by linguistics, and Noam Chomsky answered it directly. Generative grammar offered the specialized language of a science and thus presented the appearance of precise and controlled analytical thought. But these were only the trappings of science: the real successes of the sciences result from the inspired conceptual thought that guides observation and experiment, and as time went on it became ever clearer that the conceptual thinking at the base of generative grammar was profoundly flawed. The lesson has to be learned the hard way: scientific progress is not about counting, measuring, and analyzing but about knowing what to count and measure, why it is worth doing so, and what the results mean. Today, thirty-five years after the inception of generative grammar, the conceptual basis of what Chomsky initiated and of what he and his heirs (even his heretical heirs) are now doing is no clearer than it ever was.[15] In one respect, however, generative grammar did follow the prevailing habit of linguistic theory: it was yet another "begin again at the beginning" theory, and its neglect of earlier thought was only more thorough than usual, encompassing not only work in other disciplines but also virtually everything in linguistics as well.

The odd result of the strong involvement of many different disciplines in linguistic theory has therefore been not more and better thought but a greater state of confusion and a marked tendency for everyone to return to the starting point regardless of how much progress may have been achieved in previous work. The fragmentation of the field not only prevents the achievement of one area from adding to and deepening that of another but has actually led to a devaluing of everything. The mood can be summed up thus: There is Saussure— but that does not really work, for it seems to suggest that categories of things are a fiction of our language, and it is unable to deal with our strong intuitive sense that there are natural kinds of things in our world; there is Wittgenstein— but that, though suggestive, is full of enigmas; there is Chomsky, but the latest model of generative grammar is constantly being recalled for redesign of structural flaws, and it still breaks down regularly after it is supposed to have been fixed; there is Whorf—but that is imaginative without being sound. Therefore, given this much confusion, we may as well start at the beginning all over again. This mood weakens the sense of obligation that scholars usually have to know and build on their predecessors; first, because there is so much that has been said in so many contexts that no one could master it all, and second, because the only result of all this activity seems to have been a confusion that suggests that there is something wrong with all of it. Thus we arrive at the strange condition of linguistic theory at present in which, no matter how much sophisticated thought has taken place in the past, we are still constantly asked to consider yet another attempt to begin again at the conceptual beginning with a theorist who wants us to look at his or her version of the basic language situation in which there are speakers, listeners, sounds, things, and so on, to see how he or she will build the conceptual base of linguistic theory from the ground up.[16] Predictably, the proliferation of these new beginnings means that they will all suffer the same fate as their forerunners: they do not achieve the sought-for basic conceptual clarification but instead add to the confusion.

Just as in any election hotly contested by too many parties, the winner is the candidate that is most familiar. The beneficiary of this state of confusion in the case of linguistic theory is the theory with which we all start, the one that is virtually there in the language we speak. It is the default condition of linguistic theory to which everything reverts when all else fails, as it has seemed to do most of the time: we have a word for cats because cats exist and we need to talk about them and communicate information about them. We have words for the things we want to communicate about cats because the facts we are talking about exist too. Semantics is about matching words to what exists; and syntax and grammar is about a particular language's ordering and structuring the process of communicating these facts. The relation between the world and language is then simply stated. The world has a structure, and language adjusts itself to that structure. It does so imperfectly and untidily, largely because we are an imperfect and untidy species. This is the commonsense point to which we return, over and over again, whenever any attempt to depart from it finally fails. And yet it never works very well either.

In a field of inquiry that operates in this way, the habit of ignoring the great thinkers of the past seems to be accepted practice. Nothing showed this peculiar feature of linguistic theory more clearly than the massive compendium *Semantics: An Interdisciplinary Reader in Philosophy, Linguistics and Psychology*, which appeared in 1971.[17] Paradoxically, this collection of essays was intended to remedy that very condition of fragmentation I have been speaking about by bringing together work in three of the relevant fields—philosophy, linguistics, and psychology. Yet the results of this laudable intent were not to improve a bad situation but instead to demonstrate just how bad it was and would continue to be. The essays by individual members of the three disciplines showed that they inhabited separate universes. The philosophers talked about Wittgenstein, but the psychologists and linguists never even mentioned his name; it was as if his thought did not exist.[18] Whorf is mentioned by the psychologists, but there is not a single reference to him by the linguists or philosophers. (The same is true of Piaget.) A volume designed to combat the effects of compartmentalization in fact only showed and continued those effects. But as if to demonstrate that neglect of essential thought on the part of some groups of linguistic theorists because of disciplinary barriers can lead to the possibility of total neglect by all groups, the compendium showed a startling omission. In six hundred pages of articles by thirty-three different major scholars surveying various areas of work in semantics there is not a single mention of Ferdinand de Saussure, arguably the most influential of all linguistic theorists. Another startling omission is that of Charles Sanders Peirce, one of the most original and creative minds ever to have wrestled with the problems of meaning, but mentioned only once in the entire compendium (and then only in passing) by the linguist Uriel Weinreich. (It is worth noting here that Weinreich is not a generative grammarian.) For the philosophers and psychologists, and for all the linguists in the MIT mainstream, Peirce could be ignored. The complete omission of seminal thinkers like Peirce and Saussure from a survey of modern thought on semantics is an especially bewildering demonstration of the strange condition of linguistic theory,[19] and yet no conscious judgment of the importance of those thinkers is being made here; this is simply the common pattern of neglect and ignorance of prior thought that comes with and is encouraged by the habit of reverting to and building up from the primitive commonsense view.

What this compendium also showed, however, is that the ill effects of compartmentalization in linguistic theory are felt even within the same discipline. Howard Maclay, for example, introducing the essays by linguists, remarks that "meaning has come to be widely regarded as a legitimate object of systematic linguistic interest only within the past decade [i.e., the sixties]," a statement that, if taken literally, must seem absurd to any knowledgeable reader.[20] What Maclay means of course is that generative grammarians have only recently come to this view. It is as if the general confusion of too disorganized and far-flung a field of inquiry is dealt with by creating an artificial enclave that can then be treated as if it were the entire universe of linguistic thought. Maclay's further remark that "a collection of papers such as this one would hardly have been conceivable in the mid 1950's" is even stranger, for the first publication in generative grammar did not occur until 1957.

This blinkered attitude has been a matter of deeply rooted belief for generative grammarians, and it is fairly clear why it has been so.[21] Chomsky's *Syntactic Structures* was hailed as a revolution in linguistics, and this claim dictated an even more aggressive "begin again at the beginning" stance than usual—and so an intensification of the unhealthy attitude that had always been typical of linguistic theory. Anything that is announced as a revolution must involve a conscious break with the past, and that in turn will bring with it a resistance to learning from that past.[22] But to claim a revolution is also a separatist gesture vis-à-vis the rest of one's own discipline, and it thus involves an even more extreme version of the tendency of linguistic theory to fragment. It is, moreover, a stance difficult to reverse. When things began to go badly wrong for the theory of generative grammar and it turned out that the recalcitrant and untidy area of meaning it had tried to exclude had to be faced after all, powerful emotional resistance stood in the way of a recognition that this avoidance of semantics had been the result of the revolutionary attitude itself, with its built-in determination to ignore all other thought in linguistic theory. As a result, the turn to semantics had to be seen, not negatively as the acknowledgment of an ill-informed error through a belated coming to terms with and accepting what many earlier thinkers had argued, but positively as yet another intellectual breakthrough for which the MIT school of thought could take credit.[23] (This is somewhat like the behavior of those die-hard Marxists who welcomed perestroika as a bold new phase in communism, and thus the latest of its achievements, rather than as an admission forced by bitter reality that their entire system of thought had been mistaken.) Once more, the internal politics of a discipline work to preserve the destructive fragmentation of linguistic theory through a kind of selective amnesia.[24]

The situation in linguistics is to be sure an extreme one, but a similar fragmentation and amnesia has occurred within the discipline of philosophy. Striking evidence of this can be seen in the practice (which had become common at least twenty years ago) of giving a philosophical account of meaning as if Wittgenstein had never existed. For some time, philosophers have regularly taken positions that Wittgenstein's arguments seemed to have long since made problematic, without acknowledging or dealing with the fact that those arguments had ever been made.[25] It is one thing to disagree with Wittgenstein; no thinker is immune from that. It is quite another to use ideas that have been seriously undermined in classic accounts by prominent thinkers as if to do so raised no questions of any importance. Thus H. P. Grice (in some articles that have been very influential) uses the notion of mental events in his account of meaning apparently in just the same sense that Wittgenstein seemed to have decisively undermined, but without bothering to comment on that fact.[26] That amnesia about Wittgenstein's intellectual legacy is especially conspicuous follows from what I have already said about the way in which the recurrent "begin again at the conceptual beginning" favors one kind of theory at the expense of others. Labeling, denotation, and reference are ideas that benefit from this habit, and it is thus to be expected that the thinker who did most to throw doubt on those ideas will be the most likely to be neglected because of it.

The most conspicuous recent development of this kind is the so-called theory of direct reference, which has achieved the stature of a distinct school of thought in modern philosophy of language—one that its proponents consider a major intellectual breakthrough in philosophy. (It derives largely from philosophers whose orientation is to mathematical logic—yet another fragmentation effect—such as Saul Kripke and Hilary Putnam.)[27] I shall discuss this theory in more detail below, but for the moment it suffices to note that it sticks rather closely to the default condition of linguistic theory. It holds that for a significant number of cases words refer "directly" to natural classes of things in the real world, that is to say, not through the enumeration of criteria or characteristics but in much the same way that is true of proper names. What we have here, therefore, is a quite elementary "labeling" theory. That being the case, we should expect to see all of the classic arguments against the labeling theory immediately confronted and challenged by those who advance this view, but that does not occur. And so we are left to wonder: are these philosophers struggling with all the same logical problems that their predecessors struggled with but in a different way, or have they instead just not noticed some of those problems? It is only in the strange world of linguistic theory that such questions constantly arise.

Even when the ideas of seminal thinkers are suddenly resurrected, this is often done in a way that is so arbitrary and so unaware of the context of those ideas in the historical development of the field that the general impression of fragmentation and selective memory is heightened rather than diminished. A good example is the recent interest in Bertrand Russell's Theory of Descriptions on the part of generative grammarians. Russell's theory was an attempt to take certain classes of statements that occur naturally in the English language (which means that they are not very clear or tidy from a logical point of view) and to analyze them so that the component parts of their meaning are all laid out in a way that is both complete and explicit. Looked at in historical context, this is clearly part and parcel of the complex of ideas that includes both logical atomism and logical positivism, since it seeks to break down complexity of meaning into its smallest component parts, those components themselves not being further reducible. We should then have "simples"—atoms of meaning. In the history of philosophy, as we have seen, this kind of thought gradually declined in importance after Wittgenstein showed that the idea of simples was untenable, and yet many linguists have recently reached back into the history of an adjacent discipline to resurrect these ideas, oblivious of how they fared in the subsequent history of that discipline. This is surely a case of being condemned to relive history because one will not learn from it, the same steps being retraced many years after they first led to a dead end.

However, it is not difficult to see how this interest in Russell relates to the internal requirements of generative grammar. The generative tradition in linguistics began with Chomsky's setting out to systematize linguistic form and claiming that it could be done without regard to meaning: meaning seemed to be a source of untidiness that would ruin any attempt at a relatively clean systematization. When that plan could not be made to work, meaning was at last allowed into the picture, but the reduction of meaning to irreducible simple elements was the next best thing to excluding it, the step most consistent with the original impulse of generative grammar.[28] Given this mind-set it was predictable that the belated search of the history of thought about language for help would be conducted in entirely the wrong spirit. What was sought was not a way of learning how to really get to the bottom of a difficult conceptual problem but, on the contrary, a way to shore up and preserve a flawed position. Help was sought not where it was needed—that is, from those thinkers who would have shown that this approach would never work—but precisely from those who should have been avoided, from theorists whose thinking was reassuringly similar (because similarly flawed) to that of the generativists. Here the trouble was that the reassurance was entirely superficial: nobody who knew what had happened next in the history of philosophy would have been reassured. And so this retracing of the earlier steps of the logical atomists continued, with the inevitable result. As we shall see in subsequent chapters, a new attempt to go down a rather similar path yet one more time is currently underway, this time with the formidable heavy armor of symbolic logic. Once again, however, in important respects the basic assumptions are still Russell's, and there appears to be just as much innocence of the powerful counterarguments as ever.[29]

Another curious effect of this dislocation and fragmentation of linguistic theory is that the disjunction between different groups of scholars both across and within disciplines is finally also found in the minds of individuals: a surprisingly large number (including many distinguished scholars) express allegiance to piecemeal collections of insights and dogmas from this confused world of linguistic theory which are clearly inconsistent with each other. Geoffrey Sampson noticed that while Max Black (in a well-known essay) rejected Whorf's account of meaning, he seemed quite happy to accept much the same account when it was found in the later Wittgenstein.[30] Sampson was correct; this was indeed a strange inconsistency. But similar inconsistencies are found everywhere. There are many who think that analyzing meaning is a matter of setting out truth conditions on the one hand and yet accept Wittgenstein's game analogy on the other, apparently unaware that one idea contradicts the other. Much of "speech act" theory begins from Wittgenstein's insight that language does a great deal besides naming and referring to things, but soon contradicts his real thrust by relying on an account of meaning that is at its core still denotative and referential.[31] It is indeed not at all uncommon to find a respectful exposition of Wittgenstein's ideas followed by arguments that proceed as if the writer had never read what he himself had just written.

It seems merely a natural next step, given this growing invisibility of Wittgenstein's ideas, that on occasion we should see an implicit (even if unacknowledged) denial that he really stood for anything at all—for this is the thrust of the not uncommon view that he is above all a therapist of language. This bizarre notion avoids the content of Wittgenstein's arguments as a matter of principle rather than simply of practice.[32] But perhaps the most comic expression of the unreality of the scene was the appearance of a study of Wittgenstein by A. J. Ayer, whose position Wittgenstein's remarks on language had helped to demolish so many decades ago.[33] Ayer's book was generally received quite seriously, but this response seemed eerily unaware that this was rather as if Moses had appeared to write a biography and intepretation of Christ.[34] But such is the theory of language, an area of inquiry in which powerful ideas are often soon either ignored or else revered without that reverence being accompanied by any sense of what those ideas would commit us to.

The result of all this confusion is that beginning again at the conceptual beginning is the norm and there is no sense of a common thread of inquiry such that a new contribution orients itself by looking at the insights as well as the dead ends and the mistakes of its predecessors, unless by "predecessors" we understand simply the immediate circle of the newcomer. As a result there are bits and pieces of the larger puzzle of theory of language strewn everywhere, together with much wreckage of failed attempts from which a great deal is to be learned. Indeed, our first task in approaching the theory of language will be to look at some aspects of the starting point to which so many have wanted to return, though not in order to emulate them by starting again from scratch: the point of this exercise is rather to look at where the blind alleys begin, and to see exactly why they lead nowhere, so that a more productive path can be taken.

It is worth remembering that theory of language is an exceedingly intricate and subtle area of thought, full of tricks and traps that seem benign until they have done their damage, and that are difficult to spot even then. Small and apparently insignificant differences of formulation can make an enormous difference to the further course of an argument.[35] Saussure had evidently thought deeply about this characteristic of linguistic theory when he gave us a warning that is among the most important things he ever said: "It is often easier to discover a truth than to assign to it its proper place."[36] Consider just one example: Wittgenstein's notion of language games has seemed suggestive and intriguing to many of his readers even though they were evidently not at all clear what its point was and where it really leads. The result is that with the passage of time this idea becomes more and more neglected—not because it is felt to be inherently fruitless but because its proper place in linguistic theory is not clear. It is not obvious how it should be used and how it might affect all the other ideas we might entertain about language.[37]

TWO

Initial Missteps in Theory of Language

The most important steps in any theoretical inquiry are the initial ones, but this truism must be more than usually important in a field where so many feel the need to go back to the beginning to set out what seem to be the indisputable facts before proceeding on what then seems like a secure basis. For this attitude already contains an important theoretical mistake: given the decision to formulate them in a certain way, facts may well seem indisputable, but that does not mean that the formulation itself is above scrutiny. It may have embodied far-reaching decisions about how to conceive those facts and thus have determined what kinds of things facts are to be. This decision may already have committed us in ways we ·might not have wished to be committed had we thought it through before the decision was made.[1]

There are a small number of initial missteps in theory of language that are so subtle that those who take them never recognize that they have made any move at all, but so destructive and far-reaching that, once taken, they make it impossible to achieve a coherent theory of language; and these missteps are virtually universal. They are all classic theoretical traps that involve assumptions built into what look like statements of the obvious that make no assumptions at all. They are so simple and apparently harmless that the reader may well wonder what could possibly be wrong with them, but it is precisely in such situations that lurk the kind of wrong turns that lead time and again to a complete theoretical impasse and breakdown. There are three such missteps relevant to my argument, but of these one is recognizably a version, specific to theory of language, of a much broader problem found in other fields of inquiry. I shall state all three briefly before going on to show in more detail how they work.

The first of these missteps can be stated very simply: it is the assumption that the purpose of language is communication. This is perhaps the most important of the three, since it immediately misdirects all subsequent effort in linguistic theory. The specific version of the second consists in the assumption that descriptive words like *square* or *cat* are simpler and easier to understand than evaluative words like *good*, and that the former are therefore more basic and thus a better model to take for understanding how language works than the latter. This beginning, if I am correct, makes it impossible to understand how evaluative words work and provides only a highly misleading account of how descriptive words work. The more general form of this second misstep embodies an important misconception about scientific thought and procedure: the assumption (it was Chomsky's as he began the book that initiated generative grammar in 1957)[2] that science begins by taking the clear cases and then generalizes from them to formulate the principles that are used to deal with the difficult cases. The movement of thought is assumed to be from simple to complex, where the simple will explain the complex but not itself be altered by what the complex shows. The third misstep is the assumption that the verbal categories of a language serve to group like things together. The odd thing about this instance is that while there is a kind of truth in it, the exact reverse is the important truth for linguistic theory: verbal categories group *unlike* things. A semantics that begins from the first of these opposed statements can only break down into complete mystification.

It is so important to understand the way in which these assumptions and attitudes have crippled the theory of language that I shall devote the whole of this chapter to them before beginning my own exposition and analysis in the following chapter. These missteps are the most important reason for the impasse found today both in linguistics and in philosophy of language; and conversely, what is characteristic of the thought of the great thinkers of the past on whose work we can still build is that in their very different ways they were beginning to work around and beyond these traps.[3]

The "communication" model of language exists in a variety of different formulations, not all of which use the word *communication* itself. The most common and simple version looks at language in terms of its information content: a piece of language means whatever information it contains, and an adequate analysis formulates as completely as possible what that information is. The variant that uses such words as *message* and *encode* is essentially similar: language is a code that conveys messages through the twin processes of encoding (by the speaker) and decoding (by the listener). A more philosophical version of essentially the same view speaks of the *truth claims* made by a piece of language. This terminology keeps the underlying notion of the message or information content of language, changing the focus only to the extent that it speaks of what is asserted to be true; that is to say, information is still said to pass from speaker to listener, and to this is added only the notion that the speaker is also assuring the listener that it really is genuine information. These different emphases tend to be distributed somewhat according to discipline: semiotics tends to use *code* while linguists more often use *information content* and philosophers *truth claims*. As generative grammarians have begun to look to symbolic logic to solve their perennial problem of meaning (which derives, it will be recalled, from Chomsky's initial assumption), this working distinction between the two disciplines has eroded somewhat. "Semantics," writes the veteran generativist Emmon Bach in his *Informal Lectures on Formal Semantics*, "assigns to sentences and other expression [*sic*] interpretations that are something other than language, in particular, it assigns to sentences the interpretations that have to do with whether they are true or false."[4] Truth or falsity, meanwhile, is a question of whether "some situation in the real world...corresponds to the meaning of the sentence." (Here we see again that MIT linguistics, in its endless search for a solution to its insoluble problem of what is to be done with semantics, retraces part of the history of philosophy in the thirties and forties, for the logical positivist could have said much the same thing.)

Nothing seems more reasonable than the assumption that the purpose of language is communication. But there is a subtle trap here: granted, a particular act of language use may result in communication between two people, but much must have happened before they could get that far. Suppose that the two were without a language; do they lack simply the means of communicating or something more? Surely the latter: without a language, they barely have anything to communicate. Language must first have had something to do with what there is to communicate and with what will be counted as communication. It is not just a means of transferring information, it is also, and far more importantly, the locus of the process of deciding what information is to be, and of instituting the kinds of information that will be available for communication.

The distinction I am making will become clearer if we go back to the vocabulary used by scholars who think of language as the transmission of information, and therefore use the vocabulary of *code, encoding,* and *message.* This language certainly fits well with that of *communication* and *information,* the latter term substituting for *message* without difficulty, while *coding* and *encoding* seem to describe well enough the process by which the message is conveyed from one person to another.

Nevertheless, as soon as we look closely at languages and codes it becomes clear that they are very different things, so much so that the linguistic situation is completely distorted if we speak of it in this way. Codes are only devices for disguising pieces of language so that their meaning is not immediately recognizable without removal of the disguise. When we put a message into a code— say, Morse code—we are not putting nonlinguistic information into a language so that it can be transmitted in linguistic form and then decoded into pure nonlinguistic information again. On the contrary: we simply rewrite a piece of English (German, French, or any other language) in an unfamiliar way. It never stops being a piece of English in disguise, before and after this process. What is in Morse is informative only because it is English. The surprising fact is that the very common vocabulary of code and message, used so often as a model of how language works, has *nothing whatever to do with language.* Imagine our two would-be communicators again. Suppose that they have no language. Now offer them a code, whether Morse, a military cipher, or any other kind. *They will be no better off.* Having a language is a prior requirement for the use of any of these information-communicating devices; taken only by themselves, none of them can be used to transmit information from the mind of one person to another. This example shows again that language cannot be thought of only or even primarily as a means of transfer of information because without it there is no such thing as information.

It might be objected that all of this shows a difference only of degree, not of kind, and that even between human beings without a language some primitive acts of communication could take place; for example, danger signals or threats. Now these are the kinds of primitive signals sent by animals, which, as we usually say (and most linguists addicted to the information theory vehemently insist),[5] lack anything that should be called language. But even these acts would be meaningless without a preexisting convention as to what the meaning of the acts was to be. No Morse code would help without that prior convention, that is, without a prior language, however primitive. To have singled out "danger" and "threat" is to have provided a structure that allows information to exist, and before this is done information would not be available for transmitting. Notice, too, the kinds of significant decisions that the convention would have had to assume and embody before it could be used: it would have had to decide how experience was to be analyzed so that disparate events would be reduced to types of event; which types were important enough to be talked about; and how they were to be talked about. Even the most primitive system must have far more in the way of presupposition, preparation, and analysis than we can conceive of at first glance, and it is only when we understand this that we realize why a code such as the Morse code has nothing to do with language: it lacks everything that makes a language what it is. But it is the converse of this truth that is the crucial point. The essential and distinctive feature of language is not its ability to transmit information—for this would not distinguish it from the Morse code— but a logically prior attribute, the process of analysis, evaluation, and organization of experience which must have taken place before communication can occur. It is because a code lacks this stage that it is not a language. To function at all, a code has to latch onto something that has already done what languages do. Codes encode messages; languages do not. Codes merely transmit information; languages make information what it is.

Because the really distinctive features of language lie in such things as the creation of the possibility of information and the implicit decisions as to what will count as information, linguistic theory should begin with them, and that is accordingly where I shall begin my analysis proper in the next chapter. Before leaving the topic of communication, however, I should note how interesting Wittgenstein's "language-game" analogy becomes in this context. It is not just that a set of rules must exist before any move in the game can be meaningful, or that the meaning of one move is derived from its being a choice from a finite set. Thoughts like these were what was important for Wittgenstein largely because of the philosophical context that determined the questions he was pursuing, but had his interest in linguistic theory not been limited in this way he might have seen that his analogy implied an even deeper point. The experience of one particular game (hence language) is quite different from that of others, each one being a creation *for which there was no blueprint in reality* but only an arbitrary act of creation by a particular set of human beings with a particular set of interests. Such thoughts lead us even further from the notion that information is simply there in the world and that languages do no more than pick it up to carry it to a particular destination.

No misstep is more pervasive than this one; virtually all organized schools of thought are permeated by it. It is pervasive in philosophy of language.[6] It is ever present in the field of linguistics, whether one looks to the mainstream of the predominant school of thought, that initiated by Chomsky; to its heretical splinter groups, or even to those groups of linguists who reject Chomsky altogether. The influential Penguin introduction by David Crystal (generativist in outlook) simply tells us that the purpose of language is communication.[7] Chomsky's own position is the same; but the antigenerativist Wallace Chafe, while distancing himself from MIT, also soon settles for the information-transfer model, in which language links meaning to sounds.[8] Even a work that is welcomed as a bold and innovative attempt to emerge from the impasse regarding semantics that has long bedeviled the MIT tradition, such as the recent *Situations and Attitudes* by Jon Barwise and John Perry, stands flat-footedly on the same old ground: "Our claim is that the primary function of language is to convey information and that the meanings of expressions are what allow them to convey the information they do."[9] (Here one might observe that it is not at all clear why it is necessary, or how it is possible, to assert ownership of such a claim when it has been common property for such a very long time!) Still broadly within the MIT tradition, the heretical attempt to solve its unsolved problems by the recent *Generalized Phrase Structure Grammar* (the title refers to the viewpoint of a group of linguists) is not at all heretical on this point: it focuses on truth claims of sentences and says quite simply that "in order to know whether a given sentence is in fact true or not, we need to know two kinds of things: what the sentence means, and what the facts of the world are."[10] Which is as much as to say: a sentence is true if its meaning represents true information about the world. (Again, logical positivism could have said as much.)

The same kind of looking down a blind alley (a very old and well-traveled one) is characteristic even of those who are consciously trying to look for a solution in new places—for example, in physiology—in the hope that the key will be found in some fundamentally new place. For the trouble here is that it is no good looking at neural states if one is simply looking with the conceptual apparatus that has failed elsewhere; to do this is not really to look in a different place, any more than is the case when symbolic logic (to which many generativists are now attracted) is invoked. It is, on the contrary, to look in the same conceptual place, for these neural states are recognizably the beginning and ending points of the information model.

The number of those who have used the "code and message" version of this misstep is very large: it includes semioticians like Umberto Eco and Thomas Sebeok, information theorists like Colin Cherry and their German counterparts in *Kommunikationsforschung*, and even French structuralists such as Lévi-Strauss.[11] It is used so naturally and unthinkingly that it is even seen on occasion in expositions of thinkers such as Saussure whose thought is completely incompatible with it.

The number of writers on linguistic theory who have largely avoided this error, on the other hand, or whose thought moves clearly in the opposite direction, is quite small: Wittgenstein, Saussure, and Peirce were all moving away from it in various ways. But one thinker was quite explicit about the mistake of thinking that language is essentially communication: Benjamin Lee Whorf. All we have, however, is a cryptic marginal note: "Conclusion—error supposing function of language to be only the COMMUNICATION of thought."[12] Sadly, this logical insight slipped from sight as Whorf was discredited by the romantic notions imposed upon his work by his critics, and he himself never elaborated it.

So much for the first of these missteps. I turn now to the second, which, as previously noted, has a form specific to language theory as well as a more general form that relates to inquiry in general. This broader form consists in a mistaken attitude that can be found in any field; it is the habit of assuming that one begins by taking simple cases and generalizes from them to derive principles that can then be used to break down the hard cases. The most important specific manifestation of this attitude in theory of language occurs in semantics; the easy starting point will be the descriptive words that appear to have clear correlations in physical reality—say, *round, square,* or *mile*—while evaluative words are the hard cases, to be approached only when the basic principles of how words work have been abstracted from the easy cases. The consequence of this way of beginning is that descriptive words will come to be seen as more basic to the functioning of language than evaluative words; this, as we shall see, is a mistake that has devastating consequences, for *it has the hierarchy of descriptive and evaluative words the wrong way round.* Another manifestation of the same underlying attitude to inquiry can be seen in the generative grammarian's whole approach to the understanding of language: syntactic patterns are easier to systematize than semantic ones, and thus syntactic analysis comes before semantics. Soon enough, this temporal priority has become a logical one, in which it is syntax that shows us how language really works.

It should not really be a surprise that this approach always grinds to a halt: the difficult cases just stay too difficult. The sense that we should be slowly moving up the ladder of the complexity of problems gives way to frustration; no matter how much the philosopher looks at words like *square*, he never seems to be able to use what he sees there to handle *good* in an intuitively satisfying way. Even the philosophical view that (despairingly) hypothesizes that the two are totally different in kind—with only one having cognitive value—is never really convincing; this was, after all, also the basis of the positivist solution. The same kind of result is reached in the case of generative grammar's decision to make elementary syntactic patterns the starting point and basis of its approach to understanding language: no matter how sophisticated the syntactic analysis becomes, semantics seems just as much of a mystery as it always was.

We should first examine the broader problem of method before looking at its specific results in linguistic theory. The logical error at this general level can be easily diagnosed: easy cases are easy because they do not test very much— they are not critical cases for theory.[13] They will seem easy either because they could be handled in a number of different ways (while the difficult cases demand a much more specific solution), or because they are the obvious examples that fit and thus do not challenge the current state of understanding and its assumptions. The "difficult" cases, in contrast, are the ones that constitute a challenge to the limitations of current understanding and to the theory that embodies that understanding. Once we see things this way, it is clear how we must proceed: if we want to extend our understanding and theory beyond its present state, we must look above all to those cases that challenge that present state—the cases that make things hard for us given our current attitudes. To go beyond Newton, Einstein looked at the very few phenomena that Newton apparently could not handle; but once a theory was developed to deal with those hard cases, the easy cases began to look different too. To allow theory to coalesce and be settled *before* getting to the hard cases is, in fact, a recipe for making sure that you will never progress beyond the understanding that you already had before you started.

In 1957 Chomsky assured the linguistic world that it was a "commonplace" of science to proceed in this way, and since that day the aggressively claimed "scientific" status of generative grammar has served as a buffer against any recognition of conceptual failure. No matter how problematic the theory of generative grammar became, the group always consoled itself with the thought that it alone was founded on scientific principles. Generativists could thus believe that whatever problems they had and whatever mistakes they had made were simply on a higher plane than those of nongenerativists; even when their critics were proved correct, as happened rather often, they could treat this unfortunate state of affairs almost as an accident, for only those who had gone through the rigorous scientific thought processes of generativists could have reached the right answers for the right reasons.

The problem with all of this was that the notions of science and scientific procedure on which it was based were simply wrong. What Chomsky claimed to be a commonplace of modern science was in fact the antiquated and long since discredited methodology of Descartes, for whom science moved from the known to the unknown and from the simple to the complex, building on the immutable basis of the former to get to the latter. But already in the nineteenth century, Charles Sanders Peirce showed that something was badly wrong with this idea.[14] Peirce saw the crucial point here that new knowledge may profoundly change our understanding of old knowledge rather than simply build on it. We may suddenly find (as with Newton and Einstein) that what we thought we knew was not really understood properly; in principle, there can never be any stopping point where we can simply bank what we know, once and for all. Peirce concluded from this that all knowledge is in the nature of a hypothesis,[15] and it is this that has become the commonplace of philosophy of science to replace the Cartesian scheme of building upon certainty. Anyone who was really in touch with the daily life of scientists would have known that it is the unclear cases that are expected to provide fundamental new insight.

Generative grammar was founded, therefore, not on scientific method, but on a then popular delusion about science that had been especially common among humanists.[16] The decision to start with what seemed easier to deal with given the broad framework of prevailing attitudes to language meant choosing to concentrate on the systematization of syntax (which looked relatively easy to systematize) but avoiding meaning (which did not). That in turn led to the temptation to assign much more importance to the one than the other for the understanding of language, and even to pronouncing meaning to be outside the framework of science altogether. In this way, a particularly "unclear" case was shunted aside; but getting rid of problem cases is actually a practice that modern scientists think very sinful and unscientific indeed.

Maintaining this exclusion of meaning eventually proved too embarrassing for generativists, but it is important to see that the fundamental shape of their starting point was not altered by this reversal. The basic orientation to beginning with the clear issue (syntax) and the accompanying bewilderment over the sheer difficulty of the difficult issue (semantics) are still there. When later generativists decided that the original exclusion of meaning was too severe a measure, they were objecting to *a particular way* of dealing with the inevitable frustration caused by a theory that had forged ahead with what looked easy while brushing aside those problems that had not been thought through; but they still remained exposed to the same frustration by the same initial shaping of the theory. Chomsky's claim that his method was a scientific commonplace, though completely erroneous, was never challenged: on the contrary, it was met with enthusiasm. John Lyons, in his little book on Chomsky in the Modern Masters series, actually singled out this misconception about scientific procedure for commendation.[17]

An important consequence of this misstep was a correspondingly limited view of linguistics, the goal of which was now said by generativists to be the construction of grammars.[18] The limitations imposed by a starting point that took and ran with those things that looked like "clear cases" had now congealed into an extraordinarily limited view of the study of language itself, one that reduced significantly the intellectual ambitions of the field. And yet there was never any serious attempt to justify this drastic reduction of the central task of linguistics, which surely ought never to concern less than the nature and function of language.

If semantics was initially excluded from study by this misconception about scientific procedure in the generativist camp, the same basic schema—proceeding from the clear to the unclear, the simple to the complex—is also at the bottom of the most important of all missteps within semantics itself: that which takes descriptive words as the clear and typical cases and leaves evaluative words as something then to be struggled with. The distinction between descriptive and evaluative words is widespread, and that is not surprising, for it follows naturally from the notion that communication is the point of language: the descriptive content of a piece of language is its communicative content. But once we have gone this far the difficulty arises of what we are to do with evaluative words. You can see squareness and point to it, but goodness is not identifiable in the same simple way; this makes goodness seem more complex than squareness and even somewhat mysterious. Once this point has been reached, there have been two ways forward. One of them regards evaluative words as highly complex versions of descriptive words (Leibniz was convinced that complex observations and calculations would result in clarity about a factual basis for value judgments), while the other removes them from the cognitive sphere altogether to accord them only emotive content (the positivist solution). Other versions of this removal from the cognitive sphere followed (for example, evaluative words as appraisive rather than simply emotive), but while the details varied, the basic hierarchy remained, one in which some words gave us information about the world, others only attitudes of the speaker.

A full discussion of evaluation and ethical issues in relation to linguistic theory must wait until chapter 6, after other matters have first been clarified. For my present purpose it suffices to say that this hierarchy of words—descriptive words as simple, basic, and central; evaluative words as complex, difficult, and less central—will instantly seem dubious once we point to a single fact: the words that this model makes the more basic and simple of the two kinds are evidently *newer* than the others, while the second group must be very old indeed. Geometric shapes have always been popular examples of descriptive words in these kinds of arguments: square, round, triangular. And similarly, from the very beginning of the tradition of analytic philosophy, elementary scientific observations were used as the prime examples of informative statements. (Logical positivism even made this explicit when Ayer went so far as to equate "ordinary" and "scientific" statements, opposing both to "judgments of value.")[19] But what should have puzzled everyone, though it never did, is that words like *good* and *bad* have a very long history, while the vocabulary of science and geometry is newer and more artificial. If we were to judge on the basis of a presumed historical sequence which kind was likely to have been basic or typical in language (because there from the beginning) and which derivative and thus possibly atypical, we should surely have to assume that things were the other way round. Words like *good* and *bad* would then have to be central to the model of how language works, while the language of science and mathematics might even be peripheral.[20]

And that, as we shall see in the following chapter, is indeed the case: what we think of disparagingly as merely "evaluative" words will turn out to be a better key to the understanding of language than those we have thought of as "descriptive." In point of fact, we can only fully understand the character of the latter by seeing that they are a *specialized development of the former.* The hierarchy will then be reversed: words like *good* are prior to words like *square*. If we are to develop an adequate view of linguistic categories we must start with the "unclear" cases, but once we have understood those we shall also see that our understanding of the clear cases has changed, for our assumptions about them were not quite correct after all.

The last initial misstep which we must consider is the assumption that linguistic categories group like things together. Here we face an odd paradox: if we look at the books on our bookshelves, we see immediately that they are all different in content, size, coloring, length, and so on. They are then not the same, but we still say that they are like each other. How are they similar? They are similar in *all being books;* and yet they are still all dissimilar. Categorization is the most fundamental operation performed by a language. To describe how it works means using ideas such as "similarity" and "dissimilarity" very carefully indeed, so that they are assigned their correct place in the understanding of categorization. This crucial matter is the subject of my next chapter, during the course of which it will become clear that this third misstep has prevented those who have taken it from understanding how categorization works. Categorization, it will be seen, will remain a mystery as long as we see it as the grouping together of like things; we grasp the essence of the process of categorization only when we see it as the grouping together of things that are not the same in order that they will count as the same.

THREE

The Heart of Language: Categorization

The argument of the previous chapters looked first at some general weaknesses of the field, and then at a few specific initial missteps that have misdirected its effort. I now turn to what seems to me the most central issue in linguistic theory: categorization. Categorization, not syntax, is the most basic aspect of language, and it is a process that must be understood correctly if anything else (including syntax) is to be understood; and categorization, not communication, is the most important function of language, one that is prior to all others.

In the previous chapter I showed that before either communicating or coding could occur something else must have happened, and that something must be fundamental to the nature of language: a framework that could allow operations such as coding and communicating to take place must first have been established. This framework must presuppose categorization and abstraction. The task of this chapter is to analyze the process of categorization in natural languages: how do linguistic categories arise and how do they work? It is a truism to say that no two languages implement this process of categorization in the same way, but it is a truism that puts the emphasis in the wrong place. Every language is a *particular* system of categorization, and thus each system, since it is particular, must be unique. It will be most convenient to begin by using individual words as examples illustrative of categorization. I should note, however, that a deeper level of this question will emerge in the following chapter, where I shall show that there are processes of abstraction and categorization that must have gone on even before these individual categories can arise. The next chapter will thus modify and to a degree throw a different light on what will have been said in the present one.

Imagine again the situation in which there are two individuals who do not as yet have a language. As we saw, a code would be useless to them, for without a language there is nothing to encode. If we were to begin with a simple view of language as communication of a state of affairs in the world from one person to another, we might assume that all the two would need are names for the different states. If that is really all that is needed, they should soon be able to invent some. Then we should have speaker A looking at a situation, labeling it, and using that label when he wants to recall it to speaker B. Now it is important to see that the result could not possibly be a language, and that what I have just postulated is in reality an absurdity—but an absurdity so instructive that it is worth looking at very closely. The problem is that the facts of experience are infinitely variable: no two situations are exactly alike. The notion of a different label for each different situation is an impossible one. First, the label would be meaningless to speaker B unless he had been present at and had witnessed all of the situations himself. This would mean that no communication could ever take place unless every speaker of a particular language had been present in every situation and had memorized and labeled it similarly, an obvious impossibility. Second, the number of labels would soon become so large that neither A nor B could possibly remember their reference. But third, and most instructive of all, this language would have no real uses. It would be limited to the mere recall of past situations,[1] but in an important sense *nothing would have been said* about those situations.

For this primitive linguistic (or rather: would-be linguistic) situation to achieve any coherence one more thing is necessary. Nothing about a situation is available for communication until it can be said to be one that is like this rather than like that. To say something about a situation is to place it among other possible situations, and this requires not a set of labels but a system of categories.[2] Imagine, again, our individuals without languages, and that they are in a situation that we who have the English language might describe as being both hot and located among large trees with jays on them; and then imagine our language-less people trying to produce labels for these aspects of the situation. As they try to label "largeness" we shall soon see that it is impossible for them to do so without invoking experiences of other sizes and comparisons with them. "Large" taken only as a label of something in this one situation would have no meaning because the meaning we want cannot exist without a scale derived from a number of experiences, and a place on that scale. Similarly, a simple label for "hot" in one situation is logically impossible; to have meaning it too would have to indicate a place on a scale and thus a placing of this situation among others. What would it mean to make a label for "jay"? Once again, nothing at all, if reference to the content of *this situation alone* was all that was to be reflected in the label. How could we possibly even know what part of the situation the label referred to—blueness, a thing that moves, a thing that flies, a large bird, a living thing—the list would be endless. To use the word *jay* is to place the thing we are talking of among things from other situations, to compare and contrast it with other birds, in short to know something about it.

If situations themselves present a limitless variety, a language can only have a finite set of categories. It follows that language functions as the instrument of human knowledge and communication only because it simplifies the complexity of experience by reducing an infinite variety to a finite set of categories—the categories of a particular language, that is, for no two languages use the same set. This *simplification* is the central fact and process of categorization, and thus the central fact of language and the knowledge it affords us of our world. For communication to be possible, then, there must first have been a considerable degree of processing of experience—of analyzing it, abstracting from it, focusing and shaping it. It is in this complex process that the essence of language is to be found, not in communication per se. Indeed, communication is only of value to us because this prior process creates something that can be communicated and is worth communicating. Words do not label situations; they must relate one situation to others in order to be able to talk about them at all. Only a prior typology of situations and their aspects allows communication about any one of them to take place, because what is communicated is *not the facts of the situation merely in itself* (again, that is an impossible notion) but the place of that situation within the set of categories of the language.

There are many ways of describing this initial stage in language, each illuminating the situation in a different way. To say that words are categories is to stress the fact that they assign a very large number of cases to a much smaller number of groups. To say that they are abstractions stresses their role in analyzing experience and in drawing out patterns in it. To say that they are simplifications is to draw attention to the way in which they reduce limitless complexity to an ordered and thus manageable state. But however we look at this crucial basis of language, it is clear that we are dealing with a process that is far less passive than the idea of labeling would suggest. Before communicating facts about the world, a language must first have established what facts are to be.

How, then, does language set up its categories, and how do those categories relate to the real world? The one thing that is clear is that a language can only use a number of words that is greatly smaller than the number of situations we encounter. Linguistic categorization therefore means in one sense a reduction of the variety of experience: situations that are not quite the same may be assigned to the same category and thus will count as "the same." But what does this really mean? Much in the theory of language depends on our seeing what is and what is not implied by this *imposition* of equivalence.[3]

There are two ways in which we might approach the question. One would be to say that situations are grouped as they are because of their real similarity: in spite of small differences they can share certain characteristic features. The other would be to say that, for the purposes of the speakers of this language, all the situations categorized in a certain way (by the use of a certain word) are treated by those speakers in the same way, that is, treated *as if there were no difference between them*. Both of these formulations seem reasonable enough, and we might therefore think that either one will work. But, alas, it is characteristic of theoretical inquiry that what is involved in choices of this kind is well hidden, and that unexpected disaster can result from the wrong choice. In this case the first choice leads to the theoretical impasse of much current thought, while the second does not. In what follows I shall show why this is so. It is not necessary to deny that the first formulation will work much of the time; the crucial point is that the second can subsume and give the proper framework to the first, while the reverse is not possible. This means that the first can deal with some cases, while the second can deal with all of them. To recall a theme from the preceding chapter: the first formulation can deal with the clear cases but makes the unclear cases a complete mystery. Because it can deal with the unclear cases, the second can account for all that is involved in categorization.

Categorization, as I have already noted, involves simplification and a reduction of uniqueness and diversity to a finite number of types. The word *simplification* may seem to imply something negative, even distorting, and it will therefore be important to recognize its positive function in this context. We might be tempted to think that the greater the number of categories, the more sensitive the system of such categories will be to everything that is in situations, and the more useful it will be in affording us knowledge of the world. But this is not the case. To understand why, we must imagine two kinds of languages, one with a very small number of categories, another with a *very* large number. The first would obviously not be very useful: to put all experiences into, say, two categories would not do much justice to the particular features of any of them. But the second would also not be useful, though for a different reason: as the number gets larger and larger, it would begin theoretically to approach the same number as the total number of possible situations. That is, there would be one category for one situation—but that would mean no categories at all; the idea of categories will have vanished. From this we can see that the simplification of experience through the creation of categories has a positive value, one that creates the possibility of a knowledge that arises only through our knowing aspects of situations as particular *kinds* of things.

Through categorization a *working* equivalence is established for a particular set of cases, and this equivalence in turn establishes a working difference between those cases and other sets of cases—not just any kind of difference, but the categorical difference established by the set of categories. What is the source of the principles of equivalence and difference? Their primary origin must lie in the purposes of the speakers, for the categories originate from them: they are the ones who have set up the system for their own use. A word in a language embodies a decision to treat a particular range of things as if they were the same, and then to treat everything that falls outside that range as different. The word *mammal*, for example, depends not on the fact that whales, cats, and people really are the same but on the fact that they are equivalent for the purposes of that category. This is why it is important to see that linguistic categories establish what is to count as equivalence, rather than merely taking it passively from like things.

It is here that we must confront an old argument and explain why the alarmed realist loses nothing that he or she should really care about in following me this far, for my argument differs significantly from the older one that frightens realists. The realist is generally averse to anything that seems to depart from the notion that linguistic categories simply recognize what is there in the world: thus we have a word for rabbits and group rabbits together because rabbits exist and because they are like each other, and the linguistic category *rabbit* recognizes the natural category of rabbits that exists in the world outside our language. But there is no need for alarm here over the question whether rabbits really exist and whether they really are similar to each other. What is at issue here for linguistic theory is (1) whether a *particular* set of similarities that may exist among certain creatures (or any other phenomena) is sufficient in itself to dictate and justify the categories of a language, and (2) whether it is necessary for a category to be based primarily upon such similarities at all. It is not difficult to show that the answer to both questions must be negative.

The second is the easier to disprove. Realists often suppose that the only cases of words that do not show clear and defining physical criteria for their use are the grosser evaluative words such as *good* or *bad*, but this is by no means the case. Most of the basic words we live by are from this realist standpoint amorphous categories: food, shelter, clothing, poison, weeds—all of these are categories clearly held together not by physical identity but by functional equivalence. Food items have no defining physical characteristic other than that they are useful to eat. Poisons are not substances that can be analyzed into a single distinct chemical class; they constitute a grab bag of chemically quite dissimilar things that share a functional propensity. They all (though in very different ways) interfere significantly with the functioning of the human body. A table is not defined as anything that measures x by y inches but rather as something that affords a useful surface—again, equivalence of function is the point. We can take Wittgenstein's example of games and say that not all games have a defining characteristic, but then proceed to say what he did not say: that in spite of their having no common feature, the category of games does have a functional equivalence that emerges if we contrast games with serious pursuits. (Once again, Saussure is needed to supply a gap in Wittgenstein.) In all of these cases it is clear that a physically disparate group of things forms a coherent category because we make them form it; all serve a similar purpose for us.

The first point is a more subtle one, and it is where the realist's anxiety will arise, though in fact needlessly. We can easily grant that there are real similarities between things in the natural world, but are these similarities the unique basis of the categories of a language? The answer to this is that they cannot be so because there are far too many of them. Take *rabbit*:[4] does it simply recognize a natural kind, a neat division in the natural world that has nothing to do with our language? English recognizes the distinction between rabbits and hares. Is that natural too, or should we instead adopt as "natural" the system of those languages that treat both as rabbits, that is, jackrabbits, bush rabbits, and so on? It will not help to say that we should call everything in the same genus by one name, for dogs and wolves are in the same genus, just as widgeons and mallards are. Conversely, some common names—for example, *bear, owl,* or *hawk*— are used with complete confidence for animals that are *not* in the same genus. For the word *duck* we can go higher still in the biological hierarchy: animals from different tribes are all ducks. The realist is fond of saying that there is a word for cats because cats exist. But while the animals and their differing kinds of similarities do exist, the categorization *cat* is ours. Our language might have used a word that categorized these animals in a different way and that assigned them to a larger group, as it does with bears, or a smaller one, as with lions. But, the realist may finally say, the scientific designation by genus and species is *real.* To which the answer is, yes and no. The arrangement by genus and species is also arbitrary. To the question, are all genera equally distinct from other genera, and all species equally distinct from other species? the answer must be, of course not.[5] Only our language reduces the complexity of the biological world to a uniform degree of relatedness and unrelatedness. W. Haas has said aptly that "a doctrine of 'natural kinds' is the last refuge of a denotational theory of meaning.…What this amounts to, on closer examination, is just a naive belief in the divinity of one's own language"—in other words, a belief that the categories of one's own language have a unique and necessary status.[6]

A vivid practical test of this is now in the making: as biologists do comparisons of individuals, species, genera, families, and so on, in terms both of the percentage of DNA shared and of the variability among individuals assigned to the same grouping at each level of the hierarchy, it will inevitably become clear that the natural world contains only a great continuum; there will be no uniform percentage differences separating different genera, different species, or even the variety of individuals within species. It can even be predicted with confidence that a few cases will eventually come to light in which the DNA differences between certain classes at one level of classification are greater than some of the differences obtaining at higher levels of classification at other places in the system; that is, sometimes different species will be further apart than different genera.[7]

Could we invent a system that did not involve any distortion of this kind? Even to suggest this, and to put the matter in terms of distortion, is to misunderstand the nature of categorization in language. Suppose that we tried to invent a more refined system of classification, one in which words like *genus* did not refer to distinctions of so variable an extent. The trouble is once more that beyond a certain point the more complex we make the system, the less its information content would be. Imagine a system in which the particular degree of difference between each species and the next had its own unique term: now, it might be thought, we should have a really precise system. But we have only to imagine the resulting chaos of complexity to realize that we should in fact have nothing. We are back to the fundamental point of linguistic categories: they reduce the complexity of the world to make it manageable for its speakers so that they can orient themselves in it, that is, know it. This is only possible given a certain amount of distortion: language can only work by treating *this* as if it were the same as *that*. And paradoxically, it is this distortion, this making equivalent of things that are not the same, which makes language *and knowledge* possible. The odd result of insisting that linguistic categories match what is there would be a dissolution of the realist's world into one in which nothing can be known; and this should demonstrate that the naive realist has nothing to fear in accepting all linguistic classification as arbitrary. Consider, once more, the case of temperature.

Temperature can be measured with great precision: any number of people can measure a particular body of air and all find that it is at sixty-eight degrees Fahrenheit. The fact that they all get the same answer makes it seem that what they have is the "real" temperature. But now suppose that someone else says that it is twenty degrees Celsius. Has he found the real temperature too? Yes and no. Both are correct, but only given their systems of measurement. What, then, is the *really* real temperature? But what figure could that possibly be—sixty-eight, twenty, or some other number? To this, of course, the answer is that there is no real figure if by that is meant a figure that is not part of an arbitrary system of measurement. Our realist might have one last attempt to stick to unaided reality by saying that the reality here is that we have a temperature one-fifth of the way from the freezing to the boiling point of water. But even if we were to let him get away without specifying that this is true only at a certain altitude (sea level), we can still ask him why his choice of water as the basis of the system is so inevitable: why not another substance? And to this there can be no answer, for the arbitrary choice of water is a part both of the Fahrenheit and of the Celsius systems. We must at last recognize that there is indeed no such thing as an inherent temperature of a substance considered only in itself.

It is often said that *hot, warm,* and *cold* are different *in kind* to measurements in degrees of Fahrenheit and that they are instead subjective responses; but this is not so, and if we are to understand language it is important to see how and why it is not so. These terms are simply a very primitive system of measurement, no different in kind from any other; they share the arbitrariness of the Fahrenheit system but have far fewer terms and thus do less work for us. More important, these are all equally systems that have to impose a framework on reality in order to be able to talk about or know it. The realist has no more reason to doubt that things are really warm than that they are really sixty-eight degrees Fahrenheit, and the arbitrariness of calling the temperature twenty Celsius, sixty-eight Fahrenheit, or warm should not make him or her think that the physical world is an illusion because it is not *really* anything at all. It can still be true or false that the temperature is sixty-eight Fahrenheit, but only given the arbitrary classification we must create in order to be able to know such a thing.

What I have been arguing is that linguistic categories are primarily the reflection of the collective purposes of the speakers of a language rather than direct reflections of the structure of the world. In other words, the equivalence created by the categories of a language is a functional one: those things included in a category can be and are treated as equivalent for the purpose of the category even though they are not identical. Conversely, what is excluded from a category is treated differently even though some excluded things may be more similar to some members of the category than those members are to many other members of the category. For example: in the great chain of Romance language dialects stretching from northern to southern Europe, a dialect of French spoken close to the Italian border could be (especially before the effects of standardization were felt) more similar to the dialect of Italian spoken the other side of the border than either is to its respective standard language; even so, they are still categorized as "French" and "Italian."

Let me return now to the choice that had to be made between two views of the nature of linguistic categories: the one, that they are determined by and reflect the facts of the real world; the other, that they are determined by the interests of the speakers of a language. There is one great advantage enjoyed by the choice I have made: it can handle all cases equally well, while the "realist" choice is unable to do anything satisfying with a large group of words that it sees as evaluative rather than descriptive. If we say that the equivalence created by linguistic categories is primarily functional, this does not prevent us from saying that the purposes served by them are sometimes more and sometimes less focused upon particular physical properties. The continuity between *sixty-eight degrees, warm,* and *good* can be handled perfectly well by one of these two views, therefore, but not by the other. And it is precisely when *sixty-eight degrees* is misconceived as a purely descriptive fact that words like *warm* and *good* become a mystery.[8]

The prevailing view of meaning has therefore been a case of generalizing prematurely from the easy cases and then being baffled by the difficult cases. The "descriptive" words have been the easy cases from which principles were derived with which to handle the difficult cases. The fact that the difficult cases were persistently not just difficult but actually impossible to handle in this way should have been a hint that it was the analysis of the easy cases that was wrong, and that the difficult cases, properly analyzed, might yield a different attitude to those apparently easy cases too. The archetype of the linguistic category is in fact the relatively pure attitude word *good*, not derivative and atypical words like scientific terms, but even these can only be properly understood, as we have seen in the case of biological classifications, if we remember that they are also still linguistic categories.

The assumption that linguistic categories classify only and simply on the basis of physical similarities is clearly among the most destructive mistakes in linguistic theory, and it is one that seems able to pull back into its orbit even those thinkers who were on the verge of escaping from it. Rose Olver and Joan Hornsby, for example, got as far as seeing that language simplifies a complex world, but wasted this useful beginning by then saying in effect that it does so by grouping things that really *are* equivalent.[9] Only a small reformulation would have been needed here to avoid a large pitfall. We need only say that things that are grouped by linguistic categories are treated *as if they were* equivalent and that the reasons for this equivalence will vary. Others seem to have stumbled across a part of the truth without recognizing it when they saw it. Geoffrey Sampson, for example, recognized (and complained) that man-made categories are ill defined, and then wasted this insight by telling us to look for well-defined classes to use as the basis of linguistic categories.[10] It might have occurred to him that since language is a man-made thing, those "ill-defined" categories should be central for linguistics. Moreover, if what is central to language is ill defined by one kind of standard, then we should of course be looking for some other standard. Sampson had things exactly the wrong way round: if we want to look at what is typical of language, it is the precise, stipulatively defined term that we should avoid.

Even those who have seen that concepts cannot simply be derived from the structure of the real world have wasted this insight by looking for the origin of concepts not in the organizing activity of language but in an inherent structure of the human brain. Wallace Chafe, for example, says that concepts arise in the neural system, while Janet Fodor talks in an alarmingly incautious way of "mentalese," its structure, and the need to discover what that structure is.[11] Fodor's is an attempt to create a kind of hypothetical universal mental metalanguage with its own categories built in—an evident impossibility. In the case of an English speaker, we can be sure that mentalese will turn out to have the categories of English. For what this dubious notion cannot deal with is the fact that languages are different from each other; if mentalese really existed, that is, a structure of concepts preexisting in the human brain, then all languages would use that same set of concepts, and they do not. Fodor is really looking for those semantic primitives for which positivist philosophers searched so diligently and so fruit-lessly, but she searches for them in the mind rather than in the world.[12]

The finite nature of language is easily explained by the finiteness of choice that is a condition of human life. The typical linguistic category calls up choices: good or bad, black or white, criminal or not, edible or poisonous. The notion of a single category is an incoherent one: the minimum required for categorization is two because the essence of this process is the human need to distinguish one set of cases from one or more others. But once we dwell on this point it leads us again to the conclusion that the basis of linguistic categories must be functional: we distinguish one set of cases from another because we want to treat them differently, to do something different with them, to behave differently toward them. Once again, the necessary conclusion is that categories relate to our purposes primarily, and to the actual differences of the real world secondarily.

The natural world, then, offers a great variety of degrees of relatedness between individual phenomena, and to say only that it offers us "natural" kinds is to miss the fact that the definition of a kind is a linguistic process. Though the naive realist might fear that this way of looking at the world slights the real qualities that exist there, the reverse is the case: only if we conceive of the world in this way can we recognize the existence of the overwhelming complexity of its real qualities, which—paradoxically—the realist cannot do justice to or even acknowledge because of his fixed view of linguistic terms. His grasp of reality is thus determined by the way language reduces that complexity to a set of kinds that we can manage.

What can we say about the content of categories? In terms of the charac-teristics of the members of a category, some categories are relatively amorphous while others are more strictly organized. The class *good* is the most amorphous of all, while scientific terms are the most tightly organized. *Triangle* is a highly organized category, with seemingly a single criterion for membership; but it is a mathematical term, and as such specialized, derivative, and atypical.[13] Languages must have existed without such terms for a very long time, and it was during this time that their basic character must have been formed; that fact should tell us that it is dangerous to make such terms the model of how words work. And thus arises another paradox: if we are to be truly scientific about the study of language, we had better avoid taking scientific terms as examples.[14] More typical of our speech are categories such as *food* or *poison* that include a multitude of very different things while also, however, displaying some loose patterns among the membership of the class. For example, no one kind of chemical structure is found linking all poisons, but there are probably several distinct types, so that the category is not completely shapeless as far as the characteristics of its membership are concerned. Thus we see different degrees of patterning within the membership of different categories, and this is not surprising if the overall unity of the category lies in its purpose. A given purpose or function may be served by only one basic kind of thing or two or several; and that fact explains why trying to set up a single set of necessary and sufficient factual criteria for the definition of a word sometimes works but more often does not.

We can now see how a certain class of categories—namely, those in which a category contains only things all of which share a single characteristic—can mislead us, presumably because its function is a fairly simple one. It follows from the theory I have outlined that some cases of this kind must exist; these are those "easy" cases, always tempting us to think that all categories have so simple a structure and thus deflecting our attention away from the function of categories to the properties of their members. But if we yield to this temptation, we make it impossible to account for anything else in language, and we actually distort what is happening in these cases too.

This is, however, not the only factor that draws us to the naive realist's attitude to linguistic categories. More important is the fact that the categories of our language are the categories of all our mental operations; we organize our world to fit these categories and are used to behaving *as if* there were a real equivalence between the members of our various categories. Small wonder, then, that we accept its unavoidable simplifications so fully that we mistake them for the structure of the world, for as speakers of this language we have virtually given it that structure. A Frenchman once said that it was a remarkable fact about the French language that words occurred there in exactly the order in which thought occurs. What escaped him was that the same is true of all other languages.

I have outlined a theory of linguistic categories that has obvious points of contact with that of earlier theorists such as Saussure, Peirce, or Wittgenstein, and many equally obvious points of conflict with current viewpoints. It will help to round out the logic of this view of language and to explain further its rationale if we now examine the points both of similarity and of contrast with previous thought. I shall turn first to points of contact with some of the seminal thinkers of the past. As we shall see, whenever particular bits of the general picture I have set out emerged, the fragmentary quality of their presentation did not allow their full force to become apparent. Fruitful beginnings have obviously been wasted, for example, when the ideas concerned were embraced by scholars whose standpoint in linguistic theory remained a realist one.[15] Not all of the blame in these cases, however, is due to incompleteness of exposition—it must also be shared by careless readers.

Let us begin with the contributions of Wittgenstein and Saussure to the analysis of linguistic categories. Each suggested a part of the total picture but stopped well short of a rounded theory, and so neither had the impact that he should have had on linguistic theory; both could have used the insights of the other to advantage. Wittgenstein gave us the idea of family resemblances, Saussure that of contrast and differentiation. Neither idea is sufficient by itself, and more important, neither idea was fully comprehensible even in itself because of the lack of a fuller context, part of which could have been provided by the other. Wittgenstein had evidently seen that not all categories are defined by some particular property that all its members have in common, but it was the next step beyond this insight that was really crucial in his account. His first step seems to have removed the sole basis of the coherence of categories, but what Wittgenstein then managed to do was to suggest—with his idea of family resemblances—that a different kind of coherence was possible. This was a remarkable feat of observation and abstraction. The idea of a family resemblance enables us to say that one kind of trait is prominent in some games but that in others a different one predominates, the result being an overlapping series of traits such as those found in families. There is a typical Smith chin, but not all its members display it; and the same with eyes, coloring, and so on. Looking at a family as a whole, one sees the coherence of the overall group, though it is not located in any one obligatory trait.

Wittgenstein's idea is a striking demonstration of the fact that categories do not need to be built on rigidly defining features to be coherent, but it also has serious limitations: it does not explain *why* this should be so. That kind of explanation would have required Wittgenstein to look in an entirely different direction. He would have had to transfer his and our attention away from the characteristics of the members of a category to the more basic question of its function. Only thus could he have shown why categories can be as loosely organized as he correctly sees they are. To be sure, he hints at the issue of function—when he says that a language is a form of life—but the reader could only understand how such a hint relates to the idea of family resemblances if he had already found the answer for himself.

There is still another way in which the idea of family resemblances is misleading. Wittgenstein presents this idea almost as if it could be paradigmatic for categories that do not have simply defining characteristics. But it is not. The idea of family resemblances will handle some categories but not very many; its importance thus lies, not in its paradigmatic quality, but in its demonstration that categories can achieve coherence without necessarily having defining features shared by all members. It is only when we see that functional differentiation is the basis of categories that we can really understand the point of family resemblances as one example of how that differentiation might work in a particular case.[16] Categories in fact vary enormously, ranging all the way from very tightly organized to very loosely organized.

When he hit upon the idea of family resemblances, Wittgenstein was in effect taking a single point on this spectrum to show that there was a kind of category that did not work as all categories had previously been thought to work, but he did not deal with the whole spectrum, nor did he have anything to say about the nature of and reason for the spectrum, probably because he did not fully understand it. In fact, then, "family resemblances" was a splendid idea with which to break down one particular, very common attitude to definition by showing that we can find coherence in categories without defining attributes, but it was much less valuable as an indicator of where we should go next to find a viable alternative theory of the nature and structure of categories.[17] And in this regard it was actually something of a hindrance, for it kept our attention where it should not have been: on the physical properties of the members of a category instead of on the purpose of the category in differentiating one set of things from another. As a result, Wittgenstein has been at one and the same time admired and ineffective; it has been all too easy for his readers not to see the importance of what he did.[18] Perhaps Wittgenstein himself thought that simply with this idea he had redefined the nature of categories; others have certainly thought so.[19] But he had not explained why the world should be organized in what looked a rather untidy way, and without such an explanation to back his idea up it was bound to have little effect on linguistic theory.

The extent of the misunderstanding that Wittgenstein made possible can be seen in cases such as that of Humphrey Palmer's exposition of the notion of family resemblances, where it is suggested that the problem this notion illustrates might be solved if only it were possible to stipulate the meaning of all the terms we use.[20] It should have been clearer that Wittgenstein's thought on language is absolutely inconsistent with such a suggestion.

Saussure went at the same problem from the opposite direction with his idea of contrast as the basis of concepts.[21] Again, the basic idea was a penetrating one. What Saussure had seized upon was the way in which no word can be meaningful by itself but only in relation to a system of terms and a choice between them. (That, as we have seen, is an essential consequence of the notion of "simplification.") He thus saw that the meaning of each term was defined primarily by its place in the system. Saussure had grasped the crucial point (one Wittgenstein seemed to grasp only fitfully, though his idea of family resemblances needed it very badly) that the unity of a concept was to be sought not primarily in what it referred to but rather in its being differentiated from other possible choices in the language. Saussure's gap was the reverse of Wittgenstein's. He had highlighted well the differentiation of one concept from another, but he also needed to deal with the internal structure of categories if his account of language was to be convincing. He needed to deal with the objection that it is possible to look at chairs and find the concept *chair* to represent a perfectly coherent grouping of apparently similar objects. Saussure has therefore always seemed vulnerable to the elementary arguments of naive realists because he never dealt with the first objection they were likely to make: what about the real world of objects?[22] Indeed, so serious is this gap in Saussure that he is occasionally discussed and his ideas expounded using the vocabulary of denotation and reference, which runs directly counter to his notion of contrast.[23]

For similar reasons, other inspired suggestions by Wittgenstein and Saussure could suffer the same fate. Saussure, for example, made much of the arbitrariness of linguistic categories, and this was indeed an important idea—but only if it is clearly assigned to "its proper place" in the larger context of linguistic theory. Its real point could only become apparent if it were related to the way in which linguistic categories reduce an infinite world of experience to a finite and thus much smaller set of categories that, by simplifying and organizing experience, make knowledge possible. In choosing a word like *arbitrary*—which out of context might suggest incoherence—and then failing to explain clearly enough its positive value in a larger theory, Saussure left the impression that he saw much less coherence in language and in the world than was really the case. He even made it possible for people to confuse the very important point inherent in his use of the word *arbitrary* with the entirely trivial one that the choice of a particular set of sounds to denote a particular concept is also arbitrary.[24]

Still other major issues in Wittgenstein's thought were presented in fragmentary ways that obscured their relation to a larger theory of language and left the explanation of their consequences unfinished. This is true even of his central notions of "game" and "use." When he says that using a word is like making a move in a game, and that certain words seem to be defined not by their reference but by their use, Wittgenstein raises fundamental issues in linguistic theory, but he never explains fully what those issues are. It is here that he moves closest to Saussure (he was in fact reinventing Saussure's own analogy), for to think of the use of a word as being like a move in a game of chess is to see it as a choice from a finite set of possibilities, where meaning is a product of the choice. But Wittgenstein stops short of the next step, one that should have taken him to the question of the function of categories. The attentive and well-informed observer can probably see that a view of language as embodying its own conceptual scheme is advanced by this analogy, while the code-and-information view loses ground. But Wittgenstein himself does not draw out these implications, and because he did not do so the game analogy was often to be drastically misinterpreted.[25] Once again, the fragmentary nature of Wittgenstein's remarks allowed them to be ineffective. I have suggested above that this probably occurred because of his being concerned largely with disputed issues in philosophy; those issues set limits on his interest in pursuing for its own sake the theory of language that was beginning to emerge from his train of thought.[26] But this narrow focus proved self-defeating; if Wittgenstein wanted to use insights about language to change philosophy, the full logical basis of those insights would need eventually to be explained if he was to be successful. The evidence of recent developments in philosophy and linguistics suggests that he did not succeed.

The fate of the idea of "use" is the most extensive example of how Wittgenstein's ideas were misconceived after his death. There have been two major developments, both resulting in the trivialization of the idea, though in different ways. In the first, generative grammarians thought that attention to use would allow trivial variations in actual speech ("performance") to be taken as part of the essential structure of a language ("competence"). This missed Wittgenstein's real point, which had nothing to do with unsystematic individual variations in speech; it concerned instead the fundamental logic of how words did their work—not by labeling things but in an entirely different way.[27]

The second of these developments consists in the entire branch of philosophical thought about language known as "speech act" theory, which has its origin in Wittgenstein's demonstration at the beginning of the *Philosophical Investigations* that words do many kinds of work in addition to referring to or standing for an object.[28] Speech act theory takes this opening quite literally and as a result looks at the different kinds of work that language does—including referring and denoting. Now in the broader context of the argument of his book Wittgenstein's point is surely *not* that these notions can be retained as they are and *supplemented* with others but rather that they are inherently inadequate notions. But speech act theory assumes the first of these interpretations, which, if I am correct, avoids the major thrust of Wittgenstein's argument. In effect, this interpretation takes Wittgenstein to be saying, not that the denotation theory does not work, but instead only that it works fine for information content and needs to be added to for other kinds of content. Since the core use of language that is to be supplemented is always the central (i.e., cognitive) one, and the theory to be used for this cognitive function is the pre-Wittgenstein theory, the entire thrust of Wittgenstein's theoretical advance is lost. The odd result has been that the potential advance in language theory afforded by Wittgenstein's fragmentary remarks has been smothered in part by the existence of an apparently Wittgensteinian school that is in reality fundamentally anti-Wittgenstein.[29] Thus many scholars were able to go back to their familiar denotational theory of meaning still thinking they were Wittgensteinians.[30]

While Wittgenstein points in the direction of a functional view of categories, then, he did not in fact expound such a theory; had he developed and explicated systematically all the implications of such notions as "language game," he might have produced a rounded theory of language. Charles Sanders Peirce is another case of a thinker who saw an isolated piece of a viable theory of language without being able to support it adequately with the other pieces of the puzzle. Peirce understood the enormously important point that to know something is not to have a direct intuition of it but to classify it and relate it to other things. Why this must be so can be seen once more with the example of temperature. We can know the temperature of something in relation to the boiling point of water or in relation to other things, but we could not know it simply by itself: there would then be nothing to know.[31] But Peirce, too, was driven by his own particular interest (the theory of knowledge), and so he went no further toward a fully formed theory of language.

The most serious attempt to explore a functional view of categories and to relate the categories of language to human behavior is that of Benjamin Lee Whorf, but Whorf did so without providing the logical grounding for this step, parts of which are present in Peirce, Wittgenstein, and Saussure, for example, in their discussions of the content of categories, of the gamelike status of linguistic rules, and of the origin of categories. Had he provided that kind of logical framework for his ideas, his comment on the "metaphysics" of a language might not have been so easily dismissed by skeptics as fanciful.[32]

All of these failures to work out and complete a fully coherent theory of categorization have contributed to the resilience of the familiar realist view of categories; the related ideas of reference and semantic primitives seem always ready to bounce back, no matter how bad things have seemed for them. If logical positivism managed to discredit semantic primitives for a while through the backlash it provoked, we were soon back to the same ideas in the generativists' lexical decomposition;[33] and when that in turn fell out of favor we moved quickly back to the same kind of thing yet again in the universal typology sought by Barwise and Perry, an idea possible only if one has not seen and thought through the implications of the fact that such a typology would need to be finite without being (in Saussure's sense) arbitrary. (Once we understand the process of categorization through simplification that is fundamental to all languages, we easily see that this is logically impossible.) But the largest-scale example of the resilience of denotation and reference (and at the same time the clearest indication of the recent invisibility of Wittgenstein) is the theory of "direct" reference, which was developed by Saul Kripke and Hilary Putnam in the seventies.

"Direct reference" is essentially a labeling theory according to which words are names for things. With this view Kripke and Putnam in effect take us back to an earlier and more primitive era of linguistic theory—the general world of Russell, Carnap, and Ayer, and of positivism with its logical basis in the denotation theory.[34] But theirs is actually a more extreme and reductive version of labeling, for in "direct reference" words are thought of as labels analogous almost to proper names—they give names directly to natural kinds that exist in the world, without the mediation of criteria for their use. Evidently, to treat words as proper names requires a heavy reliance on the notion of natural kinds, which must be seen not just in a very restricted set of physical phenomena (say, oxygen) but almost everywhere, for only thus can this theory have the kind of broad applicability that will be required if it is to be a general theory of language and meaning.[35] Kripke sees natural kinds everywhere: "Certain general terms, those for natural kinds, have a greater kinship with proper names than is generally realized. This conclusion holds for certain for various species names, whether they count as nouns, such as 'cat,' 'tiger,' 'chunk of gold,' or mass terms such as 'gold,' 'water,' 'iron pyrites.' It also applies to certain natural phenomena, such as 'heat,' 'light,' 'sound,' 'lightning,' and, presumably, suitably elaborated, to corresponding adjectives—'hot,' 'loud,' 'red.'"[36] The idea that words like *water* refer directly to a natural kind instead of having a meaning that we learn by abstracting criteria for the use of the word from our experience (e.g., fluidity, clarity, etc.), is supported with reference to the "microstructure" of the phenomenon. Thus *water* refers to the substance with the chemical formula H_2O, and *tiger* not to an animal with stripes, etc., but to things with a certain *internal* (DNA?) structure. Another implication of direct reference is spelled out by David Kaplan: "When using a directly referential term, the *mode of presentation of the referent*...is no part of what is said. Only the referent figures in the content. Directly referential expressions are *transparent*."[37]

It can be seen that this is not at bottom a new theory but only an exceptionally rigid and uncompromising version of the age-old one, from which it follows that it is also more than usually incautious, and so more vulnerable than ever to quite simple logical objections. And yet in certain quarters it has had something of a vogue.[38]

Avrum Stroll has made a series of devastating criticisms of the Kripke/Putnam theory. In answer to the claim that the microstructure of water determines the meaning of *water*, Stroll draws our attention to the fact that steam, ice, and water are all composed of H_2O and "since both water and ice have the same chemical composition, it follows that *the difference between them cannot be accounted for in terms of their chemical composition*."[39] He also notes that the chemical composition of water is in any case a relatively recent discovery, and that the Kripke/Putnam view would thus commit us to the obviously absurd view that the word (*not* the phenomenon) *water* was not understood until that time. (Here we see yet another reason to avoid the error of taking the atypical, highly specialized language of science and mathematics as a general model for language.) Stroll also shows that the theory of direct reference must rely on an incautious faith in ostensive definition that is immediately vulnerable to the problems that Wittgenstein saw in that notion.[40] Direct reference is in fact an inherently impossible notion: some form of mediation is unavoidable. A subtle observation by Leonard Linsky is relevant: "Of first importance here is the consideration that it is the users of language who refer and make references and not, except in a derivative sense, the expressions they use in so doing."[41] Once we grasp this point the whole idea of a reference theory of meaning becomes questionable, for what Linsky's point implies is that words and their meaning must *already* be constituted before they can be used to refer to something, and thus that the meaning of a word cannot in any ordinary sense be what it is used to refer to.

The most serious problem in the Kripke/Putnam theory, however, lies in its misunderstanding of categorization in general and its consequent indefensible and almost indiscriminate reliance on the notion of natural kinds. Even those who have some sympathy with the theory object to this excessive reliance, believing that the notion has a much smaller scope than Kripke and Putnam take it to have.[42] Two examples chosen by Kripke are among those I have dealt with above: *cat* and *hot*.[43] From the analysis given earlier in this chapter, it can easily be seen that Kripke is wrong to think that these are natural kinds. The first case ignores all the problems I noted in connection with our words for animals: for example, the highly variable scope of such terms and the arbitrary choice of the particular extent of that scope in any given case, as well as the variability both within kinds and between kinds. Kripke thinks that precise specification of genetic makeup would really tidy things up, but on the contrary, it would complicate things intolerably by removing the simplification that our categories impose and that alone makes the entire natural situation manageable and knowable for us. His use of *hot*, on the other hand, ignores the fact that a particular and arbitrary *range* of temperatures is gathered together with this word,[44] and that far from referring directly to a single natural phenomenon that simply exists and can be pointed to, its use presupposes a whole set of assumptions about reference points and a scale instituted in a language, without which it could have no meaning.

The history of recent theory on the subject of categorization is thus, on the one hand, one of promising beginnings left incomplete by their authors and, on the other, one of a continual revisiting of the dead end of reference and denotation as soon as the very short memory span of the field has allowed the last such fiasco to be forgotten. With each reprise of this universal fallback theory there are new terms and thus a new clothing, but the ideas remain the same. There is a good reason for this. Our use of the categories of our own language is a fundamental part of us. It follows that we are likely to revert over and over again to the illusion that these are all simply "real" categories. To this point I shall return in a later chapter on epistemology; meanwhile, it is time to move on to a look at the more fundamental questions about linguistic categories that arise when grammar is considered.

FOUR

Grammar

The most well-known practical distinction in the study of a language is that between grammar and lexicon: we are all used to the fact that when we learn a language we buy a grammar on the one hand and a dictionary on the other. Convention and habit therefore present us with a kind of primitive theory of two basic aspects of language which has its origin in these two kinds of practical knowledge. But one of the tasks of a theoretical analysis is to take a hard look at any theory (especially one based in so mundane a distinction) that we find given to us by our everyday language itself. In addition to asking the obvious questions (What is grammar? How does it relate to language as a whole?), we must also begin by looking searchingly at this conventional starting point and at the basis of its separation of grammar from lexicon: can it be justified, and not only as a matter of practical convenience but also theoretically? Whenever a theoretical inquiry fails to begin by looking hard at the position inherited from common thought and practice, the most likely outcome will be a passive acceptance of that position followed by a desperate struggle to deal with its inconsistencies, which, however, never go away.

This essential first stage of thought has always been conspicuously absent in the MIT tradition in linguistic theory. Chomsky began his *Syntactic Structures* with a chapter entitled "The Independence of Grammar." The dogmatic assumption that both the concept of grammar and its separation from the lexicon can be accepted as a given has generally been compounded by the even more dogmatic assertion that the task of linguistics is the construction of grammars. There is a classic and very simple answer to such assertions: why? For it is not at all clear why we should not take the study of language to require an investigation of all aspects of the nature and function of its object. The reason for these assertions, however, is not difficult to find: they arise not from new thought but, on the contrary, from a strict adherence to the old. In the common practice of separating grammar and lexicon, a grammar book is conceived of as a set of rules, and the emphasis of such volumes is on formal correctness or incorrectness.

In contrast, the lexicon is a set of individual words with meanings stated individually for each separate case. Given this state of affairs, only the former seems capable of being systematized and formalized; what then could theory do with the second? Previous chapters have already suggested the flaw in this approach: if theory sets out to systematize only what looks capable of being easily systematized, it does no more than retain the conceptual structure with which it started. The almost exclusive focus of generative grammarians on syntax is therefore the consequence of combining, on the one hand, an aggressively no-nonsense, formal, and "scientific" attitude to linguistics and, on the other, a passive acceptance of the basic conceptual structure of ordinary, everyday talk about language.

Once the common distinction between grammar and lexicon has been accepted as a starting point that need not be questioned, it becomes necessary to find a difference corresponding to that distinction. Again, a candidate is readily available: the distinction between form and meaning is one that is traditional, and once more, Chomsky endorses it: "I think that we are forced to conclude that grammar is autonomous and independent of meaning."[1] This fateful beginning has caused enormous problems for generative grammar throughout its history, and to these I shall return, but two points are worth noting immediately: first, that this was the very foundation stone of Chomsky's entire system, so that later attempts to modify the system by repairing this flaw while keeping as many as possible of the system's essentials were always bound to underestimate how profound the problem really was and how deeply embedded in the system; and second, that the drive toward formalization (almost as an independent value) has remained too strong for this basic tenet to be questioned for very long. Thus, for example, the latest variants and descendants of the MIT tradition once again assert Chomsky's basic starting point on the independence of grammar and meaning.[2]

There are a few well-known arguments in support of this position which achieve some plausibility, but one has only to generalize those arguments to make them seem questionable; pushed too far, they will even appear absurd. For example, Langacker argued that gender is a purely grammatical category that has nothing to do with meaning, that is, with actual sexual identity.[3] In support of this, one can say that in French "la cage" has nothing female about it. But even at first glance this argument does not appear watertight, since "la belle" certainly does, and the bare contrast between it and "le beau," or that between German "die Alte" and "der Alte," is sufficient to establish the difference between a man and a woman. Another of these common arguments claims that noun and verb are also purely grammatical categories because the traditional explanation that the one represents a person, place, or thing while the other represents an event can easily be made to break down. And indeed it can. A storm, for example, is more like an event than a thing, though it is a noun. Arguments such as these, again, result in the claim that grammatical categories are purely formal rather than semantic. One linguist even went so far as to want to replace the terms *noun* and *verb* with "Class 1" and "Class 2" words, and so to remove from us the temptation to think in terms of persons, places, things, and events.[4]

There are, however, at least three devastating counterarguments here. First, the category of gender and the noun/verb distinction are just about the only cases that make this line of argument even barely plausible. To say, for example, that the future tense has nothing to do with the future, or the plural number nothing to do with number, or the adjective nothing to do with qualities would be very odd indeed. Would it make any sense to say that someone understood the grammar of English who did not know the meaning of number or tense? Rather than be forced into this position, it is surely preferable to look again both at gender and at the noun/verb distinction to see whether they are in fact so very difficult to accommodate to an analysis that includes meaning. As we shall see, gender in the Indo-European languages is an odd and atypical transitional case.

Second, the distinction between the grammar and the lexicon cannot be restated as one between form and meaning because this second distinction has to be made on *both* sides of the first. The word *cat* has both a phonetic form and a conceptual content, just as the future tense has a form and a conceptual content, and it is by no means clear that these two cases are different in kind. *Cat* contrasts formally with *mat* but conceptually with *dog* (among others).

Third, the attempt to make a clear distinction in kind between grammar and lexicon runs foul of the fact that there is a continuum running from the one to the other, with transition cases where the one category flows naturally into the other. A sharp distinction in kind between grammar and lexicon misrepresents this situation. Take, for example, the case of such words as *yellow, red, blue,* etc. We usually assign these adjectives to the lexicon, and thus to the kind of knowledge that we get from that source rather than from grammatical knowledge. In fact, however, this somewhat misrepresents the situation. Color adjectives do indeed have a place in the grammar of English; there is a place reserved for them in the structure of the nominal phrase. We can say "the old red barn" but not "the red old barn." The former is grammatical, the latter is not. This phenomenon is not fundamentally different from the place reserved at the beginning of the phrase for a category of words that includes *the, a, some,* etc. We cannot say "red some apples" any more than we can say "red large apples."

There is some irony here in the fact that Chomsky made the sentence "colorless green ideas sleep furiously" famous as an example of a grammatical sentence that was not meaningful, in order to advance his argument that grammar was a formal matter that was completely separable from meaning. In subsequent years there has been much debate about whether the sentence was indeed meaningful, but all of this debate missed the real issue. The sentence is actually quite clearly *ungrammatical*, a fact that Chomsky completely overlooked; it violates the structure of the English noun phrase. Consider, for example, the phrase "the some red apples." This is not grammatical because the first position in the phrase may contain only one of the category of words that occur there: to have two violates that rule. We can have either "some red apples" or "the red apples" but not both. Now consider the two phrases "reddish green apples" and "red green apples." Only the first is grammatical, because once more only one color word may occur in the color word position. In the first case "reddish" is felt to modify "green" and thus to be part of the single unit "reddish-green," while in the second case the independence of the two words makes the phrase ungrammatical.[5] When he included "colorless" and "green" in his sentence, Chomsky evidently thought that the issue he was raising was purely one of the semantic contradiction between colored and not-colored. But the case would have been the same had he used "orange" instead of "colorless," and this is therefore an issue that is both semantic *and* formal. The English nominal phrase does not allow two different colors to be asserted at the same time, as a matter both of structure and of meaning.

Many other transitions between the lexicon and grammar can easily be found. In English, we need to know that the grammatical treatment of inanimate and animate nouns is different; unless we have sufficient understanding of the lexicon, therefore, we shall not produce correct grammar. In German, a semantic difference (motion versus rest) determines whether the preposition *"in"* takes one case or another; thus what in English is a purely lexical distinction (*in* versus *into*) in German must be treated both in the grammar and in the lexicon.

In point of fact, the leakage from grammar to lexicon and vice versa is underlined by the fact that the very language of grammatical analysis is shot through with semantic terms: whether we talk of tenses, cases, modifiers, or even nouns, verbs, and adjectives, meaning is never far away. Even the difficulty faced by the traditional definitions of nouns and verbs seems to evaporate if someone asks us to explain the difference between *water* as noun and as verb. One, we will say, refers to the thing, the other to a process.

What, then, are we to do with the distinction we inherit from our ordinary language between lexicon and grammar? We need only recognize that many useful practical distinctions do not yield a corresponding theoretical distinction but on the contrary dissolve into a continuum when they are looked at more carefully. This is one such. The practical distinction is simply a convenient way of focusing on the two end points of a continuum; Chomsky's mistake was to assume that a theoretical difference of kind must also be present in such a case.

The origin of "grammar" is surely to be sought in the same basic mechanism that, as we saw in the previous chapter, underlies all linguistic categorizing: the need to simplify and render manageable an otherwise prohibitively complex environment. To recapitulate: there can be no language and no meaning without simplification of, abstraction from, and thus organization of situations we confront; the notion of a label for each and every state of affairs is neither physically nor logically possible. It follows that all meaning and linguistic form must arise from the process of sorting, simplifying, grouping, and abstracting which characterizes language. It is easy to show how what we call grammar is only a more general level of organization than is found in the case of individual words, but that it is not in theory the result of different processes.

A simple example will show how this continuity between grammar and lexicon works:[6] let us look again at the category *rabbit*. At issue here is a large number of different individual creatures that show similarities and dissimilarities. Our usage embodies a grouping that has performed a particular kind of abstraction from the animal world. Unlike the word *wolverine* or *mandrill*, it is not restricted to a single species; but unlike the word *hawk*, it does not extend over several genera. The category *rabbit* is thus in a certain sense arbitrary, as all categories are, but this does not mean that it is without a logic—it means simply that a particular logic is its basis rather than another that was also conceivable. All of these different categories make genuine knowledge of the world possible, but they do so in different ways. Knowledge would not be possible at all if we took each animal one by one as a unique new specimen, which in a sense it is; but the shape of the knowledge we can have is determined by the particular way in which our language generalizes.

Suppose now that having set up our category *rabbit* we see a number of individuals that belong to it. We could imagine a language in which we can know such a situation, and communicate it, as "rabbit, rabbit, rabbit." The same would be true of a number of hawks, and so on. But a different kind of simplification and abstraction can now arise, one that groups and relates situations in which there are many rabbits with situations in which there are many hawks. A primitive language might now have a two-word phrase to deal with these situations: "singular rabbit" and "plural rabbit." But in such a language these number words would obviously be overused; that is, while *rabbit* would occur infrequently in speech, only as often as rabbits were talked about, the words used for the concepts "plural" and "singular" might occur in every situation. Such a repetitive general usage would cry out for a more economical means. "Grammar" fills this need: instead of a separate set of words, a convention arises in which the form of the other words (*rabbit*, etc.) is varied slightly, the form of those variations being made typical and thus able to be used generally in the case of other words.

Obviously, there must be a restricted choice of meaning elements that are generalized in this way if this kind of device is to be effective. "Grey rabbit" and "brown rabbit" will likely remain as phrases with two separate words, since we should clutter the system if we varied the form of nouns also for greyness and brownness. But there is no reason *in principle* why all things should not be looked at as grey or not grey, in much the same way as they are all looked at as singular or not singular. The reason for the more economical treatment of number can lie only in the relative frequency of occurrence (and thus relative importance) of the issue of number. To put it another way, only semantic issues of great generality are advantageously treated in this economical way. The more semantic issues that are dealt with in this way, the more complex the system of grammatical markers would become, and at a certain point the advantages of priority treatment for certain semantic issues that recur with great frequency would be lost. (If everything becomes important, the concept of importance loses its meaning.) Singularity versus plurality is so general an issue that it is given "grammatical" status in English. Color is less central but still fairly important; it thus has a status lower down the grammatical scale, indicated not by variation of the form of nouns but by a reserved place in the structure of the nominal phrase.

Two further considerations arise from this example. First, it is clear that in dealing with grammar and lexicon we are dealing most importantly with a hierarchy of semantic issues. In English, rabbitness is lower down the scale of importance of semantic issues than color, since the former is wholly lexical, while the latter achieves a marginal place in the grammar. Color, in turn, is less important than pluralness because the latter achieves a much more commanding position in grammar, one that entails a marking of almost all nouns. We can put this point another way: some semantic issues are so privileged that their presence in a sentence is virtually obligatory. There is a place reserved in the grammar of English for color, but that place may well not be used, and most often it is not. The issue of number, however, is made virtually unavoidable in English. In most cases, we are forced to confront the issue of singularity and plurality of rabbits: we cannot seek to avoid the issue by saying, perhaps, "there is rabbitness." We are only allowed to say that there is a rabbit or some rabbits.

This hierarchy of semantic parameters cannot represent any absolute judgment as to what is semantically important; it is constructed differently by each language, and even closely related languages make what are in effect quite different hierarchies of importance. English and German are both Germanic languages, yet they differ fundamentally in their treatment of the relation of speaker to addressee. German, in common with other European languages, requires that a semantic distinction be made between familiarity and nonfamiliarity of the two actors, with *"du"* as the pronoun for one, *"Sie"* for the other.[7] English has demoted this distinction from obligatory status[8]—semantically the most central part of the grammar—to the outer reaches of the lexicon, where choices may be made among forms of address like "Mr. Smith" or "John" if it is wished. Similarly, some languages make more of number, with a three-way system of singular, dual, and plural replacing our two-way system; some have more, some fewer tenses; and so on.

What is important here is that we are dealing not with two different kinds of meaning (i.e., grammatical and lexical) but rather with meaning and its organization. To be sure, there is a variety, but that variety consists in differing degrees of centrality of treatment, of generalizability, and of obligatoriness. What we call grammar is the collection of those aspects of the semantics of a language which it treats as relatively central and general. The most "grammatical" are those that are so central that they are built into the basic structure of utterances and become obligatory.[9]

So far, we have been able to deal with aspects of grammar in a way that is recognizably similar to that used for the lexicon.[10] In both cases there is form and meaning, the difference being accounted for only by degrees of generality and centrality. There is, however, one very basic aspect of grammar which requires separate comment: the most central categories of a language—in a sense its first semantic choices—determine not just which semantic issues will have the highest priority in that language but what the basic framework will be for all other semantic issues.

I have argued that what is needed for language and communication to be possible is the simplification of a complex environment so that things that are never quite alike are categorized as equivalent, that is, capable of being treated in the same way for the practical purposes of the speakers of that language. But this account already used the term *things,* and that notion now needs further and deeper consideration. This stopgap usage from my previous chapter suggests that stable entities that persevere in time are a given, yet in reality there is only constant change. If no two situations are quite alike, that is in part because no one situation perseveres in the same form either. This fluidity is a further complication to be added to the problem of the inherent complexity of the world: situations differ infinitely from other situations, *and* they are not stable in their own identity either. If we are to be able to categorize situations at all, then, not only must language abstract from the variety of situations to create an equivalence that can serve as the basis of categories, but it must also abstract from the changing temporal sequence to create an identity that perseveres through time. To put the matter more simply, to talk about something presupposes *both* that it has been assigned to a category of equivalent things, *and* that a stable identity has been assigned to a changing sequence of states. Both processes impose an order; to deal with things as if they were stable and constant (which they are not) is again to simplify and thus to distort. To compensate for the distortion introduced when a fluid world is made to sit still so that part of it can be constant enough to be talked about, fluidity has to be reintroduced into the system; and thus arises the noun/verb distinction. The noun allows us to set up an identity by holding a part of the world stable; the verb is the mechanism that compensates for the unreal hypostatization by allowing for the variability of the identities that have been frozen.

Once again, it must be stressed that this distinction is a linguistic construct, a simplification imposed on our world that is necessary if we are to be able to talk about it. To talk about change, we have to postulate a stable identity that can change, but there is no such thing as absolutely stable identity; this is an arbitrary but necessary assumption of language.[11] The noun/verb distinction allows us to fix a part of our world and then to use that fixed point as a reference point to which process, change, and variability can be related. But it also gives us the fundamental shape of the semantic content of language—one so fundamental that it is virtually impossible for us to imagine whether another was possible. Other basic categories of grammar easily follow from this initial semantic split of nouns and verbs; for example, nouns can be either analyzed or specified more closely with adjectives, verbs with adverbs.

Does the noun/verb split exist in reality, or is it simply a construction that is needed to make language possible? Dealing with questions that ask us to imagine a mode of thought that is inconceivably remote from our own is a very difficult thing to do, but it is easy to see how heavily the odds must favor the latter rather than the former. First, the distinction often becomes quite arbitrary even within our language, as the struggles of linguists with words like *storm* show. Here what is abstracted and made a fixed point is quite obviously a complex series of events and changes. And second, the fact that less central categories can all easily be shown to be arbitrary (e.g., some languages have two categories of number, some more than two) tends to suggest that the same arbitrariness must pervade all linguistic categorization, at whatever level of grammar it occurs, and no matter how hard it is to imagine what thought might be like without it. Moreover, the assumption that the noun/verb distinction is a linguistic construct probably makes sense of a variety of otherwise puzzling features of modern knowledge. For example, in physics it is often said that it seems to make no difference whether analysis of light is done in terms of particles or waves, the same results being obtained. This looks suspiciously like the noun/verb distinction, and it may be that we have here reached a point where the arbitrariness of the distinction finally becomes unavoidable.

Traditional arguments against viewing noun and verb as semantic categories have missed the point because "semantic" was always viewed in referential terms: if a particular verb did not correspond to an action or an event, then "verb" could not be defined semantically. Once we see that the distinction is instead one of attitudes built into language, so that nouns treat aspects of our world as if they had a stable identity, while verbs contrast with nouns in being their opposite in this respect, this objection loses its force; no particular problem is posed by a few examples of verbs that do not appear to refer to an event or change. The point is that a primitive distinction cannot possibly deal with reality very well across its entire spectrum. No two-way categorization could. Language orders and organizes, and the noun/verb distinction is its most fundamental means of doing so; we fail to see this if we stumble over the fact that the distinction becomes problematic in some cases. The real key to understanding the noun/verb distinction is the recognition that language has to make a beginning somewhere, and that a simplification is always involved in that beginning.

Many of the classical puzzles and paradoxes of philosophy both illustrate and stumble over the basic mechanism of linguistic simplification. Is the river the same one today as it is tomorrow? The answer is that this is not a paradox once we understand the process that leads to the abstraction *river*. The river will be the "same" because that is how language works—it has abstracted from the many different states of affairs that are involved. Only a bad linguistic theory (for example, one that takes *river* to refer to a particular body of water) has any trouble here. The ancient argument about whether the essence of a thing is separable from the sum of its qualities is a muddle about the relation of adjectives to nouns; different kinds of abstractions are being made by the two grammatical categories. In both these cases, the paradox has reached the limitations inherent in the initial linguistic simplifications. Logical problems that are apparently insoluble will arise if we lose sight of the fact that nouns, verbs, and adjectives are of necessity a somewhat rough-and-ready means of dealing with a complex world by reducing that complexity.

There is one loose end to be considered before we go on: why is it that gender is such a strange matter in the Indo-European languages, one that seems to invite the interpretation that here there is an important aspect of a grammar that is purely formal, without semantic content? The answer, it seems to me, must be sought in the fact that a transition is involved, let us say from a very ancient state of affairs early in Indo-European history when this feature had its full semantic force; through intervening stages where to varying degrees an atrophy of the system can be seen; to a language such as modern English, where the atrophy has advanced so far that the system has virtually disappeared aside from a few fossils, for example, when speaking of ships: "God bless her and all who sail in her." The historical facts of the Indo-European languages certainly show that just such a transition has been taking place. Warren Cowgill summarizes thus: "In many [Indo-European] languages the noun genders have been reduced from three to two (as in French, Swedish, Lithuanian, and Hindi) or lost entirely (as in English, Armenian, and Bengali)."[12] This short illustrative list of those Indo-European languages that have lost the gender system is much smaller than the actual number that have done so; the phenomenon is in fact widespread.[13]

Exactly why this transition should have occurred is not too difficult to imagine.[14] The original Indo-European system developed in an environment where maleness and femaleness (together with all that that distinction related to in human experience) must have been regarded with a far greater and more naive awe and wonderment than could be the case today; the issue must have loomed very large in the lives of the early Indo-Europeans, so much so that they gave it central importance in their beliefs and outlook. That being the case, it would naturally find its way deeper into the semantics of their language, that is, into the heart of the grammar. But as those early attitudes changed over time under the impact of developing knowledge and sophistication, the former priority of gender among semantic issues would be out of place. A transition ensued, at the end of which (in modern English) a reasonably consistent system had finally been reached again. In the intervening transitional stage, however, grammatical gender is in some ways like a vestigial tail; it is still formally there, but often with much-reduced function.

Grammar, then, is the most general semantic frame within which more-particular issues are shaped, but it is continuous with the rest of the semantics of language. As such, it has the most commanding position within a language. In my next chapter I turn to the question of how all these levels of linguistic structure relate to thought.

FIVE

Language and Thought

The relation of language to thought has been extensively discussed, but the discussion itself has generally been a narrowly focused one, and dominated by a small set of questions: Does language determine thought? Does thought exist independent of language? Is the character of our experience of the world, and even our philosophical outlook, determined by the structure of our language? Almost invariably we soon reach a viewpoint that is referred to as the "Whorf hypothesis" or the "Sapir-Whorf hypothesis," at which point a well-known passage from Sapir's writings (rather than Whorf's) is often cited: "The fact of the matter is that the 'real world' is to a large extent unconsciously built up on the language habits of the group. No two languages are ever sufficiently similar to be considered as representing the same social reality. The worlds in which different societies live are distinct worlds, not merely the same world with different labels attached."[1] Later, Sapir elaborated this idea with a dangerous linguistic flourish that was to be quoted frequently in order to attack this linkage of thought and language: "Such categories as number, gender, case, tense,...are not so much discovered in experience as imposed upon it because of the tyrannical hold that linguistic form has upon our orientation in the world."[2]

Benjamin Lee Whorf is generally thought to have elaborated these ideas, or rather to have worked them out and supplied them with so much more in the way of practical examples that the "hypothesis" they are considered to embody is attached to his name more often than it is to Sapir's. The hypothesis has generated much discussion, and from that discussion there has resulted a kind of negative consensus; but for the most part this has been a strange debate in which even the most prominent detractors seem to have had great difficulty in putting their finger on and formulating just what their objections were, and even in spelling out the position they were objecting to. Geoffrey Sampson, for example, having cited the passages from Sapir quoted above, makes the following judgment: "These remarks might be interpreted as mere truisms, but if taken literally they are strong statements."[3] One can only wonder at the suggestion that a statement may be a truism, and yet that it cannot be taken literally: that would be a strange kind of truism. Yet this level of incoherence can be found throughout the controversy surrounding the Sapir-Whorf hypothesis. Here as in so many other discussions of Whorf, one sees that there is something that Sampson finds undeniable in Whorf, something that he finds unacceptable, but beyond that only a sense that these two things are so close to each other that they defeat the possibility of extricating one from the other.

This same structure recurs endlessly. John Lyons also seems to struggle hard (though not hard enough) to formulate what is acceptable and what unacceptable in Sapir-Whorf, but he manages only incoherence in describing both: he rejects the "strong sense" of something he calls "linguistic determinism," which is the belief that "our categorization of the world is totally determined by the structure of our native language," but is still willing to recognize and accept that "particular languages reflect in their vocabulary the culturally-important distinctions of the societies in which they operate."[4] Regarding the former, it is as easy to show that it makes no sense (a point to which I shall return) as it is to show that Whorf never said any such thing. Regarding the latter, Lyons's restricting culturally important material to the vocabulary of a language makes just as little sense; this arbitrary exclusion of grammatical features from cultural relevance would be simply inexplicable—there are too many obvious examples[5]—but for the fact that Lyons is obviously trying to avoid anything that is sufficiently general in its scope to lead in the direction he does not want to go, that is, in Whorf's direction.

Perhaps the two most quoted critics of Whorf have been Max Black and Eric Lenneberg, and to judge from the record of favorable citations of these two in subsequent accounts one would have to conclude that their arguments have been found compelling. And yet in both cases astonishing assertions are made, of a kind that surely indicate that an emotional zeal to reject Whorf is at work, but not the kind of logical analysis that could lead convincingly to that result. Black tells us that doubt is cast on Whorf's view by "the existence of diverse philosophical systems, all expressed with equal facility in such a language as English or German."[6] For a philosopher, this is a bewildering statement. For many years philosophers have been bewailing the fact that those among them in the English-speaking tradition can scarcely even communicate with those whose allegiance is to the Continental (largely German) tradition, so great is the intellectual gulf between them.[7] A critic of Whorf whose own field is philosophy could have been expected to be more aware than most that this puzzling phenomenon is just the kind of thing that is likely to occur if Whorf's analysis is correct; yet Black casually refers to English and German as if they were largely identical in their philosophical traditions, and as if Whorf had missed this obvious fact.

Moving on from philosophical to linguistic inquiry, we can see an analogous case of blindness on Lenneberg's part: "Now, if we believe, as we do, that we CAN say anything we wish in any language, then it would seem as if the content or subject matter of utterances does not characterize or, indeed, give us any clear information on the communicative properties of a language." No one who knows reasonably well a language other than his or her own could possibly entertain such an idea, and yet Lenneberg regards it as self-evident.[8]

Something is obviously wrong with a situation in which the most influential critics of a given view argue so very poorly; the Whorf hypothesis seems to bring out the worst in those who discuss it. As one might expect, what is wrong is that the issue is being framed in the wrong way—a way that almost guarantees that no sense can be made of it. Once more, in theory of language small and subtle changes of formulation can make all the difference. In this case it is an extra link in the chain of reasoning that has done the damage, an unnecessary extra step leading from one thing to another that then becomes an issue in its own right, and as a result a thoroughly mystifying one. The extra step is right there in the question posed by "linguistic determinism": Does language determine thought? Does it even exercise, in Sapir's unfortunate metaphor, a tyrannical influence over thought? But when looked at more closely, these are odd questions, for using language *is* thought. As we have seen, to know something is to categorize, to relate aspects of a situation to aspects of other situations. Language use is not an *influence* on this process but an essential part of it: it is the basis of the most organized and systematized version of this knowledge that we can have. It is only when theorists make language use separate from thought that they can then create the extra step of talking about the influence of one on the other, a step that is not possible if we remember that language use is a form of thought. Once we see this, it is clear that the appropriate way to put the question should not be in terms of the influence of language on thought. Instead, we should ask: What is the relation between this form of thought and others?

Once this extra step is removed, then, the right questions can be formulated, and the wrong ones (with the impasse they inevitably lead to) avoided. The most important aspect of these wrong questions can be seen in the very name given to the issue by those who have discussed it: the Sapir-Whorf "hypothesis." That word is wholly inappropriate to the situation: Whorf postulated no hypothesis. This is an idea that can only derive from the extra and unnecessary step created when we talk about the "influence" of language upon thought. If language and thought were separate processes, one could hypothesize about how the one process influences the other; if they are not, the test of Whorf's thinking must be of another and quite different kind.

The full extent of the confusion and even absurdity to which the extra step leads can be seen when Lenneberg takes this mode of thinking a stage further.

Because he has decided to separate language and thought and so to treat them as quite distinct, Lenneberg stumbles into another pseudoproblem: is language the cause of intelligence—or its consequence? A bemused struggle with this issue ensues:

> Even if species could be compared in terms of general (surplus) intelligence and man could be shown to possess more of this quantity than any other creature, we still could not be certain that his ability for language is the result of, say, general inventiveness. Might it not be possible that language ability—instead of being the consequence of intelligence—is its cause? This...suggests that language might be of greater biological antiquity than the peculiar intellective processes of recent man. Nevertheless, I do not advocate the notion that language is the cause of intelligence because there is no way of verifying this hypothesis. Instead, I would like to propose a *tertium quid*, namely, that the ability to acquire language is a biological development that is relatively independent of that elusive property called intelligence.[9]

This is an almost comic extension of the error of the extra step, but Lenneberg's suggestion that the development of language is a biological phenomenon distinct from the development of intelligence is a consistent result of his thinking. Once the extra step of the question Does language influence thought? has been introduced, then sooner or later the question will arise: Which came first? All we need do here is reject the extra step. We are then free to say what is obvious: the development of language *is* the major aspect of the development of modern human intelligence. These are not two developments but one. The complex categorizations observable in human thought are precisely linguistic in character. From simple general signs reflecting only the few major recurring issues that arise for the signers in the situations they face, through more developed and specific signs dealing with more particular aspects of human needs, to still more-differentiated ones that analyze and categorize aspects of the environment in more and more differentiated ways, human beings must have ascended a scale of intelligence in their handling of their environment in which their linguistic development was by far the most important feature.

In this passage from Lenneberg's essay we can also see how the notion of a hypothesis is used in a way that cripples rather than assists thought. The word *hypothesis* is to be sure part of the vocabulary of careful empirical science, and thus Lenneberg's announced refusal to entertain a certain idea because there is no way to verify it may well seem—at least on the surface—scientifically virtuous. But unfortunately, the difficulties his hypothesis runs into have nothing to do with the absence of a means of verification; they are instead created by the incoherence of a hypothesis that seeks to determine the relation between what it takes to be two distinct things when in reality one is simply an aspect of the other. No wonder it is difficult to test such a hypothesis.

This notion that we must locate a testable hypothesis about the relation between two distinct things has controlled virtually all previous discussion of Whorf.[10] "How are these vague, if stimulating, ideas...to be rendered precise enough for verification?" asks Max Black rather condescendingly, before concluding that "the verdict of competent anthropologists and linguists upon Whorf's suggestive ideas is that until some other 'near-genius,' with a talent for exact thought, succeeds in deriving some reasonably precise hypotheses, there is little scope for profitable argument." In like vein, David Crystal grumbles at "the Sapir-Whorf hypothesis, which distracted attention from more central and testable aspects of semantics for a number of years." Even the editor of Whorf's papers appears to think in similar terms, lamenting the fact that "extremely little research of an appropriate character has thus far been conducted on the Sapir-Whorf hypothesis."[11]

All of this is very unfortunate, for Whorf himself never spoke in a way that suggested he was formulating a hypothesis; nor did he write in a vague or metaphorical way. In spite of Max Black's smug put-down of Whorf[12] (and by implication anyone foolish enough to have thought him a "near-genius") for lack of "exact thought," Whorf's writings are immediately striking for their factual and precise quality. In those writings Whorf refers closely to the thought processes he sees at work (*not* hypothesizes) in particular languages. His emphasis is not on the relation of these processes to other processes but instead on the relation of thought processes in one language to those in another. Thus Whorf thought that in comparing the way two different languages work he was *showing*, not hypothesizing, important differences in the mode of analysis and thus of thought of the two. His most characteristic stance is seen in passages such as the following: "The statement that 'thinking is a matter of LANGUAGE' is an incorrect generalization of the more nearly correct idea that 'thinking is a matter of different tongues.'"[13] In using the idea of a hypothesis, Whorf's critics have had to misconstrue the very essence of what he said, which is that language and thought are not separable; even to speak of the verifiability of Whorf is therefore already to have rejected his way of thinking.

To be sure, even those who are sympathetic to Whorf also seem to absorb the extra step from the accounts of his critics. For example, in the middle of a generally appreciative account, George Lakoff says that Whorf "argued strongly that radical differences in linguistic structure led to radical differences in thinking."[14] Let us look once more, therefore, at the kind of thing Whorf actually said: "Many American Indian and African languages abound in finely wrought, beautifully logical discriminations about causation, action, result, dynamic or energic quality, directness of experience, etc., all matters of the function of thinking, indeed the quintessence of the rational."[15] The emphasis here is on the intricacy of thought *inherent in these languages*—not the thoughts their structures lead to.[16]

Yet another reason to doubt whether Whorf's critics really understood the character of his position can be found in the curious circumstance that other thinkers before and since have adopted similar views without their also being subjected to the condescension and scorn that Whorf encountered. Wittgenstein said that a language was a "form of life," and Saussure before him had taken a similar position.[17] Within the context of their respective systems of thought it is clear that both meant by this much the same as Whorf did: that is, a language represented an agreement between its speakers to analyze the world in a certain way. Charles Sanders Peirce made the same equation between thinking and using language when he argued that thought and knowledge must involve signs, and that use of a particular sign involves an expectation or disposition to act in a certain way.[18] Wittgenstein showed the same awareness of the dangers of separating thought from language when he warned that "nothing is more wrong-headed than calling meaning a mental activity," that is, one existing in the mind distinct from the use of language.[19]

We can now see more clearly just how dangerously misleading Sapir's colorful metaphor was, for his remark about the "tyrannical hold" of language over our view of the world was not just flamboyant—it actually misstated the logic of the situation in a crucial way. Because it did so, it became the focal point of attack not only on his own thought but also on that of his successor, who actually never made this mistake.[20] But there is still another crucial distortion suggested by Sapir's phrase. This is the implication that Lyons focuses upon in saying that according to this view "our categorization of the world is *totally* [my italics] determined by the structure of our native language."[21] And so Whorf acquires yet another liability—a virtual denial of free will and the creativity of human intelligence—and one based once more either in ignorance or in misunderstanding of what he said.

Whorf was often at pains to deny such a determinism. For example: "I should be the last to pretend that there is anything so definite as 'a correlation' between culture and language." He amplified this thought in another passage: "There are connections but not correlations or diagnostic correspondences between cultural norms and linguistic patterns." This kind of caution permeates Whorf's language. When speaking of the relation of grammar to thought, for example, he says that "users of markedly different grammars are pointed by their grammars toward different types of observations and different evaluations of externally similar acts of observation." The delicately phrased "pointing toward" aims to suggest a "connection" but not a deterministic "correlation," to use the terms of the previous passage. And when speaking of the "problem of thought and thinking" Whorf says, *not* that it is entirely linguistic, but instead that "it is quite largely cultural. It is moreover largely a matter of one especially cohesive aggregate of cultural phenomena that we call a language." "Largely"—but evidently not exclusively.[22]

The sweeping positions commonly attributed to Whorf—all thought is linguistic, or our thinking is completely determined by language—are simply incorrect attributions.[23] But it is important to see that these are positions that are of very little significance for theory of language, so that their failure has no important consequences. As to the first of these two absolutist positions: if we conceive of "thought" as any purposive mental activity, then it would have to include what goes on in the mind of a baby when it reaches for a toy; and that is not linguistic. It must be incorrect, therefore, to say that all thought is linguistic. But now if we simply ask, how important are linguistic operations in the totality of the mental processes of human beings? the answer must surely be: they are by far the most important thought processes we have. A thought that is conditional, for example, is a thought of some sophistication and complexity, and it is inseparable from the availability and use of a conditional sentence. Nothing more than this is needed to support Whorf's characteristic attempt at comparative analysis of the different kinds of categorizations inherent in different languages, or indeed to support the most general thrust of his work, with its emphasis on the central importance of language in thought processes.

As to the second position, it is certainly not true that everything in our mental life is completely determined by the structure of our language, for otherwise it would be impossible to account for the diversity of that mental life and its different manifestations in different individuals. Once again, we need to look instead at the form of the question that really matters: how serious a factor is the categorization structure of our language in our understanding of and approach to our world? To this the answer must be: a very serious one, because the categorizations that are inherent in the grammar and lexicon of our language form a preexisting set of categories of analysis that we bring *as a basic framework* to everything we do. Nothing more than this is needed to justify the approach to language taken by Whorf, Wittgenstein, Saussure, or C. S. Peirce. It makes as much sense to say that we are prisoners of our language as it does to say that we are prisoners of our planet. To be sure, in both cases these are conditions of our life that we cannot alter or ignore, but there is considerable room for flexibility and creativity within these boundaries; nothing but distortion is added by emotional words like *prisoner, captive,* or *tyranny.*

To talk in grandiose fashion of worldview or *Weltanschauung* is another way of raising the stakes to a level where absolute determinism seems to come into the picture once again. Superficial objections then easily follow: if language is said to *determine* worldview, many facts of experience become inexplicable. For example, we can observe a variability of worldview among different members of the same language group, we know that individuals can change their outlook while speaking the same language, and we also know that research changes the way we see the world. But none of these facts constitute any kind of stumbling block unless we have locked ourselves into the kind of absolutist position that Whorf always avoided. If instead we start with the view that the conceptual structure of our language contributes the major building blocks of the way in which we see our world, we do justice to the real force of Whorf's position while avoiding the pitfalls of the extremes asserted by his critics in order to reject him.[24]

There are, of course, real issues between Whorf and his detractors, but on inspection they can be found to reside at a more elementary level in linguistic theory. The bedrock source of the objections is almost always naive realism. Langacker, for example, insisted that even if you spoke a different language "you would live in the same world you live in now," a vague statement that can only be true if its content is trivial; if it is not trivial, it must imply that the world has its own inherent categories and that all particular languages do is allow us access to them.[25] Whorf's remarks about the differing experience of speakers of different languages are much more specific, for example, "Facts are unlike for speakers whose language background provides for unlike formulation of them," or, the "automatic, involuntary patterns of language are not the same for all men but are specific for each language and constitute the formalized side of language, or its 'grammar.'"[26] Here there is no vague talk of living in different worlds.

Donald Davidson's discussion in his *Inquiries into Truth and Interpretation* underlines my point. He insists that "truth" is the only real issue in a conceptual scheme: "Something is an acceptable conceptual scheme or theory if it is true." Thus for him "My skin is warm" presents only the issue whether it is or is not true.[27] But that is the reaction of a man thoroughly in the grip of English. As we have seen, even in a closely related language such as German, the concept *warm* is a different idea. Whether attached to water or weather the German word reaches further up the scale than the English word. At a particular temperature, we might indeed use appropriately both the German and the English word, but that temperature would have to be very high in the range of the one and low in the range of the other. Do the words at that particular juncture mean the same thing because they "refer" to the same temperature? No, because we have only to move a few degrees up the scale to find that while German is still using *warm*, English has moved on to *hot*, which shows that the words do not mean the same thing. The English word gives the range of comfortable temperatures, but the German word reaches beyond that to the range of tolerable temperatures, only moving on to the historical equivalent for *hot* ("*heiß*"—but meaning "very hot") when tolerability is seriously in question. Davidson thinks only of the fact that *warm* can refer to a particular state, not of how it categorizes that state, nor of what it says about that state through associating it with a range of others.

So far, I have tried to clear a path through the thicket of pseudoproblems that arise in the course of attacks on Whorf because this is where most of the confusion surrounding the topic of language and thought is generated.[28] But this attack is in any case misdirected in being aimed at Whorf, for the nature of his original contribution does not really lie in what is commonly attacked in his work. Whorf shares with many thinkers, before and since, the idea that the concepts of a particular language are unique constructs of that language and thus part of its structure of thought. To attack him uniquely on these grounds, therefore, is both to misconceive what his original contribution was and to shut one's eyes to the much wider currency of these ideas. Whorf's individual contribution lies in something far more specific than this. It has two major aspects: First, his is a unique attempt to take these theoretical ideas and make a detailed empirical study of their application to the study of particular languages, especially languages remote from the Indo-European realm. Second, he shifted the emphasis of the argument from concepts in the lexicon of a language to the broader realm of grammatical structures. The basic ideas involved were not new, but Whorf's use of them in a careful and detailed empirical study that focused above all on grammar definitely was.

Though the attack on the basic ideas that Whorf used might equally have been directed at other theorists, then, it was in fact directed at Whorf because he pressed those ideas in a unique way. One important consequence of this fact should be noted: because Whorf's importance lies in his empirical investigations, the resulting specific interpretations of his material are in principle separable from the general approach he adopts. I stress this point for the following reason: sometimes Whorf's critics attempt to question his approach by arguing that (in specific instances) he misinterpreted what he saw, or at least that other interpretations of his material are possible. But even if true, this would not give us grounds for questioning his general framework. On the contrary, a persuasive reinterpretation of Whorf's material may well be a continuation of his approach, not a refutation of it.

It was perhaps because a lexicon could more easily be identified with the "culture" of a people—that is, with the stock of its ideas and customs—that serious resistance to this thrust in linguistic theory came only at the point where grammar, rather than simply the lexicon, entered the picture. The case for cultural -transmission through the medium of language in this more limited sense is of course easily conceded by Whorf's critics, for this is a much more superficial phenomenon; it is limited to the set of very specific institutions that find explicit formulation in the lexicon of a language, institutions that may in any case change over a relatively short period of time. What is involved there is little more than the transmission of information by word of mouth (thus only in this limited sense through language) from one generation to the next. The fundamental shape of a language, however, changes only slowly, and transmission through this deeper level of categorization is more persistent. It was this deeper question of the perseverance of a categorization system in the structure of a language that concerned Whorf.

If we consider that Whorf's special contribution to the complex of ideas developed by himself and others was a more serious empirical investigation of the structure of meaning in different languages, it is ironic that the attack on him harped on his alleged failure to adhere to the methods of empirical science. If we measure him against others who took a similar view of language, this alleged weakness is in fact his greatest strength. And there is still another irony here: the great failing of almost all other empirical work on the topic "language and thinking" lies precisely in its making a fetish of the more mechanical aspects of scientific method—that is, controlled experimentation—to the exclusion of really thoughtful observation guided by a well-informed theoretical intelligence. What is really important in science is the imaginative conceptual thought that comes before observation begins. In their zeal to display and to luxuriate in the surface trappings of scientific rigor, most researchers have not first sought to learn anything about the theory of language, with the result that the questions they asked and the hypotheses they formulated were at best relatively uninteresting, and often entirely worthless.[29]

A prominent example of this generalization is the work of Jean Piaget. Piaget conducted experiments designed to show that children learn to conceptualize only at the age of twelve years, and his results duly confirm this. And yet any reasonably sophisticated theory of language should have suggested at the outset that this would be an inherently nonsensical result: since all language use involves conceptualization—even learning to use the word *cat*, which must abstract from things that are of different size, shape, and color—the notion that human beings use language for ten years before they learn to conceptualize is not just highly improbable, it is simply impossible. To use a language is to conceptualize. Unfortunately, Piaget set out to do research on language knowing virtually nothing about linguistic theory, and so he operated with the most naive version of what I have called the default theory—denotation and reference. He thought of words as labeling objects, and evidently supposed that only in the case of abstract ideas such as those involved in religion or the law was conceptualization involved.[30] It was this mistaken separation of labels and (higher) concepts that made Piaget want to look for a date in the life of human beings when the capacity for the "higher" activity manifests itself. The fact that he was able to find results that confirmed this "hypothesis" is a tribute to the ability of the empirical researcher to find what he is looking for, even when his goal is an absurdity.[31] Even granted his premises, however, one must also be completely unacquainted with children to imagine that they do not understand ideas such as "right" and "wrong," "illegal" and "democracy" long before they are twelve years old. Piaget also thought that intelligence antedates language, and that the contribution made by language to human reasoning is simply to make it "inter-personal"; these are extraordinarily primitive ideas for one who wishes to do research into language behavior.[32] An empirical investigation of the development of language function that begins essentially by deciding that no important function will be found for language cannot be expected to produce anything worthwhile.

Essentially the same complex of mistakes is found in that other apostle of the experimental method, L. S. Vygotsky, whose profession of absolute faith in experiment as the unique means of clarifying issues was, as so often, accompanied by very little knowledge of linguistic theory.[33] Like Piaget, he relied on the labeling theory: "Modern linguistics distinguishes between the meaning of a word, or an expression, and its referent, i.e., the object it designates."[34] And again like Piaget, he thought that reasoning could be separated from language, so that "inner speech is to a large extent thinking in *pure meanings*" (my italics).[35] This juxtaposition of an obsessive use of the language of scientific rigor with a theoretical framework full of primitive notions (e.g., "pure meaning") has been typical in experimental work on the topic of language and thought.

The topic of language and thought is certainly one requiring empirical study, but it is also an important part of epistemology—the theory of knowledge —since for human beings the most important means of their knowing the world is through language. Epistemology is a major area of the discipline of philosophy, to which we must now turn in the following chapters. In those chapters, however, I reverse the more usual order of priority in the discipline by looking first at value judgments and only then at epistemology. The reason for this ordering of topics has already been briefly suggested above,[36] but it will become even clearer as the discussion progresses.

SIX

The Problems of Philosophy I:
Ethics and Aesthetics

Few problems are as persistent in human life as that of conflicting value judgments. Two relatively distinct kinds of judgments have been analyzed by philosophers: ethical and aesthetic. The former are naturally considered more important than the latter, but I treat both together here because for the most part they raise the same kinds of issues for theory of language. As we shall see, many intractable philosophical problems have been created and perpetuated by assumptions made about the logic of these problems which are essentially due to misconceptions about how language works.[1]

Ethical philosophy is largely of two kinds: the first is assertive in character, and it generally gives us a particular philosopher's view of how life should be lived. The second is analytical: its concern is rather with elucidating the nature of and justification for ethical judgment. It is with the second that I am concerned here. The typical questions that have arisen in this kind of inquiry have been these: What is the relation between statements of fact and judgments of value—are they fundamentally different in character, and if so, what exactly does this difference consist in? How can statements of what people "ought" to do be justified? What does "good" mean, and how does it differ from "evil"?

The inability of the field to find really compelling answers to these questions answers that might be able to give a solid feeling of satisfaction to at least a reasonable number of its members—is even more obvious here than it has been in other areas of philosophical inquiry. The most important divergence between the various positions taken by ethical philosophers can be seen in the attitudes they have taken to the relation of factual and evaluative statements. There is a fundamental divide between those who have tried to assimilate the one kind to the other and those who, in contrast, have argued that the logic of the two is entirely different.[2] Within these two positions there is also (or at least appears on the surface to be) considerable variation, but in spite of these variations

67

within and attempted refinements of the two basic approaches, the logical problems of both have remained remarkably persistent.

Let us take some simple versions of the two sides of this argument to see what problems typically arise. The attraction of the attempt to assimilate evaluative statements to factual ones is obvious enough. We should like to be able to treat those ethical statements to which we are strongly attached (for example, it is wrong to kill) in the same way that we treat ordinary factual statements that we know to be true. We should like the one to be as undeniable as the other, and if evaluative statements are simply another version of factual statements, we have what we want. The immediate logical objection is that we can observe and verify the truth of factual statements but that no direct observation appears to verify the proposition that it is wrong to kill. In order to progress beyond this point the attempt to assimilate evaluative statements to factual ones has to claim that evaluations differ from ordinary factual statements only in their complexity but not in their essential nature. To verify them would involve far more and far more complex observing, but the essential process would be the same. Thus Leibniz, a cheerful assimilationist, thought that moral maxims would turn out to be amenable to reason, and their correctness shown, provided only that they were fully analyzed.[3] Complex calculation of consequences might be needed. John Stuart Mill's famous dictum "the greatest good for the greatest number" is essentially similar in treating a moral judgment as if it were a complex calculation.[4]

Here, then, is one attempted answer: ethical judgments are highly complex statements, and it is this complexity that makes them seem so different from ordinary factual statements. They may seem not to be directly verifiable, but that is not because verifiability is in principle inapplicable to them—it is only because the process of verification is so complex that no single look at the world (which is all that would be needed to verify, for example, that a book is on my table) can provide enough information.

The logical problems of this position, however, soon become apparent. They are already there right on the surface in Mill's dictum, where an evaluative term is *not* replaced by a host of factual ones, for those replacements are all evaluations too: "good" has been defined using the word *good* again in the definition. The general "good" turns out to be only a summary of many, many situations each of which has had to be evaluated as good or bad before they could be aggregated. The gulf between factual and evaluative statements is, then, not closed in this way; it persists even after an appeal to complexity to close it.

The only apparent alternative to an ethical theory that assimilates evaluative terms to descriptive ones is one that treats them as logically quite different kinds of words. This nonassimilationist position, in its turn, gives us both some attractive features and some very difficult problems. If evaluative judgments are completely different in kind, then their validation must also entail an entirely different kind of process. A different kind of judgment, and indeed a different human capacity, must be involved. This capacity has been variously conceived, but whether we take Kant's moral faculty or G. E. Moore's intuitionism, what is postulated is a kind of special sense that something is or is not right.[5] This kind of ethical theory finds support in our strong intuitive conviction that there is found in human beings a moral sense that is not the same thing as the ability to reason or calculate. But the problems of this position, too, are soon found. If it is assumed that we all have the same moral sense, then it is hard to account for the fact that people disagree sharply with each other on moral issues. Appeals to a moral intuition (for example, "this is obviously right to me and it ought to be to you") usually occur precisely when an argument has broken down completely and reached a bedrock disagreement, and these are therefore conspicuously *not* occasions when a mysterious light of moral truth appears. Even Kant's golden rule (i.e., do as you would be done by) is vulnerable to the fact that different people are occasionally found to have differing views of how they would be done by. Both sides of many celebrated moral arguments can embrace the golden rule without the argument being in any way changed or advanced: the dispute over abortion rights, for example, would not be resolved by the application of the golden rule, or by any other kind of ethical intuitionism.

Exponents of these two major approaches to value judgments (assimilationist and antiassimilationist) have in fact easily managed to argue devastatingly against the other's position without being able to defend their own against the same treatment. Moore, for example, was able to make life extremely difficult for those who were guilty of what he called "the naturalistic fallacy" (the fallacy of thinking that stating a moral judgment was like describing the natural world), but his own ethical theory now has virtually no followers.

The story of recent ethical theory has been a series of attempts to develop and refine these two basic positions. In the case of the assimilationist model, however, refinements have largely been confined to rather marginal issues, while the central logical problems have remained untouched. The development of the antiassimilationist model, on the other hand, has generally consisted of attempts to achieve a more logically defensible position through the costly expedient of claiming less and less for ethical theory, and even abandoning the idea of validating ethical judgment altogether. Let us look more closely at these developments.

If there is one point in ethical philosophy on which most people seem to have been able to agree, it is that John Stuart Mill's version of utilitarianism can be dismissed as logically naive; and yet later philosophers who attempted to develop and improve Mill's position actually retained its most vulnerable feature. Mill's most serious logical problem, as we have seen, was his use of the word *good* as part of his explanation of ethical judgment. A secondary difficulty for Mill is that the notion of a calculus of greatest goods for the greatest number is ambiguous at its core: is the greatest amount of goods to take precedence over the greatest number of people, or vice versa? And if neither is to take precedence over the other how do we know what the correct mix is? If capitalism produces the most goods but distributes them unequally, while socialism produces a far lower aggregate total but distributes them more fairly, which one better fulfills Mill's definition? I call this a secondary rather than primary problem because it is still dependent on the prior use of *good* to explain "good": if the primary problem cannot be solved, a solution to the secondary problem will still not achieve a workable theory. But recent attempts to refine utilitarianism have attempted to deal only with the secondary problem without touching the primary one. The paradox of recent attempts to save Mill's utilitarianism from its image of being a rather simpleminded theory is this: the attempts to refine it and to make of it a more sophisticated theory never deal with the central problem that led to that image in the first place.

Yet even these attempts to patch up the lesser problems in utilitarianism have been conspicuously unsatisfying. John Rawls's theory of distributive justice, an attempt to deal with the ambiguity in Mill's formula of "the greatest good for the greatest number," has had something of a vogue, and yet it takes only a few simple questions to undermine it.[6] Rawls's theory tries to find an answer to such questions as: What kind of distribution would be required for a just result in "the greatest good for the greatest number"? Must an irreducible minimum for the worst-off segment of society be implied, and if so, what kind of *class* is "the worst-off segment" to be? (A certain number at the bottom of the pile? A fixed percentage? And what is the precise number or percentage to be?) All of this will quickly evaporate into arbitrary assumptions that solve little enough of what Rawls explicitly tries to solve. We need only ask, for example: how are fundamentally dissimilar kinds of "goods" (material and other) to be compared and evaluated in relation to each other? (Money, love, security, family, environment, stress, and so on.) How can these apples and oranges be summated in the numerical way required by utilitarianism's formula? Rawls's theory could not even deal with so simple an issue as whether the fifty-five-mile-per-hour speed limit is justifiable. Is the worst-off segment (the extra dead on the roads?) to be regarded as a class (whose protection then becomes a sine qua non)? But in that case would even a thirty-mile-an-hour limit be defensible under the same standard? Remember, once more, that none of this does anything for the much larger -problem of the assimilationist model, the use of *good* to explain "good." Indeed, on this larger matter Rawls simply crosses over to the other side of the divide between the assimilationists and their opponents. Having started off on Mill's side of the fence, Rawls takes a leaf out of Moore's book by postulating that there is a moral sense that resides in all of us—but what is this but Moore's intuitionism once again? And if this moral sense exists in all of us, why is ethical philosophy needed at all?

The root cause of the assimilationist's difficulties is that the attempt to aggregate facts until they add up to value requires quantification on a single scale, and that will mean that it is impossible to deal with the *qualitative* differences in our experience. Must the exciting life of the race car driver be regarded as an unacceptable choice because it may well be shorter? Was the Ayatollah Khomeini simply wrong to reject Western materialism so completely? Is life in a commune a good or bad choice? What percentage of our income should be donated to charities? These are in practice the ethical choices we really have to deal with, and yet the great debate between, for example, "act" utilitarians (will this *particular* act lead to the greatest good, etc.) and "rule" utilitarians (does this *type* of act lead to the greatest good, etc.) is supremely irrelevant to those choices, for both are equally dependent on the notion of the "greatest good," one with far more serious inherent problems than the relatively minor matter that is the subject of this debate.[7]

The crux of the matter is this: utilitarianism must aggregate many different kinds of factual consequences of an action, and aggregation and summation in turn require the prior assimilation of values to facts. But what actually happens (since the planned aggregation proves to be impossible) is the reverse—the factual consequences all have assigned to them an arbitrary *value* in relation to each other. And so in the end this attempt to validate value judgments by analyzing them down to their factual basis actually requires the rampant use of arbitrary value judgments.

The developments in the nonassimilationist camp have been of a completely different kind. Instead of choosing the path taken by the assimilationists—that is, looking for ways to solve the logical problems that had been bequeathed to them by their predecessors while all the time maintaining a faith that some version of assimilationism would eventually be made to work—the path chosen by nonassimilationists was one of radical surgery. They kept the separation of fact and value intact only by abandoning any cognitive claims for value judgments. They no longer tried to *justify* value judgments, and it was in the very fact that they could not be justified that the difference between the two kinds of statements was found. This was, of course, a costly solution: what had begun as a search for the elusive rationale of and justification for value judgments now ended in the denial that any such thing could ever be found. The kind of nonassimilationist attempt to justify value judgments advanced by Moore could not be made to work; therefore, no such solution seemed possible.

Logical positivism provided the first version of this development: value judgments for Ayer are merely emotive expressions that have no factual meaning, since they are not verifiable as all genuine statements ought to be.[8] What happened next was rather like what happened to Mill. It was soon a commonplace that Ayer's view was simplistic, and yet those who (having made that judgment) tried to develop a more sophisticated nonassimilationist account ended by accepting the essentials of Ayer's logic while varying from him only in rather minor, even cosmetic ways. What Ayer had produced was at least a coherent view: judgments of value expressed attitudes, while only statements of fact could be true or false. But while coherent, it did not seem adequate to represent everything in the situation. Is the difference between a judgment I make about Gandhi, on the one hand, and an ax murderer, on the other, no more than a question of my mood and attitude? The great difficulty of Ayer's solution was that the problem seemed not to have been solved but rather abandoned.

But whether or not this is a reasonable judgment of Ayer, subsequent nonassimilationist theories are not materially different from his, even though the conventional wisdom of the field has assigned to them a degree of sophistication that his is considered to have lacked. Whether we look at Stevenson's subjectivism (value judgments are the expression of the speaker's preferences), Hare's view that evaluative statements essentially commend, Nowell-Smith's very similar view that there is a class of words that appraise and express a positive attitude rather than describe, or even the more recent formulation of the same point in the terms of speech act theory (according to which, evaluation is a matter of the perlocutionary effect of language—which really only says once again that evaluations commend rather than describe), we have essentially the same logical structure: statements of fact and evaluations are fundamentally different, and the only coherent account of this difference that seems to be available is one that reduces value judgments to a matter of the attitude of the speaker.[9] It is just as true of all these variants as it was of Ayer's original version that this conclusion can only remain profoundly unsatisfying. It leaves the nagging suspicion that the heart of the problem has been sacrificed to maintain the logical consistency of a flawed position. Who could really be satisfied with the idea that ethical value judgments are only commendations or appraisals?[10] Ayer's successors in this stance sugarcoated his point with language that did not seem to be so uncompromising as his, but once the sugar has been absorbed the ingredients of the pill are just as bitter as they ever were.

Ayer's position is surely more useful than that of his successors precisely because it does nothing to sugarcoat the point: it challenges us to look again at an unlikely conclusion that follows so inexorably from its fundamental premises. He displays those premises with great clarity: they are linguistic. It is the theory of meaning that has led us to so unsatisfying an ethical theory. Later philosophers adopted the linguistic theme more explicitly, calling themselves "ordinary language" philosophers and announcing a method that involved looking at how ordinary language worked, but this ordinary language orientation usually used the same denotative theory of meaning that had led to Ayer's impasse.[11]

The fate of aesthetic value judgments has been roughly parallel to that of ethical judgments, and the unsatisfying consensus reached by about the time of the rise of ordinary language philosophy and speech act theory was virtually the same in that area too. Only the earlier stages had looked somewhat different: the assimilationist position was represented, not by a Mill-like utilitarianism, but instead by the "criterion" theory, which looked for factual criteria indicative of a work of art's greatness. The logical weakness of the criterion theory was exactly the same as that of Mill's utilitarianism, however: the allegedly factual qualities chosen as criteria were themselves evaluative, so that the criterion theory too was using evaluative terms on both sides of the equation.[12] A favorite criterion, for example, was "complexity," but one person's complexity could be another's busyness and clutter, and in fact the quality that was diametrically opposed to this one ("simplicity") could likewise be evaluated as bareness (bad) or economy (good). The gulf between evaluation and description of works of art had not in fact been bridged; the descriptions were already evaluative.

The subsequent development of aesthetics—from Ayer's expressions of attitude, through Nowell-Smith's appraisals, to speech act theory's perlocutionary force—was exactly that which we have seen in the case of ethics, and it leaves the same disappointment. When we say that Shakespeare is a greater writer than Mickey Spillane, are we really saying nothing about the two but simply expressing our attitudes to them? Surely not.

It is scarcely too much to say that in spite of all the energy that has been devoted to patching up Mill, on the one hand, and to reformulating Ayer in a more palatable way, on the other, we have been in a massive impasse in the analysis of value judgments for some time. It is almost an axiom that an impasse of this magnitude must be due to the way questions are being posed: something must have crept into the assumptions we have made when stating the problem which makes its solution impossible. If I am correct, the source of the roadblock in both ethics and aesthetics is one of the fundamental missteps in linguistic theory I have already pointed to in my second chapter: everything in the theories we have been considering begins with the relation between factual statements and value judgments the wrong way round, and from that point onward movement is always in the wrong direction.

As we saw previously, linguistic theory has been hampered by a general misconception about scientific procedure—the assumption that we proceed from the simple to the complex, from the known to the unknown, from the unproblematic to the difficult. The result of this approach to problems in any field is that the unknown is likely to stay unknown, and that what is difficult and complex will stay that way because the concepts we have derived from the apparently simple cases were inadequate; we have in effect made sure to start out with a theory that must by definition have excluded a large set of cases. What trips us up here is an overconfident view of what we thought was "the known," that is, those cases for which we think we already have a coherent view. The trouble is that when we find a view adequate to all cases, we shall almost certainly have to face the fact that the theory that seemed to handle the easy cases got those wrong too.

Beginning with the simple and moving to the complex was what seemed to be involved in starting with factual statements such as those found in scientific observation and then moving on to the more complex value judgments. We find the former far less mysterious than the latter, we think we know what we are doing with them, and so the urge to treat value judgments as if they were a more complex version of the former seems a natural one. Once we begin in this way, subsequent paths have been firmly set: there will be theories that attempt the assimilation, and others that try to explain why assimilation never seems possible, just as we have seen. But in all of this an enormously important assumption has been made, one that has slipped by us without any analysis or justification. The framework that we have adopted has two poles, one of which is simple and basic, the other complex and sophisticated. Mill gives us an analysis of "this act is good" which makes it so complex that to analyze its content would be a never-ending task; a veritable avalanche of future facts would need to be evaluated to determine what it really means.

Yet all of this is upside-down. The key to clearing up the conceptual mess into which ethics and aesthetics have descended is this: evaluative statements (for they are statements, as we shall see) are not complex judgments that everything else leads up to but instead simple and even crude beginnings. They are not the complex end points to which everything leads but instead starting points that must quickly be left behind if thought and judgment are to become more complex. Instead of seeing our task as one of progressing from the simplicity of factual statements to the higher intellectual reaches of value judgments, we shall have to see it as the reverse: we start from the simplicity of crude, undifferentiated statements like "this is good" and move toward the relative sophistication of the more differentiated and developed statements that ensue as we make more-refined categorizations of our environment. This reversal and reorientation will lead to a surprising result: assimilation of the two kinds of statements in the traditional argument is indeed possible—*provided that the direction is reversed*. Factual statements must be assimilated to evaluative ones, not the reverse. Many years of argument have shown that it is not possible to assimilate value judgments to factual statements, and everyone has thought that to have shown this was the same thing as having shown that it was not possible to assimilate the two kinds of statements. But those two results are not at all the same; the possibility that the assimilation might be made in the reverse order remained hidden from view, owing to a prevailing illusion about the logic of factual statements. This is only the general outline of a solution, however; it remains to explain how it will work in greater detail.

To begin to understand how and why a continuum must run from evaluative to factual statements, we need first to consider that the prototype of all statements is much more likely to have been "this is good" or "this is dangerous" than it is to have been "this is triangular." When we make the precise observations of science the basis of our thinking about the nature of language, we are forgetting that they are latecomers; language was shaped long before such observations can have arisen. This temporal priority alone should suggest that we would do better to treat evaluation as the prototype of language, not the increasingly differentiated and sophisticated scientific statements that must have slowly *developed out of them.*[13] The continuity of these simple and even crude evaluations with the eventual precise factual statements is easy to see if and only if we reverse our usual hierarchy and start with the former rather than the latter.

Language, it will be remembered from a previous chapter, works with a variety of categories all of which are functionally well defined, but some of which fulfill their functions only through a tightly organized membership while others represent much more amorphous collections. A category is a simplification and thus creates a particular kind of order and structure; it is not one simply given by the world and is therefore not an unevaluated one. Since function is the basis of all categories, all are to a degree "evaluative"; even a category representing a biological species represents an evaluation of many individuals and of their relation to others.

The most amorphous category of a language is one such as *good.* Here all kinds of things of fundamentally different kinds are gathered together in a category that has only one evaluative parameter: what is advantageous from a human point of view versus what is not. This category, then—one we have been used to thinking of as a highly sophisticated and complex judgment—is actually a grab bag of the most disorganized kind: it can cover all kinds of issues relating to food, shelter, skills, entertainment, relationships, and so on. Somewhat more differentiated than this are statements like "this is a weed" and "this is food," the latter lumping together all kinds of disparate things (leaves, seeds, fruit, flowers, flesh, etc.) because they have a *particular* kind of value to us, the former lumping together a group of plants that have no value for human beings, whatever value they have for other creatures. *Weeds* represent structurally an exceptionally diverse group; without a functional analysis, the category would be bewildering and its unity impossible to find. *Game* and *vermin* are similar kinds of categories, but somewhat more differentiated and thus slightly less amorphous as to their membership. Words like *straight* and *crooked* continue along the continuum, which finally produces the highly differentiated and sophisticated terms of modern science. To be sure, a certain kind of simplicity is achieved through an increased clarity of focus as we move along the spectrum, and in comparison the content of the category *good* could in one sense be said to be more complicated. But this should not obscure the fact that the achievement of this kind of clarity of focus represents an advanced stage of the development of our thought, and that the complication of the more general evaluative category is not that of an intellectual complexity but rather that of a disorganized and more primitive phenomenon—these are essentially unsorted gatherings. As we think more precisely and in a more advanced and organized way, we must leave them behind. Yet this is just the reverse of the appraisal made by the ethical theorist of the assimilationist stripe, who in contrast thinks that we must struggle toward a more complex view of them and, when that proves impossible, finally comes to think of them as rather mysterious things.

The more general the form of a value judgment, therefore, the more primitive and unsorted it is from an epistemological point of view. The category of things or events that are "good" (without further differentiation) is one that reduces a great variety of different instances to a single parameter: favorable or not favorable for human beings. How could we expect so vague and amorphous a category to yield much in the way of knowledge?

To go back to the terms of the traditional debate: the antiassimilationists were quite wrong to say that value judgments were *in principle* not cognitive, and here the assimilationists were correct. But where the assimilationists went completely wrong was in their assumption that the knowledge expressed by such judgments was of a superior kind, for in reality it was exceptionally low-grade knowledge. To know something as a member of a very primitive, undifferentiated category is not to know very much. Here the instincts (though not the actual theory) of the antiassimilationists were closer to the truth.

It is easy to make this clear if we look at a few examples. Suppose that a man walks into a shoe store and asks for a good pair of shoes. The shop assistant will be unable to do anything for him until he asks for more differentiation. Good for what?—walking? running? for dressy occasions (but what *kind* of dressy occasions)? Good for work (but what kind of work)? Good for long wear? And so on. In practice, the customer now becomes more precise, as he must. Now imagine a situation in which the customer insists on the grandeur of the general judgment "good" and refuses to refine on the grounds that it will be cheapened by this reduction of generality. That situation is of course unimaginable in the real world in which we live: anyone who behaved in such a way might find his sanity questioned. Only philosophers behave like that: it is only in the unreal world of ethical theory that the general statement "this is good" can be felt to say more instead of less than more fully differentiated statements.

To be sure, practical situations can force the use of these amorphous categories upon us. If we are going on a vacation and there is a strict baggage limit, our mind must operate with a vague category such as "good things to take on vacation," which will compel us to compare and evaluate the relative advantages of apples and oranges: is it better to take a tennis racket, more books, or a radio? These are epistemologically meaningless choices, but it is only at this level that very general value judgments work. Only factors such as the need to close a suitcase can compel us to work at this crude level; why then should ethical philosophy want constantly to return to it?

Good is therefore a cognitive term, and a linguistic category like any other, but so disorganized a category as to be useless except as a starting point. It is only as this disorganized grouping is broken down and analyzed that useful knowledge results. We shall then reach more-differentiated statements that yield useful ethical facts and *knowledge;* these will all talk intelligibly and even "factually" of such things as the relationship between actions and results, just as anyone interested in ethics should wish.

What is the impetus for the constant return to and obsession with the undifferentiated beginning in moral matters? Frequently when we talk about the morality of an action, we analyze its effects in considerable detail. If, having done this, we finally say that the action concerned was good rather than bad, this can easily be understood as a kind of summary; like all summations, it tells us far less than what is being summarized, but as a practical matter it may serve for those limited practical purposes in which more detail is either unimportant or impossible. The curious fact is, however, that in moral judgment the reductive summary is felt to have a greater, not lesser, content than the full recitation would have had. In no other sphere should we fail to recognize that here priorities have been reversed.

If we make a distinction between action and knowledge, then we can say that while the former is more effective if based on the latter, it cannot reproduce all of its potential subtlety and complexity. The analysis of a situation may be immensely complex, but the need to act brings with it a need to choose a course from a small set of possible actions—those actions that are available to us in the situation—and thus action inevitably simplifies. Until we are forced to act, however, this simplification is unnecessary. General value judgments of the form "this is good" are obviously close cousins of actions, that is, both simplify situations by narrowing the number of categories to a very few and forcing a choice between them. General value judgments are in fact like ethical *decisions* that are required by the need to act, but they constitute a great reduction of the content of moral *knowledge.* The crux of the problem of philosophical ethics, then, is this: the field has felt the pressure to return constantly to the most general form of value judgments without understanding how that pressure originates. For this reason it has allowed the analysis of moral knowledge to become fixated upon that form of ethical judgments which is relevant only to actions but of little use for knowledge; and in the resulting confusion, it has tended to assume that the logical difficulties that then arise are due to the complexity of general evaluative judgments rather than to their crudity.[14]

Another psychological factor that favors generality is the fear that to abandon it would be to abandon general moral principles and consequently to be caught up in moral relativism. In aesthetic theory the corresponding fear is of subjectivism, always felt to be a danger if we abandon a single standard of value, since that might seem to result in multiple standards, which in turn will seem to have abandoned the possibility of validating any one of them. But this is an illusion: the fact that we can give more than one good reason for an action does not mean that those are not still good reasons, and similarly, the fact there are many reasons to estimate Mozart highly does not mean that any of those reasons lack force or that we have decided that all reasons are equally valid.[15]

We can now deal with the recurring question: what is the relation between "facts"—that is, circumstances in our world that we can point to and have others recognize—and value judgments? While the split between fact and value has given philosophers much grief, it never seems to trouble us very much in our real lives. Take, once more, the example of weeds. It is clear that *weed* is nearer the evaluative than the descriptive pole of the spectrum of categories. Weeds, to be sure, are plants, yet not a type of plant defined by structure: we cannot have someone learn the use of the word by telling him that these are plants of a certain shape or size. The meaning of the word is learned instead by looking at the behavior of gardeners: if we abstract from that behavior we shall learn that these are plants that appear when we do not need them and do not want them. So far, we seem to be referring almost entirely to our attitudes in defining the word *weed*. Does this mean that "facts" about the plants concerned are not relevant to their being weeds? Of course not. The plants that give us trouble are those that seed very easily, grow fast, thrive in the absence of cultivation, have no food or other value, and so on. None of this is at all mysterious; the facts have a perfectly clear relationship to the evaluation. Here the "is" (this is a plant that seeds well even in a drought) seems to have a clear and understandable relation to the "ought" (you ought to do your best to get rid of it). The category *weed* is functionally defined but that does not mean that we are unable to see patterns in the structure of the category. The degree of patterning in this case would turn out to be a weaker and looser version of Wittgenstein's family resemblances.

Here we can easily be reminded of what Saint Augustine said about time: we understand it until we start to think about it. Similarly, the relation between fact and value gives us no trouble until philosophers start to talk about it. To be told that we are simply expressing our attitude to a plant, or appraising it, does less than justice to the quite valid sense we have that in calling it a weed we have also said *something about the plant*. On the other hand, to be asked for the defining criteria for a weed would only confuse us, because hardiness and ease of seeding might just as well be thought of as criteria for desirable varieties of carrots or fruit trees. The close relation between our judgment that something is a weed and the facts relevant to that judgment has only been obscured by these attempts to explain them. The causes of a particular plant's being included in the category of weeds are still there at the end of all this, and they are still not accounted for.[16]

The same is true in the moral sphere. If we set out the facts of Mother Theresa's activities, we shall have no difficulty in relating those activities to the judgment that she is a supremely good person, but once we begin to look at them in terms of the criteria for goodness we are immediately in difficulties. The trouble is that many people do completely different things and are still seen as supremely good; and there are even others who did *some* of the things that she did and we think of them as supremely bad. (For example, Jim Jones.) But this problem of the relation between fact and value only arises in each case because we are trying to make our thought process lead up to and culminate in the most general form of value judgment. If on the other hand we see general value judgments as vague and indefinite and the categories they create as amorphous and disorganized, we can treat them in the appropriate way: they are a starting point to be moved on from, not an end point to return to. To ask for criteria no matter what the category is to make the mistake of dogmatically assuming a similar kind of coherence of organization in all categories, including these which are in fact the least organized of all. "Facts" (i.e., statements that are far more differentiated and delimited) should lead on naturally from these indistinct beginnings, just as they do in our real-life deliberations, where the link between values and facts is both real and unproblematic.

Wittgenstein came upon the notion of family resemblances through analyzing the category of games, but as he did so he was evidently thinking more of descriptive than of evaluative words. In that context his discovery was somewhat mystifying, because now a descriptive category seemed not to have anything very clear to describe. His exposition of what was at stake was somewhat tentative—he said only that some words seem to work in this way—and this careful, cautious approach is typical of the best in his procedure; a possibly careless generalization is avoided. But it is also probable that the real importance of this discovery eluded him. For the example he chose was clearly that of a word rather like *weed*, a word that evidently needed a more explicitly functional definition because it was much closer to the evaluative end of the spectrum than the descriptive. When Wittgenstein found that games display a variety of different features all of which are clearly relevant to the idea of a game without any one of them being essential (for example, in some there is competition, but not in all, and some are amusing, but not all), what he missed was that none of this is relevant to the *definition* of the word *game,* any more than ease of seeding is part of the definition of weed. The proper definition of *game* is functional: games are activities that do not relate directly to the purposive activities in our lives. It is the niche they fill in human life that is the focus of their definition. Wittgenstein doubtless thought that he had found a factual definition that was simply a looser alternative to standard factual definition *per genus et differentiam,* but the real point of his discovery should have been the realization that the separation of fact and value had just broken down. He had just given a kind of factual structure for a category that could only be defined evaluatively. Had Wittgenstein seen this, his thought about language would have taken a giant step forward.

It was, apparently, also possible to reach a similar result coming from the other direction (that is, starting from the attempt to analyze evaluative categories) and likewise not to understand quite what it meant. Some thirty years ago I attempted to find a structure for categories that were plainly evaluative, and used the example of a "great king."[17] Still using the language of "criteria," I suggested that there were many criteria for, say, a "great king" in English history, but that not all of those rulers whom we usually judged great met all the criteria. Some of the criteria might even exclude others; for example, kings who increased the power of their country might not be those who made the lives of their subjects better. I concluded that we should expect those that are judged great kings to excel in a number of the relevant criteria, but not all, and that no single criterion was necessary. Only some time later did I realize that in attempting to analyze an evaluative category I had arrived at a point very similar to that which Wittgenstein had reached in analyzing a seemingly descriptive one, for the logic of the result was quite like that of Wittgenstein's family resemblances. The two results, when put together, lead unmistakably to the conclusion that the opposition of facts and values is actually a continuum. That in turn should lead to the realization that we are not dealing with two fundamentally different kinds of words, and that a single logic should therefore be able to deal with the definition of all.

I conclude that there is no reason why ethical concerns cannot be treated as precise and "factual" in the sense in which we usually understand this term, provided that we realize that the form of ethical judgments which we have regarded as the most profound is actually the most primitive. The same reasoning applies equally to aesthetic judgments: if we substitute the words *great* or *beautiful* for *good* or *just,* the arguments I have set out here will lead to similar results. The logic of the subjectivists and the criteria theorists is faulty in just the same way that we have seen in the case of ethical theorists.

The "good" (or the "just") and the "beautiful" have had a long run in ethical and aesthetic theory, in both cases beguiling common sense and rendering the theory of value utterly mysterious to us. The antidote to this needless mystification is simply a better sense of how language works.

SEVEN

The Problems of Philosophy II: Epistemology and Logic

Epistemology is that branch of philosophy which deals with philosophical questions concerning knowledge. The questions that are generally taken to be central to epistemology form a closely related group: What does knowledge consist in? What can we know? What are the objects of our knowledge? What is truth, and what are the criteria for a true statement or the conditions under which it is true? To these traditional kinds of questions another was added when logical positivism introduced the idea that statements had to meet certain logical standards before one could usefully consider whether they were true or not. The test proposed—What are the criteria for a meaningful proposition?—added to the small group of central epistemological questions the further question: do all or only some propositions give us knowledge, and if only some, what is the difference between those that do and those that do not?

Much of the energy and attention of those who have pursued these questions has been absorbed by a single central problem, that of validity. How is knowledge to be distinguished from mere opinion? A claim to know something implicitly includes the claim that this is valid knowledge—but how is knowledge validated? Perhaps three different concerns arise. First, the problem of illusion: we may be dreaming or hallucinating. Second, the problem of inference: we may have inferred incorrectly from things we know to something we do not know but think erroneously that we know. Third, the problem of misinformation: we may be giving credence to, and inferring from, reports that are false. How can we be certain that we are not dreaming, not inferring falsely, and not being misled by false reports?

The result of much analysis has left on the whole a very simple answer: we can never be absolutely sure. Where did this leave the distinction between knowledge and opinion? Not very clear, it seemed, and yet here was one of those cases where only philosophers seemed to think there was a problem: the distinction between knowledge and opinion continued to be used by everyone else. In his book *The Problem of Knowledge,* Ayer offered what seemed a reasonable solution: there was no such thing as absolute certainty, but knowing something should essentially involve having the *right* to say one knew it, that right having been earned by virtue of the procedures one (and perhaps others) had gone through to reach this point.[1] What made this position seem unassailable, though also unremarkable, was that it was a practical definition, one that had all along been assumed in the everyday behavior of those whom, presumably, philosophers had been intending to enlighten. Small wonder that while it seemed a sensible solution, it also seemed one that was philosophically quite uninteresting: the philosophical business of conceptual analysis had yielded in this case to a simple description of the behavior and attitudes of the naive, nonphilosophical world. The philosophers had promised to burrow more deeply into the problem than ordinary mortals but had eventually just returned to the surface to join everyone else. I remember occasions when Ayer was taxed by students wanting to know what these answers really added to human knowledge, and his only reply was a rather defensive admission that philosophers sometimes worried about questions that nobody else worried about. But this was a considerable retreat from the importance philosophers claimed for their work in other contexts, and it avoided the question whether philosophers could offer any more broadly acceptable justification of their interests.

Much else in philosophical epistemology deals with questions closely related to this one, and the process we have seen here of asking imposing conceptual questions but finally returning simply to describe our everyday habits is repeated in them. A celebrated example is the question of how we experience the outside world: do we have knowledge of objects themselves or only of the impressions they make on our senses? The problem is that the very notion of direct experience of objects (i.e., nonsensual) is such an odd and even impossible one that even to postulate a choice between these two possibilities seems artificial. Most people know that a sugar crystal under a microscope looks quite unlike what it seems with the naked eye and therefore that our experience of objects is a function of the equipment we have to see, hear, and touch with; and they also know that the consistency of our experiences strongly suggests a comfortable, constantly tested, and confirmed assumption that there is an outside world of objects. Therefore, when Richard Aaron in the 1986 *Encyclopaedia Britannica* article "Epistemology" still (more than thirty years after Ayer's very tidy and honest account) tells us that "of central importance to epistemology is the alleged assurance of the existence of a physical world," the reader cannot help feeling that this is a problem that has to be invented in order to be found worth solving.[2] In contrast, ethical problems seem to present themselves whether we want them to or not.

Both the starting point and the predominant emphasis of philosophical epistemologists, then, seem clear enough: speaking of the concept "knowledge," Aaron tells us that "the use that most concerns the epistemologist is knowing that something is the case."[3] But as we shall see, to formulate the aim of epistemology in this way is to ensure that it remains the uninteresting topic it has so often been; this opening move sidesteps the infinitely more important prior question of what knowledge consists in, with the result that epistemology remains tied to relatively trivial questions. Once again, the source of this intellectual failure lies in inadequate ideas about language.

If the major concern of epistemology were really a matter of our knowing or not knowing that something is the case, then its focus would quite naturally be on examining and attempting to specify the conditions under which we can have reliable access to whatever is "the case." But to see the situation in this way is in fact to have already bypassed what should have been the core area of epistemology. If we begin with the naive realist's theory of language, as most unwittingly do, then whatever is "the case" is a fact independent of linguistic formulation and thus of categorization. From this it would follow that to speak of "knowing" is to speak only of the process of our gaining access to the facts, and this in turn will lead naturally to the attempts made by many analytic philosophers to purify the linguistic instrument through which we refer to them so that the act of referring can be purged of any ambiguity or imprecision. If states of affairs *as they are expressed in propositions* exist independent of the knower, our problem is only one of making sure that the knower does his job of locating and specifying them cleanly and precisely. But if all of this is so, a large puzzle arises: if this really were the sum total of the epistemological problem, how could we account for the fact that it has caused us so much trouble? The character of knowledge would be crystal clear, and the only problems remaining would be laziness and sloppiness—yet neither of these is a *theoretical* problem.

All of this misconceives in a fundamental way the role played by language. While undoubtedly *something* exists independent of the knower, to know anything about it is to have done something to it: to categorize it, to relate one situation to others, to place it among others, to situate the experience of it among other experiences. An individual with a language can know a situation in a way that is not possible for an individual without a language. To use language, in particular *to state through means of language that something is the case,* is to process the immediate experience and relate it to other experiences, not simply to receive an impression from the outside world and express nothing but the inherent structure of that impression. To return to the discussion of my third chapter: if we attempt to think of knowing as the direct apprehension of something before us, in itself and taken by itself alone, we should know nothing and be able to say nothing. If we look at the temperature of a substance, we cannot say what that temperature is without relating it to something else, because the very notion of putting a figure to it will presuppose a relation to the temperature of something else; in the case of both the Celsius and Fahrenheit scales, what is given is the relation of the substance being measured to the freezing and boiling points of water at a certain pressure. If someone asks us what the temperature of the substance is *taken only in and by itself*, we can only say that he is asking an incoherent question. Speaking about phenomena is a matter of relating them to each other, and if we do not wish to do that we cannot speak at all. We can say that something in front of us is a cat or a mammal or a female or grey or an animal or a pet or a nuisance or many other things. But if we ask the question what it really is, taken in and by itself, before we get to linguistic categories, no answer can be given. This is not to say that these categorizations do not give us knowledge of the thing we are looking at; it is simply to say that to know is to categorize, and that our language is the system of our categories, and thus of the instruments of our knowledge. To look at a thing and to try to know it as something that "is the case" simply by itself is impossible. To know something and to speak of that knowledge is to organize and analyze experience, not simply to receive it. From this it must follow that the focal point of epistemology should be, not on what is true and false, but instead on how and why this categorization rather than another is used.

We can now see why the obsession of so much philosophical epistemology with "truth conditions" is beside the point,[4] and why so potentially fruitful a study should have bogged down in questions that never seem very interesting. The manufactured problem of whether the external world exists and the surely minor problems of guarding against illusion and misinformation pale in comparison with what should be the real problem of epistemology: what is it that we do with experience when we perform the action we call "knowing"? Granted that knowing is analyzing and processing experience, and that the framework for and instrument of that analysis is the structure of a language, with its preexisting overlapping levels of categorization, what can we say in general and in particular about the process of knowing? Since we know that the central role in that process belongs to language, any answer to this basic question must begin with the structure of categorization in particular languages.

To be sure, conventional epistemologists also routinely acknowledge the importance of language; Aaron himself says that "what distinguishes contemporary epistemology from earlier studies in the field is its profound interest in linguistic problems." What such a "profound" interest consists in, however, can be seen in the comment that immediately follows: "Some writers have spoken of the need for a special, technically exact, philosophic language." But that is tantamount to saying that epistemologists are not really interested in language at all.[5]

Chomsky, too, has linked epistemology with the structure of language (for example, in his *Language and Mind*), but not in a profitable way. His view that syntax is a structure built into our minds is not one the truth or falsity of which need concern us very much, for it lacks any real content; from the point of view of epistemology, it is inconsequential. It tells us nothing about the structure of knowledge other than that we are constitutionally able to deal not only with individual categories but also with hierarchic and overlapping arrangements of categories, and we know this well enough already. This position is not simply a harmless irrelevance, however, and it does more harm than just to deflect attention from more productive ways of thinking. Chomsky makes explicit some destructive implications of his view when he goes on to say that "the theories of philosophical grammar, and the more recent elaborations of these theories, make the assumption that languages will differ very little, despite considerable diversity in superficial realization, when we discover their deeper structures and unearth their fundamental mechanisms and principles."[6] In other words, all languages are fundamentally the same because they can all be reduced to a highly abstract schema. By the same token, all creatures (or houses, or books, and so on) can be said to be fundamentally the same. Thus the great diversity of human languages and of their ways of categorizing experience is ignored; and this encouragement to ignore the diverse substance of languages comes from—of all people—a linguist.

One last point needs to be cleared up before we proceed: it is as well to see what the position we have arrived at does *not* commit us to. One common development out of the conventional focus in epistemology on the "facts" of the external world is a skeptical leap to a diametrically opposed view: we then have knowledge only of our own thought processes and/or language. This position is the result of a mistake that arises in many different situations. Essentially, it sees that there are overwhelming and irremediable problems in a standard view but retains the terms of that account, with the result that a radical skepticism is the only possible outcome. This thought process never leads to an intellectually coherent position because it essentially gets no further than telling us that there is no genuine knowledge of the external world *if we define knowledge as the standard account defines it.* Yet since we know very well that we do have considerable knowledge of the external world, this skepticism must obviously have missed the point: knowledge of the external world will have to be formulated in some other way.

Richard Rorty provides a good example of this misconception. Rorty sees well enough the triviality of the common emphasis in epistemology and recommends that we turn our attention elsewhere, but his alternative consists only of a knowledge of our own thought processes.[7] What Rorty never sees is that he has accepted more and rejected less of the standard account than he thinks. He uses the terms of its flawed analysis, and that analysis is thus the essential basis both for the position he criticizes and for his own. We need only look at the implications of his position to show this. Even if, with Rorty, we confine ourselves to statements about our own thoughts, it would be impossible to conceive of any useful statement about those thoughts except insofar as they refer to our experiences of the world around us. If, on the other hand, thought processes really are to be restricted to their own inherent character (that is, if Rorty's position is to be *genuinely* different from that which he criticizes), Rorty will have left himself unable to deal with the fact that we can plausibly be said to know more about the external world than people did in earlier times.

The suggestion that language is all and that "there is nothing outside the text" is a wilder and less cautious version of the same point, but one with a similar logical structure.[8] Here we should recall once again that when we look at the vocabulary of temperature differences, the words concerned can have no meaning without some variation in our experience to which they can relate: it is just as wrong to say that forty-five degrees Celsius is simply a fact of our language as it is to say that it is simply a fact of the world. In point of fact, these are two sides of the same mistake.[9]

Well-thought-out positions that avoided this premature skepticism were already available, however, to anyone familiar with the history of linguistic theory. Whorf, for example, saw that subject and object are both needed to account for language and meaning, and Peirce held that words imply actions with regard to things and expectations of them, not just reference.[10] Either could have been the starting point for the valuable new approach to epistemology that was possible after the shortcomings of the prevailing approach had been understood.

A similar attempt to break loose from the problems of the defective epistemology of brute "facts" arose in the realm of aesthetic theory, where a recognition that referential definitions cannot work with concepts such as "art" led W. B. Gallie to postulate a special kind of "open" concept, one that is "essentially contested." This kind of concept, Gallie thought, arises to provide a locus for contesting the nature of art. But this is on its face an inherently implausible idea: the concept of art has important work to do in our real world besides getting good arguments going.[11] Gallie's theory is ingenious but wholly mistaken, and the source of his error is evident: "art" is a concept that is especially hard to deal with using the standard theory of definition.

Although nothing very useful can be done in epistemology if we restrict ourselves to the narrow question whether something is or is not a fact, there is much valuable and interesting work to be done in what should instead be its central area: the analysis of how facts are constituted by different languages. Goethe's dictum is again useful here: the most important thing is to grasp that everything that is "factual" is already theory. To understand facts we must look at the system of categorization that produces them. It will then certainly be possible to ask whether a particular fact is the case, as long as we remember that it can only be the case given the system of analysis that constitutes it. No fact is ever irrevocably "solid," because the system of which it is a part can always be questioned. That does not prevent us from saying that facts are facts, however; for in leaving open the possibility of reshaping the facts we cannot be waiting for any *ultimate* system that will finally correct our misconceptions. We have to use a particular system, and whatever that system is, it will still have to categorize as others do: it will still simplify and make equivalent things that are not identical. But can we say that one system is more useful than another for particular purposes? It would seem that we can, but this too must not be misunderstood. Facts as understood within the Newtonian framework apparently can be stated in a way that is suitable for most uses. Those facts are all subject to reformulation in the Einsteinian framework, which seems to work better for some purposes and not worse for any. Does this mean that Einstein is the truth while Newton is not? Not at all. The fact that a well-observed body of data has already had to be reanalyzed from start to finish on one occasion should tell us that the same could happen again. We can never rule out a need for a new system, and it is in this kind of transition that we can see the really interesting work of epistemology, not in the overblown concern with verification and truth.

The most practical work that might be done in epistemology at the moment would lie in the comparison of the epistemological structure of different languages. A sense of what this kind of inquiry could do might emerge, for example, from a look at the differences between the German and English languages in light of the different kinds of philosophical thought that have been characteristic of the two linguistic communities since the German language began to be used for learned purposes in the late eighteenth century. We seem to enter a different universe when we go from Anglo-American to German philosophy, and this fact is almost a source of despair to many who have to deal with both. The Germans lean heavily to abstraction and to metaphysical speculation, while the English are more empirically minded. Is this simply an accidental cultural difference? Many observers have said that German philosophical language itself is a barrier, and that simply to speak German is to enter a different world of thought. Yet to relate the two kinds of thought to the two languages could not simply be a matter of a different vocabulary, for that gap could be bridged by inventing or importing a few new terms. One could surely guess, therefore, that the relevant linguistic differences would have to be of a broader and more strategic character— that is, the differences would likely be at the more general level we call grammar. Do strategic differences in categorization exist that could be important enough to have any bearing on such large differences in philosophical thought? Indeed they do.

There is a crucial difference between the two languages in their treatment of abstractions: while both have at a primary level the standard Indo-European array of grammatical features with which to abstract from experience, that is to say, nouns, verbs, and adjectives, German has an important area of flexibility that allows easy movement between these different kinds of abstraction. Any adjective can be converted into a noun merely by capitalizing it and providing it with a definite article. We know this in English only through translation from languages that allow it: "the Good" is for us an uneasy usage that is recognizable as philosophical talk and thus alien to common usage in our language, but it is quite ordinary German to shift adjectives to noun status in this way. This is a profound difference in conceptualizing. The basic model of thought common to both languages is one of a three-way system of abstraction: a part of experience is held constant (noun) so that change or variation (verb) in particular aspects or parameters (adjectives) can be expressed. But in German, an expression that originates in order to deal with variation of a fixed point can itself become fixed. In other words, the arbitrary three-way separation of different kinds of abstraction is complicated by the fact that two of the three can be readily converted to the other. English can of course manufacture particular examples of such a crossover from one basic category to another, for example, from *good* to *goodness*, or the other way round, from *book* to *bookish*. But these are relatively clumsy devices that draw attention to the origin of the new words in grammatically different ones, and in any case the resulting meanings are of quite different and much narrower scope: a *bookish* person is a much smaller category than that of people who read books, and *goodness* relates only to a particular kind of *good*. No easy transition is available that works in nearly all cases and that also retains a comparable scope of meaning, as is the case in the shift from *good* to "the Good."

It is not difficult to imagine that this difference in the way abstractions are handled might have something to do with the characteristic difference between German and English philosophy. German is more at home with a greater variety of abstract ideas than is English, and a connection between this feature of the language and a more speculative, idealistic philosophy is easy to see.[12] The English language, meanwhile, is more likely to talk of "good things" than of "the Good," and this proclivity seems to connect well with the fact that philosophizing in English is in general much more empirical. Both sides commonly claim to have the advantage: the Germans that they are more abstract and philosophical(!), the English that they are more analytical and less prone to ill-defined abstractions. There will be more to say on at least a part of the substance of this dispute later in this chapter, but for the moment it suffices to say that the philosophical difference between the two language communities is no longer surprising even after we have only looked at this single epistemological difference between the two languages. There are of course many others: to look at this one feature would only be a beginning of the serious comparative study of the epistemology of the two languages.[13]

Individual words and ideas may well be more or less transferable from one language and culture to another, but differences in the way ideas are framed are a quite different matter. Much more profound cultural differences may be embodied in this deeper level of the conceptual system of a language: here we are dealing with those fundamental aspects of a language that give its meanings their general shape and that therefore can change only over very long periods of time. They are in a sense basic institutions of a culture, ones that will persevere while others that reside merely in individual words can change in a single generation.[14]

The obstructive effect of a misconceived theory of language on philosophical epistemology cannot be overstated. The restriction of the field to questions that are relatively unimportant has made the field a stagnant one with very little new thinking of real substance since at least the 1950s, and what innovations there have been over that time have themselves been heavily infected with the same problem. Once again, we can see an example of this in the recently increased interest (both in linguistics and in philosophy)[15] in Bertrand Russell's Theory of Descriptions. That theory sets out to "make explicit the information which is implicitly contained in the use of proper names or left to be picked up from the context."[16] More generally, it seems designed to reformulate propositions so that all their implied information content is clearly and exhaustively stated. The impulse we see at work here is the familiar one: since knowledge is all about reliable access to what "is the case," what is most important is that we should pin down exactly what is being asserted in any particular proposition. Russell's theory is a first cousin of logical positivism, the only difference being that there the analysis is turned toward distinguishing those propositions which genuinely assert that something is the case from those which do not, while here it is turned to making the content of the former clear and precise. In both cases, epistemological purposes are thought of as being thwarted by linguistic complexity or obscurity, and a process of purification is therefore advocated that will leave us face-to-face with a clear statement—on the one hand, of what kinds of statements assert facts, and on the other hand, of just what those facts are. In neither case is there any doubt about the solidity of facts.

It is not difficult, then, to interpret the recent upsurge of interest in Russell's theory; if the theory worked, it would solve everything and avert the pain of reconsidering theoretical commitments. But those who refuse to learn from history really are doomed to relive it, for this was also the motivation of logical positivism and logical atomism. There is much irony here in the fact that the underlying motive—to reach statements of the facts so simple and basic that epistemology would then become a simple matter—is part of a theory that actually makes life very difficult for philosophers: the more problems encountered in the pursuit of this simple solution, the more frenzied and confusing the search becomes. A related development in some parts of the MIT tradition in linguistics has been a turn toward the language of symbolic logic, a recognizably Russellian response to the impasse in the field. Once again, we are seeing "truth conditions" as the leading idea in semantics, and the concomitant assumption that what we have lacked until now has been a more rigorous kind of analysis of the content of propositions, rather than a different and better general theory. This will only mean that greater and more precise efforts are to be devoted to the same *kind* of activity within the framework of the same basic ideas. This misdirected effort does not appear to be producing the long-sought solution, but it is certainly verifying one well-known maxim quite conclusively: all the rigor in the world will not make up for an initial bad assumption.

As all these examples show, the recurring problem for theory of knowledge is that semantic primitives and uninterpreted facts always sneak back into the picture no matter how many times they have been discredited. The result is that in all kinds of circumstances people are using, or are responding positively to the use of, the essential logic of positivism, though most would be genuinely distressed to realize they were doing so.[17] One of the latest attempts to fix semantic theory, for example, is the recent volume of Barwise and Perry, *Situations and Attitudes*. There are glimmers of hope early in the book, when although the authors announce a concern with communication in general, they also tell us that their central concepts will be "situations" and "attitudes," which sounds more promising. They even make some remarks that are critical of Russell's logic. But soon enough, the two are looking for salvation in a universal typology, which takes us back to semantic primitives yet once again.[18] The promising beginning followed by eventual return to the same familiar error is a pattern repeated by many.[19]

Even that seemingly sophisticated and modern development, speech act theory, repeats this pattern. As we have seen, Wittgenstein begins the *Philosophical Investigations* by setting out the semantic theory that makes words denote or stand for things, then goes on to show that there is far more to meaning than referring, denoting, and asserting, and gives a long list of things this limited theory cannot deal with. (The list includes giving orders, playacting, asking, thanking, greeting, and many others.) This is another good beginning, with a move away from assertions and their concomitant truth conditions. The beginning could be built upon if we took Wittgenstein to be saying that there is so much that the labeling and asserting theory cannot deal with that it must be rethought *in its entirety*. But it will be wasted if, on the other hand, we keep the basic denotative theory and merely *supplement* it, taking Wittgenstein's point to be only that we should look at other things language does too, for the entire thrust of the argument demands the first of these two interpretations. Speech act theory takes the second path and so gets back to square one all over again, for if we ask which is the most important of these various functions of language there will be no doubt that asserting facts will count as the most central, and that function is still conceived in the way it was before speech act theory, that is, in the way Wittgenstein rejected.[20] To believe that his work really leads in this direction we should have to ignore all the rest of the *Philosophical Investigations*, especially those parts of his argument that question the idea that there are simple facts, or that the basis of categorization lies in the simple apprehension of common properties.[21]

This regression to older and more-primitive positions and the neglect of more-promising ones is one of the signs that philosophy as a field is not in good health. After its brilliant progress in the earlier decades of this century, analytic philosophy has bogged down and stagnated; the field has lost its momentum and excitement, its concerns have become somewhat routine and in many cases even trivial, and it now has a distinctly parochial air. The philosophical vacuum thus created has predictably been filled both by a resurgence of Continental metaphysics and by an anxious search for new areas—medical ethics is one— that would formerly have been regarded as backwaters. Formerly, analytic philosophers seemed to like to maintain a high public profile, to make claims for their work that went well beyond their own discipline, and in general to meddle to their hearts' content in work in all kinds of other fields. But to communicate with this larger academic world they had to speak a language accessible to it. In contrast, recently we have seen the rise of highly technical language that insulates the field from its neighbors, and yet that technical jargon often clothes thought based in an underlying linguistic theory that is not correspondingly complex but on the contrary quite unsophisticated. The character of the claims that philosophers make for and about what they see as their most important recent work tells us the same kind of story: what is most striking about, for example, the common claim that "direct reference" is the most important new idea in analytic philosophy in recent decades is that this (even if sound, which is very doubtful) is an unusually limited idea to make the subject of so wide a claim: at best, it is a refinement of little interest to anyone besides the scholars who debate it. Philosophers usually put forward far broader claims for their best ideas.

If I am correct, the key to the descent of analytic philosophy into a routine and pedestrian state lies in the wrong turn that occurred when Wittgenstein's new ideas in the theory of language—ideas that should have fundamentally redirected epistemology—were instead allowed to degenerate after his death into the uninteresting world of ordinary language philosophy, which offered little more than the occasional piecemeal corrective to premature generalizations about the meanings of individual words.[22]

Theory of knowledge should concern itself above all else with the organization of meaning and the structure of categorization in languages, for these phenomena are at the center of epistemology. We know something only by relating it to other things in the way that our language alone makes possible through its hierarchy of categories. This general recommendation for a new and more useful direction in epistemological study would doubtless raise new issues and problems for epistemology; however, some new light on older concerns might also be expected, for example, the matter of distinguishing valid knowledge from invalid and meaningful from meaningless propositions.

Take the case of new philosophical coinages, that is, new concepts (whether or not they use existing verbal forms)[23] introduced specifically as part of a new philosophical argument or set of ideas. If we look at proposed philosophical concepts in light of an adequate theory of language, some important considerations will be suggested. New coinages are not part of and are thus not given their meaning by the highly complex set of agreements embodied in a natural language. New terms (or distinct new usages suggested for existing terms) are artificial ones created in the single moment and act of their proposed definition. It follows that when they are compared to existing words in a natural language these artificial words can have only a rather simply stated meaning, since the complex set of agreements developed by many individuals over a considerable period of time (e.g., the case of *game*) is replaced here by a single act by a single individual at a particular time. Since it lacks the backing of a well-tried place in a larger structure of concepts, such a definition must constitute a clear and complete stipulation without any ambiguity, something only possible in the case of concepts with the simplest structure. As a consequence, any stipulated definition that is in any way unclear or ambiguous fails, since there is no other source outside the initial definition from which more about the meaning of the word can be learned.

Given this requirement for successful new coinages, then, it is quite likely that much of what logical positivism wanted to do—to rid the philosophical world of unclear concepts and arguments—could legitimately be done by invoking it. All branches of inquiry need to be able to introduce new concepts as they become necessary, and introduced concepts with clearly stipulated definitions play an especially important role in the physical sciences. But it is important to see that these are linguistically atypical in that they are exact; in contrast, Wittgenstein showed that in ordinary language there is no single ideal of exactness.[24] The command "Stand over there!" is successful though it does not specify a precise distance away from the speaker or the boundaries of an area. New coinages in a field of study, on the other hand, must make up in precision what they lack in an established place in the system. Many of the coinages that the logical positivists tried (eventually unsuccessfully) to reject using the verifiability principle would fail to meet the test of precision.

There is another important conclusion to be drawn from the fact that new terms with clearly stipulated definitions are artificial usages: it is that since the terms of logic and mathematics occupy this same place in our language, they are similarly artificial within the linguistic system. (Once again, the archetype of language is to be found not in artificial terms like *triangle* but rather in words like *good*.) This means that logic and mathematics must be a very poor model for natural languages, and that those who want to analyze natural languages as if they were formal languages make a very serious mistake.[25] It is easy to show why this is so.

In the real world, a set of things that is based upon the absolute identity of those things is as a practical matter very rare. In an infinitely varying world, the decision as to what level and kind of similarity/dissimilarity will count as equivalence is an arbitrary one: it depends among other things on how many or how few categories will be the most useful to us. The decision is dictated therefore by human considerations, not simply by the structure of things. From the infinite number of possible groupings that are available, a linguistic community has chosen those that (for good reason) it is interested in, and our language is structured accordingly. In formal logic, on the other hand, the meaning of each term is precise only because the system of terms has no reference outside itself: it is cut off from those functional concerns and categorizations that make language what it is.

This remoteness of formal logic from our actual use of language can be seen in the fact that, for example, a set (not a category) is designated by a letter (x); since none of the particular organizing principles inherent in a specific real-world category can now be relevant (because they cannot be known), all subsequent argument must be based on an absolute identity of all members of the class. But this means that the most important and most central feature of language is not present in this kind of artificial language: it has been completely bypassed. In our speech, categorization is based not on absolute but on functional equivalence; the members of a class are not identical but are equivalent for the purposes of a given category, and those purposes vary greatly. We know that stealing is a crime, but the concepts "stealing" and "crime" are functional categories with greatly differing members. Marginal members of such categories are also still members. Now if we try to use a formal kind of logic that assumed that each member of a category were identical with all of its other members, we should misrepresent the situation and not be able to reason correctly in the real world of experience.

Many linguists and philosophers have tried to push language toward logic and mathematics in order to make its working more precise and thus (as they have thought) more unambiguous and more useful to us. There could be no greater misconception about language than this. Logic and mathematics are specialized, restricted forms of language that lack its essential reality—its arbitrary and yet fixed system of making equivalences. This is what makes language useful to us, and what makes knowledge possible—not a regrettable imprecision and untidiness, but on the contrary a means of managing our world through organizing it that is quite alien to the completely controlled *real identities* of logic. That is why logicians are always frustrated with real language, and why the positivist view of logic as the cutting edge of language always leads to disappointment. Modern logicians like to think of their field as the science of reasoning, but I have never seen anything but disappointment whenever a newcomer to the scene finds out how limited the applicability of formal logic to real language and real life actually is. The tired old syllogism rarely seems to help—all men are mortal, Socrates is a man, therefore Socrates is mortal—for most of us use the result to explain the syllogism, not the reverse.

It is important to see that the irrelevance of formal logic to language is not a matter of language being too imperfect or too corrupt to match up to the ideal of logic: on the contrary, if we understand this inapplicability correctly, we shall see that we are dealing with the limits of conventional logic,[26] not of language, and even with that very feature of language that makes it what it is, and that makes it so important to us. And yet it is also true that a different kind of logic would indeed be useful to us, one that studied how reasoning with human languages works. It would have to be based, *not* on the artificial view of categories basic to mathematic terms,[27] in which all x are identical, but on that of natural languages, in which they are *functionally*, though not *actually*, the same. That would be a very different kind of logic, but it would be a genuine study of the logic of human reasoning and of its central instrument—the languages we speak.

EIGHT

The State of Linguistics

The problems of linguistics as a field at this point in its history are to a large extent the problems of the school of thought that has dominated it during the last three decades, that which derives from Noam Chomsky. That school is now so fragmented and scarred by past and present internal disputes that some of its offshoots think of themselves as quite distinct from Chomsky and MIT; but even when central tenets of Chomsky's thought are challenged by linguists who grew up in that tradition, more of its assumptions and general mind-set remain than they think.[1]

It will help to begin by contrasting an outline view of the history of these years which might be given by those from within the MIT tradition, whether orthodox or heretical, with a quick sketch of the contrasting view of that history which I shall develop.

The insiders' view would be roughly as follows: A breakthrough in linguistic thought occurred with the publication of Chomsky's *Syntactic Structures* in 1957, one so profound that linguistic theory for the first time achieved a wholly new level of sophistication and scientific rigor. This new starting point represented so great an advance over previous linguistic thought that everything that had happened beforehand could for practical purposes be ignored. To be sure, in the years since 1957 many unsolved problems in the theory have come to light, and attempts to solve them have been made at different times by different groups. Progress has been made, it is still going on, and the MIT tradition in linguistics remains the only one in which both the necessary brainpower and a basically productive orientation ensure that progress will continue to be made.

A more realistic account, I shall argue, would go like this: *Syntactic Structures* captured the attention of a then theoretically stagnant field by offering a sense of rigor, purpose, and scientific precision, but it was based on theoretical mistakes that were so basic and so disastrous that recovery from them was scarcely possible short of abandoning the entire theory and beginning anew. The series of attempts to solve the problems of generative grammar since its inception could not succeed

97

because they were driven primarily by the need to patch up a fundamentally flawed position; they did not constitute real progress. Bitter schisms within MIT linguistics have arisen because choice among the suggested amendments was arbitrary, since none could have made the system work. What continues to stand in the way of facing up to the extent and depth of the initial mistakes is a commitment to the notion of a 1957 "revolution" and the psychological benefit that idea brings—a sense of belonging to a special group of linguists with higher and more scientifically rigorous standards of thought. A pervasive gloom has now set in; since so much has been questioned, many have begun to ask what the revolution consisted in—though mostly to reassure themselves that there was one—and others wonder whether convincing solutions will ever be found for the theory's problems. Morale in linguistics departments is low.

* * *

In *Syntactic Structures* Chomsky was concerned chiefly with how to systematize syntax, and that has remained the emphasis of the MIT tradition (including its various splinter groups) to this day. Because of this concern he quickly-brushed meaning aside with the assertion that it was entirely separate from grammar: "Grammar is best formulated as a self-contained study independent of semantics."[2] (This was not an entirely original view; Bloomfield, for example, had said as much.) As we have seen, this separation was a fundamental error. It was later questioned from time to time within the tradition, but even then the disturbing thought was never faced: how could a distortion of this magnitude in the foundations of the theory have failed to produce associated weaknesses through- out the entire edifice? The absence of any place for meaning in the theory immediately became an embarrassment, and a long but unsuccessful series of attempts to remedy this failing ensued. The felt need to deal with this problem kept the theory in perpetual turmoil over the coming years, but even in 1957 it should have been obvious that the arguments used by Chomsky to support his position were weak.

In *Syntactic Structures* Chomsky used the sentence "the fighting stopped" as an example from which to argue that the "grammatical relation subject-verb" does not have "the 'structural meaning' actor-action" (p. 100). But he was picking a quarrel with an obviously inadequate version of the relevant distinction. His example might instead have led him to conclude that "actor-action" needed replacing by something more like "subject entity" and "action or change of state." Here, as so often in *Syntactic Structures*, Chomsky carefully picked weak positions to argue against. What he really needed to confront was something that would have made his rigid separation of grammar and meaning much more difficult to maintain—the fact that grammatical concepts are *routinely* semantic in nature. We talk of past and future tenses of verbs, of singular versus plural for both nouns and verbs, of possessive and objective cases for nouns, of conditional sentences, of active and passive mood, and a host of others. It would have been hard to argue that past and future tenses have nothing to do with the past and future, that plural forms are not about number, that imperatives have nothing to do with commands.

Even the famous sentence through which Chomsky attempted to demonstrate that grammaticality was independent of meaningfulness ("colorless green ideas sleep furiously") should have shown just how wrong he was. This was, as we have already seen in chapter 4, a plainly ungrammatical sentence, and for reasons that demonstrated again the link of grammar and semantics: the structure of the English noun phrase has a place for a color word, but only for one and this sentence had two. The grammar of the noun phrase cannot be described without reference to the position occupied by color words, which constitute a semantic category *and* a grammatical one. Not only did Chomsky's pet example show how superficial his grammatical analysis had been, it also pointed to an alarming tin ear for language: "he is sleeping furiously" is a well-understood paradoxical juxtaposition in English, a commonly heard modern version of which is "he is sleeping up a storm."

Chomsky does, to be sure, acknowledge that links seem to exist between semantic functions and grammatical structures, but it would not be quite correct to say that he gives us an argument against the importance of those links; what happens is more like a sleight of hand. First, he admits that there are "striking correspondences between the structures and elements that are discovered in formal, grammatical analysis and specific semantic functions" (p. 101). There is already something odd about this way of stating the point: who has ever found it *striking* that the plural form of a noun indicates that it is plural? What then follows is not an argument against the significance of these correspondences but instead a series of restatements of the same point with a gradually increasing level of negativity, until at last it seems not to exist in any really important way. In the first restatement the idea of such correspondences is said to be "very nearly true." The next sentence then downgrades them to "only imperfect." The last formulation steps up the skeptical language to deliver the final blow: the correspondences are now "so inexact...that meaning will be relatively useless as a basis for grammatical description." And thus the real argument that would have been required by such powerful evidence to the contrary is sidestepped: Chomsky has not argued against it but only talked it into unimportance.

The kind of grammatical structure most often cited as evidence of the separateness of grammar and meaning is that seen in "it is raining." Here it is plausible to say that the "it" is a grammatical but not a semantic subject. But this case is quite easily dealt with. English allows for a "dummy" subject where meaning does not require one. It plugs the usual space with a kind of zero. When Chomsky considers dummy elements he argues that unless we accept his view of a grammar independent of meaning, these forms would all need independent reference to things; but this is a willful misunderstanding of what it means to have a dummy element (p. 100). Various other oddities are commonly cited for the same purpose of separating grammatical form and meaning, but all are easily dealt with. For example, in the expression "a four man boat," we have a singular form and plural meaning, but this is simply explained: the numeral already carries the idea of plurality, and undifferentiated noun forms are common in such situations. The same avoidance of redundancy can be seen in the way German uses present tense for future time in such expressions as: "Morgen fahren wir ab" ("We shall leave tomorrow"). The adverb already announces a future time, and so the verb need not.

Now that MIT linguistics had separated grammar from meaning, there arose one of those mischievous and destructive situations that I have described earlier: an unnecessary extra step had been inserted into the very foundation of linguistic theory, and some intelligible function needed to be found for it. Thus an unreal problem came to haunt the field: if grammar and meaning were quite separate things, how were they then to be related to each other? How, in other words, could one deal with "striking correspondences" that were totally distinct? Finding a solution to an imaginary problem now became the goal of an entire field.

The separation of syntax from semantics soon produced a language all its own, a language that, though designed to solve a problem, ensured that it could not be solved. Linguists began to talk of the "components" of a linguistic theory: the syntactic component, the semantic component, the phonetic component. This seemed to make clearer the job that had to be done: it appeared to be a question of how to stack the components so that they fitted together. Sadly, those who used this language did not seem to understand that the language itself had already made the most important decision for them. The talk of components led next (perhaps because it contained a hint of stereo components and the wiring diagrams showing how they should be plugged into each other) to diagrams with boxes and lines connecting them. Linguistic theory became for a time a series of rival diagrams in which were set out the competing ways of linking the boxes. The diagrams put up a brave front of clarity and explicitness, but that was an illusion, for no genuine conceptual clarity accompanied them; at a more real level they represented a defense against conceptual chaos and floundering.

John Lyons's book on Chomsky was a typical case. While Lyons's tone was one of uncritical adulation, he could not avoid dealing with the shifts in Chomsky's position that had occurred by 1970. He did so by giving diagrams showing how the various boxes and their relations with each other had been reshuffled. Each shift thus appeared to be firm and decisive, rather than part of a pattern of uncertainty and disorientation. Again, the neatness of the diagrams hid the conceptual confusion from view. Diagrams certainly have their uses; at their best, they show the essential shape of issues and let us grasp that shape intuitively. Here, however, diagrams were being used, not to make a clearer showing, but instead to help linguists *believe* that they had achieved clarity.[3]

To see how threadbare the theory already looked at this early stage, and how difficult the separation of grammar and semantics had made life for all concerned, we need only look at introductory expositions for beginners. Introductions must make everything simple and clear, but in situations like this clarity is dangerous. Ronald Langacker seemed rather helpless when he told his beginners that "the function of syntactic rules is to link conceptual structures with surface structures. We know very little about conceptual structures....Since linguists are unable at present to describe conceptual structures, they are severely limited in their ability to formulate definitive syntactic rules for connecting conceptual structures with surface structures."[4] Evidently, once conceptual structures have been separated from linguistic structures they become a complete mystery, since they must be looked for where they are not rather than where they are.[5] Langacker here displays another weakness of the MIT mind-set—its insularity—when he says that "we" know little about conceptual structure, for a good deal of work on conceptual structure was already available to linguists prepared to look at it. The firm belief that MIT thought was the only source of wisdom was clearly blocking off useful knowledge, even though a desperate search for ways of dealing with excruciating problems was already underway. This refusal to learn from others meant that familiar errors would be clung to much longer than was necessary.

The first attempt to deal with the problem of the absent semantic "component" was that of Jerrold Katz and Jerry Fodor, whose article "The Structure of a Semantic Theory" was greeted with virtually universal acclaim and even some relief by generative grammarians: now the gap in "the theory" had been filled.[6] But as so often in the development of Chomskyan linguistics, the initial enthusiasm soon waned, and an essay that had dominated the discussion of semantics was soon forgotten. Katz and Fodor had tried to apply the derivational tree diagrams used previously for syntax to the meanings of words. The word *bachelor* had a tree that branched into "animal" and "human" (since seals can also be referred to as bachelors); under "human" it branched again at "male" as opposed to "graduate," and so on. These divergences were called semantic markers, but at the end points of the branchings were "distinguishers," that is, phrases such as "one who has never married," which were not analyzed further. It was with the aid of this kind of analysis, then, that meanings were to be attached to syntactic structures.

Unfortunately, there were problems everywhere one looked in the Katz/ Fodor theory. The most obvious superficial problem was the arbitrariness of the distinction between "markers" and "distinguishers"; some aspects of the meaning of words were apparently to be covered by one, some by the other, but a coherent formulation of the distinction was not to be found.[7] More serious was the fact that in focusing on words and plugging them into syntax, Katz and Fodor were actually ignoring the real problem they had to deal with, which went back to those "striking correspondences" between grammatical plural and semantic plural. *That* problem did not arise from the individual meanings of words, and *it* was the crux of the mysterious relation of semantics to syntax in Chomsky's theory. All that Katz and Fodor had attempted was a way of accounting for the fact that "colorless green ideas sleep furiously" was not a well-formed sentence, and even there they were wrong.

Katz and Fodor were a disappointment even within the restricted terms of reference of the generativist school because they had not dealt with its real problem, but from any broader perspective things seemed worse still. Their theory was evidently no more than a crude version of the old-fashioned definition *per genus et differentiam;* the insularity and myopia of the generativist community had allowed it to welcome, at least for a short time, the reinvention of a very rusty and broken wheel.[8] In addition to all the usual problems of denotative and referential theories of meaning that we have seen in previous chapters, Katz and Fodor had invented some extra liabilities. Their arbitrary division of semantic features into two basic kinds was compounded by the use of tree diagrams that required the rank ordering of *all* semantic features to get the succession of branchings correct, for otherwise the analyses given could vary widely. Yet just a moment's thought should have been enough to recognize the absurdity of a universal rank ordering of semantic parameters. In all of this, moreover, the central problem of positivist logic is glaring: the need to make the semantic features "simples" incapable of further analysis. For example, "young" had to be a simple feature of the analysis of *bachelor,* but that idea could easily be analyzed further into a number of different stages and kinds of youngness; it is not simply an irreducible "marker."

In *Aspects of the Theory of Syntax,* his second major attempt to expound the theory of generative grammar, published eight years after the first, Chomsky was evidently worried about the problem of his earlier separation of syntax and semantics. He insisted that he saw "no reason to modify the view...[that] there is, at present, no way to show that semantic considerations play a role in the choice of the syntactic or phonological component of a grammar or that semantic features (in any significant sense of this term) play a role in the functioning of the syntactic or phonological rules."[9] But the hesitations and qualifications in this sentence betray Chomsky's anxiety about the logic of his position, and one senses an awareness that a future defense or perhaps even withdrawal might have to be constructed out of the phrases "at present" or "in any significant sense."

The difficulty and the vulnerability of persisting in the exclusion of semantics had evidently made an impression on Chomsky, for he now also says (with a characteristic mix of precision and vagueness) that "as syntactic description becomes deeper, what appear to be semantic questions fall increasingly within its scope," and even that "the syntactic component of a grammar must specify, for each sentence, a DEEP STRUCTURE that determines its semantic interpretation."[10] The thrust of the theory was now increasingly turned, as Newmeyer puts it, "to deep structures that exhibited semantic relations far more straightforwardly than the rather shallow ones of earlier work."[11]

The severity of the conflict that Chomsky had created within his theory was clear: he aspired to a description of grammatical structure that was free of the untidiness of semantics, but most of the terminology he had to use in talking about grammar was inescapably semantic in character. But with "deep structure" (an underlying structure postulated to account for the assumed equivalence of, for example, passive and active forms of the same sentence) the reference point of *everything* now seemed to be semantic content. "Deep structure" seemed indeed to be a factual semantic core, for it was hard to talk of the transformations that resulted in surface structure (that is, the actual shape of a real piece of language) without talking of the addition of meaning elements (for example, interrogative transformations) or the alleged nonaddition of meaning elements (as in passive transformations). Chomsky had implicitly reversed his earlier position, but because of a determination not to concede error it was a reversal clouded in double-talk, which only added to the conceptual confusion of MIT linguistics instead of providing much needed clarification and redirection.

Because of this failure to confront openly the errors of 1957 the move to bring back meaning through the idea of deep structure only brought generative grammar still more problems. These were principally of two kinds: first, deep structure had to be incapable of further analysis in order to count as deep. Second, the analysis of surface structure that resulted in the discovery of deep structure must be one that accounted for everything significant on the surface. It takes very little to show that neither of these requirements could possibly be met. As to the first, the need to make deep structure a datum beyond which analysis could not go resulted in a particularly wooden and rigid version of logical atomism, the logic of which requires atomic facts, simples, and the reference theory of meaning—with all their unhappy history and insoluble problems. For if nothing is incapable of further analysis, there can be no such thing as deep structure. As to the second, Dwight Bolinger easily showed that there was much that was meaningful in surface structure that would be lost in the reduction of every piece of language to underlying simplified shapes.[12] Active and passive forms of "the same" assertion certainly have a large element in common, but their difference is still meaningful. Once it is conceded that all *significant* elements in surface structure must be accounted for, the distinction between surface and depth will evaporate. Both will exhibit the same complexity, and the postulation of a deep structure will then have lost its purpose.[13]

In practice, the move to deep structure through the idea of transformations was bound to run into the problem of the arbitrariness of deciding what is to be counted as deep and thus the end point of the analysis. For example, should all pronouns be replaced by the subjects to which they refer? But if so, what nouns should be chosen? Does *he* need to be replaced by *man* or by a name, or by some facts identifying the individual? And what of the meaning added in an interrogative transformation, which is indisputably semantic and yet could not (by definition) be a part of deep structure, since it was added by transformation. Deep structure turned out to be a dreadful conceptual muddle.[14]

Another source of confusion in generative grammar was the introduction at about this time of a confused version of Saussure's distinction between *langue* and *parole*. Chomsky rewrote this to make it the distinction between linguistic "competence" and "performance." Saussure's distinction had had a clear purpose: *Langue* was the language shared by those who used it and as such, it was the system that could be abstracted from their speech. *Parole* referred to the actual examples of speech in that language—the concrete material from which an abstraction such as "the French language" could be derived.[15] Chomsky's attempt to rewrite this distinction only confused it, and his reason for doing so was both dangerous and unnecessary: because "performance" (i.e., actual speech) might contain errors, we need to "idealize" the data to reach the abstraction "competence." Now if all that was at issue here was the need to abstract from data to formulate general principles, this argument was unnecessary: all abstraction implies separating the wheat from the chaff. Saussure's *langue* is "idealized" in this sense. But Chomsky's distinction contained the possibility of something else: the concept of "idealizing" would eventually be used for far more than just getting rid of noise in the system. Speech impediments and outright syntactic inconsistencies can indeed be ignored when we are describing the structure of English— the linguist would falsify the system if he did not discard them. The rest of the data would easily show that these are individual idiosyncrasies. Why, then, make a fuss about a commonplace of all inquiry and waste time elevating it to a theoretical principle of linguistics?

As the distinction was used and developed within the generative camp it became clear that something far more insidious was involved. Not simply individual idiosyncrasies, but whole areas of the system of speech *shared by its users and an integral part of their speech convention* were being relegated to "performance" and thus written out of that system. Much later, Frederick Newmeyer candidly admitted that "many aspects of meaning, in his [Chomsky's] view at the time, were part of performance," and that "not surprisingly, as the class of 'grammatical' phenomena increased [i.e., to include aspects of semantics], the competence-performance dichotomy became correspondingly cloudy."[16] MIT linguists were actually using the distinction to get rid of those aspects of the linguistic system of a language that they could not deal with! The procedural virtue of filtering out the noise in the system was providing a cover for the sin of rigging the data. Without shared understandings as to meaning and the use of words, language could not exist; to treat any significant part of this aspect of language as unrelated to the speaker's competence was thus astonishing. From this misuse of Saussure's distinction another important consequence followed. The relegation of the idea of "use" to the lowly area of "performance" made it easier to ignore Wittgenstein.

As we shall see in the case of a heresy that was soon about to arise, the ill-defined distinction between competence and performance achieved virtually a moral force within generative grammar. Only competence was a fit concern for linguists, and so anyone found to be arguing from performance phenomena could be convicted of conduct unbecoming a linguist. In effect, the term *performance*, applied to someone else's theory, became one of common abuse.

By now a conviction had become firmly entrenched among generativists that the problems of Chomsky's theory could only be dealt with from within the tradition, by reference to and through a new exegesis of the founding texts.[17] On matters of linguistic doctrine only the views of those who shared the faith mattered, with outsiders being ignored as irrelevant.[18] The debate had become entirely an internal one. From an outsider's point of view, the dispute seemed inefficient and archaic; the issues were familiar ones with a long history and much was already known about them. But faith in their own unique virtue had cut generativists off from the outside assistance they needed, and they directed their energies instead into bitter sectarian disputes with each other.

The major heresy that arose in the late sixties became known as generative semantics. This flouting of orthodoxy could scarcely have been more deeply iconoclastic. What was involved was a challenge to something that, in the words of Frederick Newmeyer, the semiofficial historian of MIT linguistics, "had gone unchallenged since the inception of transformational generative grammar, the assumption that syntactic and semantic processes are fundamentally distinct."[19] (Newmeyer carefully avoided mentioning that outsiders had always challenged this unlikely notion.)

Chomsky's own revisions of the mid-sixties had in reality brought him much closer to the heretics than they were willing to see, but they wanted to acknowledge openly the error of 1957, which he would never do. There was, however, one serious analytical issue dividing the two sides: the generative semanticists saw that (contrary to the view that Chomsky had been moving toward) "deep structure" (whatever that might turn out to be) could not be identical with semantic structure because the transformations added meaning.

For example, if we assume a kind of logical atomist's simple declarative assertion as a model of what deep structure might look like, the argument that the passive transformation did not change meaning might seem superficially plausible; but the interrogative transformation was another matter. Another meaning element had obviously been added, for a question is not a statement. Abandoning the untenable view that surface structures did not affect meaning would have been real progress; generative semantics was in effect trying to rid MIT linguistics of one of its most vulnerable features.

From a broader perspective, however, generative semanticists were still only picking and choosing from among the inconsistent premises that Chomsky had given them. They abandoned his unwillingness to talk about meaning when he did syntactic analysis, but not the kind of analysis he did; they abandoned deep structure as the unique source of meaning, but not the atomist logic of meaning and search for simples incapable of further analysis which deep structure implied. George Lakoff, the most pugnacious and uncompromising of the generative semanticists, made the fundamental drift of the sect quite clear: "The theory of generative semantics claims that the linguistic elements used in grammar have an independent natural basis in the human conceptual system."[20] This was a charmingly frank yet theoretically very innocent remark that could hardly have been made by anyone who knew that the idea already had an unhappy history in philosophy. Anyone who wished to resuscitate it had to explain how all of the difficulties seen in the past could be overcome, and how powerful arguments by Wittgenstein, Saussure, or Peirce could be met. But in a world created in 1957 the past barely existed. Now great excitement and a sense of a brave new enterprise accompanied the reinvention of ideas such as "natural logic" and the pursuit of the ultimate constituents of meaning (a.k.a. "simples") by "lexical decomposition." Thus the generative semanticists retraced the steps of so many before them along a path that had always led to frustration.

The predictable collapse of generative semantics was much like that of its forerunners. Slowly, it began to dawn on everyone that both the methods and the results of lexical decomposition were too arbitrary and variable to be able to yield anything as fixed and certain as the ultimate constituents of meaning. The heretics were finally crushed and orthodoxy reasserted itself, but nothing was learned from the temporary success of generative semantics. The inconsistencies and weaknesses the heresy had exposed remained.

Katz and Bever delivered a stern judgment on behalf of orthodoxy: "This assimilation [by generative semantics] of the phenomenon of performance into the domain of grammaticality has come about as a consequence of an empiricist criterion for determining what counts as grammatical.... the generative semanticist program for linguistic theory represents, if anything, a more extreme approach than even Bloomfieldian structuralism."[21] To understand quite how harsh this condemnation was, one must look at the emotional weight of its key terms within MIT linguistics. As we have seen, it was openly abusive to accuse anyone of being concerned with performance rather than competence, but the reference to Bloomfield was even worse: Bloomfield belonged in the dark ages before 1957. Most damaging of all was the term "empiricist." That word may seem congenial enough to anyone familiar with its normal meaning in the English language, but for those who knew the MIT meaning of the word, to be accused of empiricism was devastating. In the language of Chomskyan linguistics an empiricist was a linguist without a theory—presumably one who just accumulated data. This usage is surely one of the strangest in the MIT lexicon: no empirical scientist proceeds without constantly fitting and refitting data to theory and theory to data, so that to use "empiricist" as a term of condemnation is to inhabit a very odd intellectual world. The terms of the denunciation suggested a complete loss of control, a runaway leaking of grammar into lexicon, of competence into performance. *Anything* could happen, it seemed, if a strict theoretical boundary between grammar and semantics was not observed.

From the very beginning, the problem had been where to place the boundary between the two. Specific decisions always seemed arbitrary, and yet if the theory of an autonomous realm of grammar were really correct, the boundary should have been obvious. A fuzzy boundary would suggest a continuum, and so the collapse of Chomsky's autonomous grammar. Just how desperately generativists struggled with this issue could be seen when, for example, one of them suggested that the distinction between active and passive verb moods should be analyzed as lexical, not grammatical, in nature; and, astonishingly, the suggestion was taken quite seriously.[22]

This is surely one of those classic points in inquiry where a reductio ad absurdum of a line of thought has occurred, and those points suggest that somewhere along the way something went badly wrong. What had gone wrong was this: observing the difference in scope between an individual item in the lexicon and a widely applicable grammatical structure, Chomsky had decided that they must represent distinct entities: form and meaning, or syntax and semantics. This was an error because *both* lexicon *and* grammar displayed form and meaning. The operative factor in the distinction between grammar and lexicon was precisely the thing that was most apparent in the first place— particularity versus generality. And that suggested not a boundary between distinct things but a continuum running from most specific to most general. That continuum would move from individual words, to groups of words with structural similarities, to categories of words that have reserved places in more-general structures (like words of color in the noun phrase), to regular mutations of word forms carrying categorical meanings (plural or past), to concatenations of words in phrase structures which order meanings and in so doing add extra

dimensions to them, through to the most general categorical distinctions—
that is, verb and noun.

This was why the problem of where to locate and how to conceptualize
the boundary would never go away, and why the insistence on an autonomous
grammar kept generativists endlessly searching for a way to patch up their theory
and make it work. But a patch could not be enough when the flaw in the theory
lay at its center, and if the real problem had been faced, nothing would have
been left of the theory.[23] And what made things even more hopeless was the
continued adherence to a primitive notion of meaning,[24] for this meant that even
when one group briefly set aside the destructive barrier between grammar and
semantics, they were soon overwhelmed by the problems of their semantic theory.

After the collapse of the heresy of generative semantics, a retreat to the
safety of orthodoxy ensued. The notion of performance was again invoked to
keep a stricter and tighter grip on (autonomous) grammar, and deep structure
was rehabilitated. In other words, the destructive extra step was firmly back in
place, with syntax on the one hand, and semantic interpretation on the other.
Semantics was in any case somewhat deemphasized, and the boxes in the diagrams
were reshuffled.[25] Some modifications were introduced into the "standard theory,"
and these justified the new designation of "extended standard theory." So it
looked to insiders.

When looked at from the outside, however, the changes seemed quite
minor, and they did not even deal very well with the problems that generative
semantics (whatever one might say about its own validity) had undeniably been
able to demonstrate in the orthodox theory. Nevertheless, a period of relative
calm and stasis set in, and the vigor of internal debate over minor points of
doctrine substituted for attention to more fundamental doubts.

The calm after spent fury led a number of outsiders to express the hope
that a more open and reflective atmosphere might allow linguistic theory to take
a more productive turn. W. Haas began a survey of the linguistic thought of
the last half century by observing:

> Anyone surveying the contemporary linguistic scene will be struck by a
> curious wave of unrest and uncertainty, a softening of oppositions, a greater
> readiness to listen to one another on the part of "schools" formerly exclusive,
> and an eagerness for new suggestions, however vague, as if the one sure
> thing were the inadequacy of the extant school-solutions. This may be the
> time to stop and review the most prominent trends of linguistic thought
> during the last fifty years.[26]

Haas's proposal was just what was needed: when an impasse is reached (and
this obviously was one), we should do well to look back at the path that led to

it. Though he tried to be generous to generativists, Haas's diagnosis showed clearly enough what the wrong turn had been: "It would be wrong to suppose that generative-transformational grammar will be remembered merely as an interruption in the progress of linguistic thought." Janet Sternberg also took the opportunity provided by this "crisis in linguistic inquiry" (the title of her paper) to survey the corpus of fundamental criticisms that had been made of the MIT tradition, and concluded that the "most auspicious outcome of the present crisis in linguistics" would be "replacing the TGG paradigm." Robert A. Hall, Jr., took the same tack, marshaling and surveying all the significant critiques of MIT that had been produced. Hall concluded that "the criticisms we have just briefly discussed constitute a devastating refutation of all aspects of Chomskyan theory" and expressed the hope for a better future for linguistics.[27]

After two decades, however, MIT linguistics was too institutionalized to dissolve itself so easily; the fervent commitment of so many to the idea of a glorious revolution made for a powerful emotional resistance to any radical rethinking. The bruised and weary faithful, though by now resigned to the fact that "the theory" (which still meant the only theory) had deep problems that would continue to give them headaches for a long time to come, returned to the fold. They settled for the now battered and heavily patched orthodoxy.

It was only to be expected that a stasis based largely on weariness could not last for long; the contradictions and confusions of the standard theory made it inherently unstable. A resurgence of heresy was inevitable, and yet when it came it took the form, not of mass desertions, but instead of a redoubling of effort to wring success from the same flawed premises by taking them to greater extremes.[28] Now salvation would be sought in the rigor of formal logic, but this would only intensify the already marked tendency of the MIT tradition toward positivist logic and thus reinforce the intellectual limitations that had been there from the beginning. And in another repetition of the usual pattern, this heresy also provoked the forces of orthodoxy to fresh efforts to maintain control of the tradition with new but minor revisions.

When students of language—whether they are linguists or philosophers—are drawn to formal logic to find answers to their problems, they must make the assumption stated openly by Richard Montague, the logician who influenced generativists in their next phase: "I reject the contention that an important theoretical difference exists between formal and natural languages."[29] Formal logic seemed to offer those who had for so long struggled fruitlessly with the problems of "the theory" a refuge from the untidiness of natural languages in a realm where everything is neat and controlled. Once this mood sets in, language will begin to seem like an imperfect version of mathematics, and it is even said on occasion that it is a subbranch of mathematics.[30] But as I have shown above, the reverse is the case: mathematics is a highly artificial subbranch of natural language, one from which those essential elements that make language what it is have been excluded. Language seems ragged and imperfect only if, as here, it is treated as something that it is not. Formal logic brings with it the worst features of traditional philosophical epistemology—the exclusive focus on truth conditions, an especially wooden labeling theory of meaning, and classes based on identity instead of on differentiation and equivalence.[31]

One such generativist offshoot is the book *Generalized Phrase Structure Grammar*, which begins with the brisk assertions that "a theory of meaning should define a function which, given an arbitrary sentence of English and a possible state of affairs, tells us whether the sentence is true or false in that state of affairs," and "we believe that no semantic rules whatever have to be given directly by the grammar."[32] Here is the same combination we have seen so many times: the implied claim to being at the cutting edge of modern thought plus the same old mistakes—the very mistakes that keep causing this search for a solution.[33] All that is new is the mathematical term "function," which suggests precision of thought where in reality confusion still reigns.

Faced with the challenge to his leadership posed by the inroads of formal logic, Chomsky developed "government and binding," which is at present either the majority view within generative grammar or the largest sect within the movement, depending on the stance of the observer. Curiously, Chomsky was the one now to argue that Montague grammar had nothing to contribute to linguistics, and to say, "I do not see any point in formalizing for the sake of formalizing."[34] But it is doubtful that Chomsky objected to very much more here than simply a deviation from his own emphases; for if his objections had been based on the fundamental principle that formal languages are unlike natural languages, his objections would have applied equally to his own system of thought.[35]

* * *

Where, then, does all of this leave linguistics? After so many twists and turns, the field is dominated by a theory that still tries to hold grammar separate from semantics and so dooms itself to look for an imaginary extra step (the process of relating the two) that can never be found, still relies on the conceptual muddle of the distinction between competence and performance, and still works with a primitive theory of meaning. These are huge barriers standing in the way of progress toward a richer sense of language as a complex conceptual system of categorizations and an ordered hierarchy of meanings with differing degrees of generality. For over thirty years Chomsky's initial errors have sent countless bright young people down a theoretical blind alley; during that time the field has been in turmoil as one attempt after another to deal with enormous conceptual problems ended in failure, while Chomsky himself has stubbornly held to his original commitments.[36] The result has been a dark age of linguistic theory. How could this have happened, and how could it have gone on for so long?

Throughout much of its history the study of language did not enjoy either high prestige or a high profile. Dictionaries and grammars have always seemed to be necessary but boring things. The words *grammar* and *grammarian* bring with them associations of pedantry. The advent of generative grammar seemed to offer a welcome change of image for linguistic study. Generative grammar appeared to replace the image of the dullard traditional grammarian with one of high intellectual ambition, scientific rigor, and analytical power. This complete change of image perhaps explains why generative grammar started off with exhilaration, and why its adherents promoted it with messianic zeal and not a little self-congratulation. Normally, however, this kind of mood would die down fairly quickly as a new stance is assimilated by a field and scholars start to pursue the new possibilities that have been opened up. Yet in this case obsessive self-congratulation continued well beyond the normal period. The reason for this almost certainly concerned the new system's weaknesses: skeptics were able to point to problems that insiders themselves were not secure about. The heady sense of achievement normal in the early stage of a new turn in knowledge needed constant and continuing reinforcement because it was always being questioned. But now another and far more damaging mechanism also came into play as a further protection of this sense of high achievement. Objections to this or that feature of generative grammar were proving very easy to make, and insiders were making them too. An attitude soon developed that divided objections into two classes: those which resulted from high intellectual standards should be taken seriously, but those which originated from a lower order of thought should not. Thus developed the fatal self-insulation of MIT linguistics from its critics which, more than anything else, has allowed a bad situation to go on for so long.

Critics of one's viewpoint are annoying and quite often uncomprehending, and yet they are vital to the health of an idea. Like a predator in relation to its prey species, they pick off the weak elements in an argument and thus strengthen it, making it more fit to survive—if it can. An unsympathetic critic will be the first to find the problems we have not sufficiently thought out, the concepts we have left ambiguous, and the evidence that is not yet sufficiently compelling. Thought inevitably degenerates if it operates without the very real benefits of exposure to hostile criticism. By isolating themselves, generative grammarians abandoned the most important source of help available to them. And, surprisingly, this attitude persisted even during periods of great internal dissatisfaction. Outsiders may have pointed out right away that Chomsky's exclusion of meaning from his theory was a horrendous mistake, but when many insiders were finally forced to that conclusion years later they could not acknowledge that critics outside the tradition had been right; the critics' point could not have been the same one because it had not been arrived at within the generativist framework.

And yet it was of course the same point. Part of the problem was the example set by Chomsky himself, who never seemed to meet objections squarely or to allow them to lead to serious rethinking, instead seeming concerned mainly to concede as little as possible.[37] Wittgenstein's response to a crisis of confidence in the system of thought of his *Tractatus Logico-Philosophicus* was very different: his intellectual curiosity and freedom from dogmatism easily prevailed, and he took the lead (in his *Philosophical Investigations*) in criticizing the position whose most prestigious spokesman he himself had been.

Another means of stabilizing this very unstable situation was the ritual repetition of basic beliefs; it was as if a credo were being enunciated instead of assumptions that were not beyond question. The basic truths incanted in this way were, for example, (1) that the task of linguistics was to construct grammars, (2) that semantics must pair semantic statements with syntactic ones, (3) that we must begin with the distinction between competence and performance, and (4) that generativists have shown the "creativity" of language. The ritual quality of the repetitive recitation of these pieces of dogma seemed to dull any possible awareness that one might query the arbitrary limitation of the first, the questionable separation of the second,[38] the sloppy distinction of the third,[39] or the commonplace quality of the fourth.[40] But credo repetition did help to hold things together.

The ritual included a claim of scientific rigor, but this should certainly have been a danger signal. Obsessive claims of scientific status for a field have routinely been signs of uncertainty of direction and deep conceptual troubles; they are invariably found in fields that are *not* part of the natural sciences. Moreover, the emphasis in these fields is always on the surface trappings of scientific procedure: quantification, diagrams, and a technical vocabulary.[41] Just as routinely, the really important part of science is absent—a well-developed and refined conceptual framework the basic shape of which is absolutely compelling. It should have been clear to any reasonably attentive observer of the folkways of the academy that Chomskyan linguistics fitted this pattern, for it clearly showed the two major diagnostic features: the obsessive claims of scientific rigor and the uncertain conceptual basis.

Perhaps the most important of the survival mechanisms of the MIT tradition, however, is a belief in the 1957 scientific "revolution." But here too there is a warning sign, visible in excessive discussion of what the revolution consisted in. The rule here should be analogous to that which forbids asking the price of a yacht: if you have to ask, you can't afford it. If you have to ask what a revolution in thought really consisted in, it didn't happen. Who has to ask what the Copernican or Darwinian revolutions were?

Frederick Newmeyer devotes several pages of his history of MIT linguistics to an insistence that a revolution took place.[42] His first claim is that *Syntactic*

Structures was revolutionary in its "conception of a grammar as a theory of a language, subject to the same constraints on construction and evaluation as any theory in the natural sciences." This is much too vague to convince anyone: scientific revolutions consist in specific theories that overturn other theories, not just in the desire to be scientific! Moreover, the notion that a grammar is a kind of theory of a language would have been congenial to most pre-Chomsky linguists. Newmeyer tries again: he tells us that Chomsky was revolutionary in placing "syntactic relations at the center of *langue*." But this claim has to be bolstered with the falsehood that Saussure had treated syntax as *parole*, and so it too fails. Newmeyer elaborates this point by insisting that only thus can we account for the creativity of language, that is, for the fact that a finite set of rules can generate an infinite number of sentences. But as we have seen, this is Saussure's point about "freedom of combinations." If this and the previous point are revolutionary, it must be a Saussurian revolution. But anyone who contemplates the number of words in the *Oxford English Dictionary* will easily see that the number of their possible combinations in grammatical sentences is unimaginable. Generativists try to make an obvious fact into a revolutionary discovery, but it is neither a discovery nor revolutionary.

Howard Maclay's statement of what the revolution consisted in is vaguer still: "Chomsky's work has led to a genuine scientific revolution in that his approach has redefined the goals and methods of linguistics."[43] This again says exactly nothing. Nobody would be content with saying that the Darwinian or Copernican revolutions consisted in changing the goals and methods of their fields; they would talk of the specific nature of the change. But that kind of specificity would immediately run into serious trouble in the case of the "Chomskyan revolution."[44]

The overwhelming difficulty in claiming that a revolution in thought took place in 1957 is that this fact should have become clearer with the passage of time, as those with vested interests in the prerevolutionary (presumably obsolescent) system of ideas died off. And yet just the reverse has happened in the case of generative grammar: more and more doubts have emerged. Instead of increasing clarity we have seen the entire theory in a state of increasing turmoil as even its own adherents have questioned one aspect after another. During this time the only relatively constant elements of what has been claimed as revolutionary have been either largely empty ("the creativity of language"), vague and superficial ("scientificness"), or confused ("competence/performance"). What is most striking here is not an enduring core of accepted thought but instead the questioning of so much that was thought basic in 1957.[45]

The substance of *Syntactic Structures* was in fact far from revolutionary; much of it was very familiar, and that was especially true of its most characteristic errors. Shortly after the initial publication of *Syntactic Structures*, Robert Dixon argued that the idea of "grammaticalness" used by Chomsky was based on "the worst type of traditional and prescriptive teaching."[46] Indeed, the notion of deletion transformations recalls the old idea that we should speak in complete sentences, not part sentences, for Chomsky's analysis makes the latter complete sentences with deletion.[47] The notion of the "logical subject" and of deep structure were similarly part of the spirit of the old-fashioned classroom. Faced with this criticism Chomsky admitted that these were indeed traditional ideas, but argued that they were laudable elements in a tradition that should be preserved.[48] But this admission has a most peculiar consequence: this is probably the first and the last time that a scientific revolution would be claimed for a return to the relatively unreflective attitudes of an earlier generation. Moreover, Chomsky still did not confront the arguments that had made Saussure and his successors reject these ideas as primitive.

There is only one justifiable claim that could be made about the 1957 turn in linguistics: unquestionably, it introduced a new seriousness of purpose and intellectual ambition into the field. That achievement was undercut, however, by an accompanying closed-mindedness and narrowing of scope; and that fact, taken together with a realistic assessment of the theory of generative grammar, can lead to only one verdict on the era it has dominated: this has been a most unproductive time in the history of linguistics.

Conclusion: Theory of Language

Theory of language is a field of inquiry in which progress is achieved not by making startling new empirical discoveries but instead by once more analyzing thoroughly familiar phenomena and ideas in order to rearrange and reorder them until there is at last that sense of a coherent fit between them in which the place of each is clear. That is why Saussure's observation is so important: "It is often easier to discover a truth than to assign to it its proper place."[1] In theory of language, ideas assigned to the wrong place in the larger system of ideas about language are not just less useful than they might be; they can falsify completely our picture of how language works. Then a "truth" becomes in effect a falsehood. This is as true when we are looking at widespread traditional notions such as "reference" as it is when we are dealing with the suggestive ideas of particular thinkers. Wittgenstein's idea of family resemblances, and Saussure's own notion of arbitrariness, for example, have both commonly been falsified by being assigned to the wrong place in linguistic theory. I can best summarize the theory of language that has emerged during the course of this book, therefore, by setting out briefly the way in which it reorders some basic ideas and assigns them a new place in relation to each other in order to construct a different system of ideas.

A fundamental aspect of this system consists in the reordering of such ideas as information, communication, reference, and categorizing so that the relation between them is changed. A powerful mainstream in linguistic theory relates the first three closely to each other by saying typically that language encodes information for communication by referring to a state of affairs in the real world; and most important, it takes this as the basis on which all else is built. My own view of linguistic theory begins with the perception that this conventional picture must have these basic ideas in the wrong order, because something important must have happened before information, communication, or reference could become possible: these are all ideas that presuppose the existence of a language and therefore cannot have described the basis of language. Encoding requires a language to code, and thus the message encoded is not transmitted by language but is itself already a piece of language; "code" is therefore in the wrong place in this account. Similarly, the notion of "reference" is misplaced if we try to use it in the context of an explanation of how language is constituted; it is instead a use to which we can put language. This reassignment of "reference" to a different place in linguistic theory is crucial: only when we understand that we cannot make sense of the notion of referring to a state of affairs without a language already being in place are we then also able to see that it cannot have the central place in theory of language that has been assumed. Theory only begins to take on a coherent shape when reference, communication, and information are assigned to a different place—one that comes *after* categorization. Accordingly, categorization must be the most basic process of language.

The usefulness of categorization as a central idea can still evaporate unless we make sure to give it its proper place in relation to yet other ideas. Its distinctive character in language is lost if we think of it as a gathering of what is similar; that will be too passive to capture the importance of categorizing in language. The idea that must be adjacent to categorizing is equivalence, not similarity; only thus can categorizing be understood appropriately as the creation of a finite system that simplifies the infinity of the real world. Now we reach the place in the entire system of ideas where Saussure's idea of difference belongs: a system of categories must above all ensure that the categories are differentiated from each other.

We could still leave the notion of categorizing in the wrong company and ruin the entire system unless we make one more choice correctly: does it belong next to the related idea of the categorizer or with that which is categorized? If with the world that is categorized, then all languages should be the same, which is not the case. We must therefore understand categorizing primarily in relation to the purposes of the categorizers. Only if we relate categories to their primary source can we then understand the variability of categories both in the different kinds of jobs they do and in the coherence of the groupings they create. (If instead we place the idea of categorizing closest to that of the categorized, as is usual, we shall find that we have restricted it to one type: the gathering based on similarity.) Some will look like a narrowly defined group, others (like weeds or poisons) will fulfill the purpose of the category in a number of different ways and so include very dissimilar things. Wittgenstein's idea of family resemblances belongs at this place in the system of ideas, but only as one possibility among possible category structures; we understand its place in theory of language only if we take it as breaking the too rigid mold of the conventional idea of categories, *not* as instituting another mold.

If we fail to place the idea of categorizing where it belongs—next to its logical source—and instead place it primarily with the things categorized, the structure of categories will become an endless mystery, and we shall always be trying to make every category fit the only kind that would look the same whether we look in the one place or the other: the narrowly organized one. All kinds of other errors result from assigning this basic idea to the wrong place, and all kinds of damage is done to many different fields of inquiry. In linguistics, assigning categories to the wrong source will lead to the mistake of thinking that mathematics, with its well-defined sets, is the model for natural languages. Nothing is more destructive for the study of natural languages than this idea. Once categorizing has been assigned to its proper place, on the other hand, we shall easily be able to see that mathematics and formal logic is an extreme and artificial end point of a scale of categories which is highly diverse, and that consequently the scale would be completely misrepresented if this atypical kind were taken to be the norm.

In ethics, the consequences of misplacing the idea of categorizing are just as disastrous: since value judgments, being highly amorphous categories, are at the opposite end of the scale from the putative norm of tightly organized categories, they will seem mysterious and even unfathomable. The unbridgeable split between fact and value is the result, as well as a reversal of the hierarchy of categories in which those that are newer and more artificial are mistakenly seen as more basic than those that are older and more firmly established.

A better understanding of epistemology, too, depends on what place in the overall system of ideas in linguistic theory we assign to categorizing. Here is the place in linguistic theory for Peirce's idea that to know something is to categorize it, to place it among other things. As concepts, categorizing and knowing are close relatives—"information" is merely a derivative that presupposes the system of categories that makes knowledge possible.

Giving a central place in theory to categorizing is also essential for understanding how grammar relates to the lexicon: only thus can we see that both are part of a complex and hierarchical system of categories running from most general to most specific in scope. That in turn allows us to see that grammar and lexicon form a continuum, and to avoid the highly destructive mistake characteristic of the MIT tradition of thinking that there is a formal separation of syntax and semantics.

During the course of this book I have repeatedly mentioned a philosopher whose position has long been badly outdated: A. J. Ayer. I have done so because on one point central to the thrust of their work, he and his associates were correct: they were right in assuming that a proper understanding of how language works could produce far-reaching consequences in a number of different fields when applied rigorously to the central problems of those fields. What went wrong for them was simply that the theory they used was poor and ill informed, but that had nothing to do with the more general notion of applying linguistic theory systematically in a number of areas. To that notion homage is rightly due—and the discerning reader will doubtless have observed that it has been appropriately paid.

If my argument has been correct, linguistic theory should indeed have a considerable impact on a number of fields and redirect effort in many places. Philosophy should expect less of and concern itself less with speech act theory, which results largely from "assigning the wrong place" to an idea of Wittgenstein's. Both philosophy and linguistics should expect little from the attempt to link language and formal logic and should direct their attention elsewhere. Epistemology should drop its nearly exclusive concern with truth and refocus its effort on what should be its central issue—the organization of knowledge in a particular language by its hierarchy of categories. In ethics the old arguments about the justification of value judgments, whether intuitionist or utilitarian, should no longer be central once it is seen that they are based on a sense of the relation of evaluative to descriptive statements that is upside down.

As to linguistics proper, the chief prescription that results from my analysis will long since have become clear: the series of fundamental logical misconceptions of the MIT tradition which I have set out in the course of this book leave no doubt that the most useful redirection of effort in linguistics would be a decisive turn away from that tradition. In what direction then should it go?

In general, linguistics should be concerned most with that aspect of languages which is most fundamental and most important in human life: with languages as hierarchically ordered systems of categories. And since the distinctive features of each particular linguistic system are highlighted by contrasting it with different kinds of systems, this is a study that can only be comparative in nature. To date, the most important body of work that has examined languages comparatively— though not in the sense intended here—is in the tradition of Joseph Greenberg. Greenberg and his followers are motivated by a concern with language universals, that is, with recurring features of particular languages, and this concern requires them to be seriously comparative in their approach.[2] The limiting factor is precisely the idea of universals that is the thrust of the project. Its origin lies in the urge to find the common denominator in all languages, which seems to me not a very useful idea; at bottom it is the relic of an excessive desire to formalize. It is far more important to look at the *differences* among languages—the different ways in which they construct their ordered systems of categories. But because the Greenberg tradition requires a careful survey of near-equivalent features in many languages, it could not help but find interesting differences among them. And so the results sometimes focus not on the uniformity of languages as much as they do on interesting but characteristic variations among languages. Looking closely at comparable issues in different languages was in fact, whatever its intent, an empirical investigation that was bound to begin producing interesting results.

By focusing on the systematic comparative analysis of the different systems of meaning in different languages, linguistics could move away from the extraordinary narrowing of the field that has characterized the past thirty-five years. Saussure had stressed that language was a "social fact," and by this he meant not just that language had a social use or impact but that it was itself a social fact at its very core. In excluding meaning from any central role in linguistic theory, Chomsky excluded this central and defining social function of language and reduced its scope to the exploration of better ways to systematize and describe syntax—an arid specialty whose procedures were of concern only to its initiates. This was a terrible loss. A language is a unique, highly complex, ordered conceptual system. It is the most central factor in the social life of those who share it, and it is the most crucial thing that differentiates one community from another. Generative grammar so diminished this fascinating area of inquiry that a radically incomplete study of syntax became its center, while the far more important social dimension was relegated to the peripheral status of an applied field ("sociolinguistics")—a low-status kind of concern that was beneath the leading theorists.[3] This narrowing of the study of the most central and unique phenomenon of human life to something that barely involves people and their lives has been the dubious achievement of Chomsky and his followers.

Notes

CHAPTER 1

1. Alfred J. Ayer, *Language, Truth and Logic* (London, 1936). As Ayer himself acknowledges, "logical positivism" did not originate with him but with members of the Vienna Circle such as Moritz Schlick and Rudolf Carnap.

2. Ludwig Wittgenstein, *Philosophical Investigations/Philosophische Untersuchungen*, ed. G. E. M. Anscombe and R. Rhees, trans. G. E. M. Anscombe, 3d ed. (New York, 1968).

3. Benjamin Lee Whorf, *Language, Thought, and Reality: Selected Writings of Benjamin Lee Whorf*, ed. John B. Carroll (Cambridge, Mass., 1956).

4. Charles Sanders Peirce, *Collected Papers*, ed. Arthur Burks, Charles Hartshorne, and Paul Weiss, 8 vols. (Cambridge, Mass., 1931–58).

5. Throughout this chapter I have referred to ideas such as those mentioned here only to illustrate the argument; in all cases, the content and significance of the ideas themselves will be explored in later chapters.

6. But Peirce's more recent expositors also seem to get no help from those later thinkers. E.g., in his *Peirce and Pragmatism* (Harmondsworth, 1952), p. 125, W. B. Gallie expounds Peirce's theory of signs seemingly unaware that Saussure is an obvious point of reference for his arguments.

7. Noam Chomsky, *Syntactic Structures* (The Hague, 1957).

8. See Claude Lévi-Strauss, *Structural Anthropology*, 2 vols., vol. 1 trans. C. Jacobson and B. G. Schoepf, vol. 2 trans. Monique Layton (New York, 1963, 1976).

9. Ferdinand de Saussure, *Cours de linguistique générale*, ed. Charles Bally and Albert Sechehaye, crit. ed. Tulio de Mauro (Paris, 1972), English translation: *Course in General Linguistics*, trans. and intro. Wade Baskin (New York, 1959).

10. Leonard Bloomfield's major work is *Language* (New York, 1933).

11. Only recently has a beginning been made on this topic by Roy Harris in his short book *Language, Saussure and Wittgenstein* (New York, 1989). But Harris brings to the comparison only some of the conventional ideas about these thinkers that have grown up while they have been considered in isolation from each other; this wastes the opportunity to see how the partial ideas of the one answer some of the problems of and extend the ideas of the other in a way that might form a much more powerful and complete system. Moreover, Harris often misses the real point of the ideas of these two thinkers; see, e.g., below, chap. 2.

12. That is, in Ludwig Wittgenstein, *Tractatus Logico-Philosophicus*, ed.

and trans. D. F. Pears and B. F. McGuiness, 2d ed. (London, 1971; orig. pub. 1922).

13. But this much could have been done simply by resurrecting the work of Charles Sanders Peirce—yet another case of how the fragmentation of linguistic theory impedes its progress.

14. Wittgenstein, *Philosophical Investigations*, pars. 19, 23, 241; Saussure, *Course*, p. 6.

15. For a more detailed discussion of this legacy, see chaps. 4 and 8.

16. This is true of people as different as Jon Barwise and John Perry, *Situations and Attitudes* (Cambridge, Mass., 1983), on the one hand, and Wallace Chafe, *Meaning and the Structure of Language* (Chicago, 1970), on the other. Barwise and Perry represent one of the latest strains of thought within the broad tradition of generative grammar, while Chafe is an outright dissident who is hostile to that tradition.

17. Danny Steinberg and Leon Jakobovits, eds., *Semantics: An Interdisciplinary Reader in Philosophy, Linguistics and Psychology* (Cambridge, 1971).

18. To be sure, generative grammarians have occasionally mentioned Wittgenstein's name, usually in order to attack an aspect of his theory that is anathema to them, namely, that words are defined by their use. But the attack has rarely focused on what Wittgenstein meant by this dictum, instead being largely concerned to protect a key generativist dogma—the distinction between competence and performance. To give central theoretical importance to the idea of "use" has always been felt to be a threat to this distinction, which was introduced to support the notion of "idealizing" data, that is, to allow us to get rid of what could be regarded as "noise" in the system. Too great a concern with actual usage might seem a threat to this train of thought. But (as shown in the discussion below, chap. 3) the two sides in this dispute are really at cross purposes; what Wittgenstein meant by "use" is not at issue in these attacks. And so this misguided attack on Wittgenstein only serves to reinforce my contention: there is no serious concern with Wittgenstein's thought among generativists.

19. The Steinberg and Jakobovits compendium is not aberrant but typical in this respect. A similar compendium edited a decade earlier by Kelly Thurman, *Semantics* (Boston, 1960), also managed to omit all mention of Peirce, Wittgenstein, Whorf, and Saussure—and many others. Another, more recent compendium edited by Ernest LePore, *New Directions in Semantics* (London, 1987), doesn't do much better, with only a tiny number of references to these thinkers shared among its many contributors, and one omitted altogether.

20. Howard Maclay, "Linguistics: Overview," in *Semantics*, ed. Steinberg and Jakobovits, p. 157.

21. Ronald Langacker, *Language and Its Structure* (New York, 1967), allows a revealing look at the mind-set that operates here when he tells us that his book "is an introduction to language, not to the discipline of linguistics. Consequently it does not attempt to examine and contrast the views of competing linguistic schools...but rather to present...the fundamental insights about language to which every well-educated person should be exposed" (p. v). What then follows is a strictly Chomskyan analysis. There is, apparently, no "fundamental insight about language" to be found elsewhere. The invocation of a "well-educated person" is hard to square with such carefully cultivated narrowness of reading and outlook.

22. Frederick Newmeyer's article "Has There Been a 'Chomskyan Revolution' in Linguistics?" *Language* 62 (1986): 1–18, is much concerned to make the case that there has been a revolution, and to silence the doubts that have recently arisen on this score. His arguments are highly implausible: for a discussion of the specific claims made by Newmeyer as to the nature of the "revolution," see below, chap. 8.

23. Geoffrey Sampson, *Schools of Linguistics* (Stanford, 1980), notes, as many others have, that "much research by members of the Chomskyan school...consists of time-wasting rediscovery of facts or principles that had long been common knowledge outside the Chomskyan camp" (p. 160) and that "their lightest speculations are taken as significant contributions to scholarship while the work of others is largely ignored" (p. 155). His bluntest version of this point is the charge that "the most half-baked idea from MIT is taken seriously, even if it has been anticipated by far more solid work done in the 'wrong' places" (p. 235). What Sampson did not see was that this behavior is inevitable once a revolution in linguistic theory has been claimed—that is, a sharp break with the past in all important respects. The important theoretical problems of generative grammar must be cleaned up from within, since to do otherwise would be to admit that no genuine revolution has actually taken place.

24. It might be said here that Chomsky had indeed learned from Saussure, in that his distinction between "competence" and "performance" is recognizably similar to Saussure's between *langue* and *parole*. But, as we shall see, the two distinctions are quite different; indeed, Saussure's, when rightly understood, shows that Chomsky's distinction is incoherent. See below, chap. 8.

25. Charles Caton, introducing the philosophical contributions to *Semantics*, ed. Steinberg and Jakobovits, expresses concern about this problem ("Philosophy: Overview," pp. 12–13), but in a strangely muted way, calling it only a "worry of my own." It is as if he were unable to face the puzzle of a practice so widespread and yet so indefensible.

26. H. P. Grice, "Meaning," *Philosophical Review* 66 (1957): 377–88, and "Utterer's Meaning and Intentions," *Philosophical Review* 78 (1969): 147–77. These articles have achieved enormous prominence in the field, not an encouraging indicator of its general health if my view of the essential slightness of their content is correct. Crispin Wright, in a review of Simon Blackburn's *Spreading the Word* (Oxford, 1984) in *Mind* 94 (1984): 310–19, has evidently reached a similar conclusion, saying that after reading Blackburn's book he was able to see that there is "little point in certain celebrated theses and projects, or at least far less point than would justify the attention which they have actually commanded. Such is the fate here of Grice on meaning" (p. 312).

27. I argue below (chap. 7) that it is a serious mistake to think that mathematical logic has anything to do with the logic of natural language; thus if I am correct, the origins of the theory of direct reference make it dubious at the outset. The major sources here are Saul Kripke, *Naming and Necessity* (Cambridge, Mass. 1972; expanded ed. 1980); and Hilary Putnam, *Mind, Language and Reality*, Philosophical Papers, vol. 2 (Cambridge, 1975), esp. the essays "Is Semantics Possible?" and "The Meaning of 'Meaning.'" A collection of essays devoted to this idea is *Naming, Necessity, and Natural Kinds*, ed. Stephen P. Schwartz (Ithaca, N.Y., 1977).

28. The impulse to analyze meaning into its simplest components was visible quite early among Chomsky's associates; the well-known article by Jerrold Katz and Jerry Fodor, "The Structure of a Semantic Theory," *Language* 39 (1963): 170–210, first attempted a semantic theory of such a kind, and it enjoyed for a time a great vogue among generative grammarians, though it is now regarded as something of an embarrassment. The slightly later "lexical decomposition" (similarly concerned to analyze words into their ultimate simple components) also eventually died out after much wasted effort that could have easily been avoided. As I will show in later chapters, the same impulse persists, from the Katz/Fodor article through lexical decomposition down to the present day.

29. The collection of essays edited by LePore, *New Directions in Semantics*, is a convenient recent example of these generalizations.

30. Sampson, *Schools of Linguistics*, p. 88; Max Black, *Models and Metaphors* (Ithaca, N.Y., 1962).

31. For more on this point, see below, chap. 7.

32. This is only one of a number of ways of avoiding the point of Wittgenstein's mature thought. Another can be seen in the case of Colin McGinn, *Wittgenstein on Meaning* (Oxford, 1984), who sees Wittgenstein's exegesis of what happens when we follow rules as "a sort of *anti-intellectualism* about the activity of using signs in a rule-governed way: he wishes to emphasise the *habitual* character of rule-following and to discourage an overly rationalistic conception of the nature of this form of behaviour" (p. 24). Jane Heal, "Wittgenstein, Kripke and Meaning," *Philosophical Quarterly* 144 (1986): 415, surely understates when she remarks that "this cannot be quite right": it would be more apt to say that it is a disastrous misunderstanding. The thrust of Wittgenstein's argument is to replace one kind of rational understanding with a better one. This kind of misinterpretation of Wittgenstein generally results from so strong a commitment to the view he is questioning that rejection of its logic is felt to be a rejection of any logic whatever. A contrary tendency in Wittgenstein scholarship, which originates in the same commitment but reaches a diametrically opposed result, can be seen in the case of Roger Scruton, in his review of Saul A. Kripke, *Wittgenstein on Rules and Private Language* (Oxford, 1982), in *Mind* 93 (1984): 592–602. Scruton tries to assimilate Wittgenstein's mature analysis of language and reality to the model he finds acceptable, which is to say the *Tractatus* model of the early, Russell-oriented Wittgenstein: "Whatever the differences between the *Tractatus* and the *Investigations* concerning the structure of language, it seems to me that Wittgenstein never wished to displace the concept of truth (or, if you like, the 'language-game' with the concept: correspondence with reality), from the central place that it occupied in his earlier philosophy" (p. 597). But that is exactly what he wished to do. This response may originate from a fear that Wittgenstein is trying to deprive us of a relation between language and reality, but if so this is a needless anxiety. Wittgenstein's argument concerns the inadequacy of ideas like "correspondence" to deal with that relationship. McGinn and Scruton thus agree in being unable to abandon that idea and differ only in that one thinks that Wittgenstein meant to reject it (and hence becomes intellectually incoherent) while the other thinks it impossible that he can have meant to do so.

33. Alfred J. Ayer, *Ludwig Wittgenstein* (London, 1985).

34. But see also the judgment of Malcolm Budd, *Mind* 95 (1986): 389–92: "[Ayer's book] makes no significant contribution to our understanding of Wittgenstein" and "gives the impression of a greater concern with his own philosophical ideas than with those of Wittgenstein" (pp. 390, 392).

35. See, e.g., Max Black's analysis of Whorf (below, chap. 5), where careless formulations of Whorf's views introduce seemingly tiny changes of wording that fundamentally change his views and show the careful observer that Black completely misunderstood what Whorf was saying.

36. Saussure, *Course*, p. 68.

37. This particular example is dealt with in more detail below, chap. 3.

CHAPTER 2

1. Chomsky has often been particularly insistent in refusing to allow for this possibility; see below, chap. 8.

2. Chomsky, *Syntactic Structures*, p. 14: "A certain number of clear cases, then, will provide us with a criterion of adequacy for any particular grammar."

3. An indication of how much is missed by Roy Harris in his comparison of Saussure and Wittgenstein is his statement that both assume that "language is primarily a form of communication and that languages are to be viewed as communication systems" (*Language, Saussure and Wittgenstein*, p. 97). As we shall see, much of the importance of these two thinkers lies in their having moved beyond the limitations of this view. Harris goes on to say that "from a 'games' perspective, no other assumption is admissible"; but, on the contrary, such a perspective offers the distinct prospect of seeing beyond the limits of the communication model.

    4. Emmon Bach, *Informal Lectures on Formal Semantics* (New York, 1989), p. 8.

    5. E.g., Eric H. Lenneberg, "A Biological Perspective of Language," in *New Directions in the Study of Language*, ed. Lenneberg (Cambridge, Mass., 1964); Noam Chomsky, *Cartesian Linguistics* (New York, 1966), p. 78. Generativist orthodoxy came to locate in syntax the crucial test of whether a particular set of signals merited the term *language*; see this view repeated quite recently by Lord Zuckerman, "Apes R Not Us," *New York Review of Books*, 30 May 1991, pp. 48–49. This proposition requires that syntax be given a unique status in language; for a discussion that rejects this view, see chap. 4. Note, however, the more cautious (and surely more intelligent) approach of R. A. Gardner and B. T. Gardner in "Teaching Sign Language to a Chimpanzee," *Science* 165 (1969): 664–72: "Theories of language that depend upon the identification of aspects of language that are exclusively human must remain tentative until a considerably larger body of intensive research with other species becomes available" (p. 672).

    6. See, e.g., the recent collection of essays *Themes from Kaplan*, ed. Joseph Almog, John Perry, and Howard Wettstein (Oxford, 1989), in which this assumption is still repeated by many contributors in a manner that suggests that it is simply obvious and unproblematic. Scott Soames, in "Direct Reference and Propositional Attitudes," for one, speaks of meaning as "the information encoded by a sentence" (p. 395).

    7. David Crystal, *Linguistics* (Harmondsworth, 1971), p. 239: "What is language's main function? The answer is clear, and generally agreed: language is the most frequently used and most highly developed form of human communication we possess."

    8. Chafe, *Meaning and the Structure of Language*, chap. 2, "Symbolization." Although Chafe gained an occasional convert for his approach (see, e.g., Alan Kaye, "Schools of Linguistics: Competition and Evolution," *Studies in Language* 10 [1986]: 198), his approach to meaning and language (and his challenge to MIT) has not in general been seen as successful.

    9. Barwise and Perry, *Situations and Attitudes*, p. 31. See also the even more frank and innocent admission "Information is prior to language" (p. 29). The openness of this remark suggests that in the minds of its authors it is, once more, something that could not possibly be doubted; it appears for them to be just the same thing as saying that the world and all of its manifestations exist before we talk about them. But it is not at all the same: "information" is an organized thing, organized in the way that only *language* can organize.

10. Gerald Gazdar et al., *Generalized Phrase Structure Grammar* (Cambridge, Mass., 1985), p. 7.

11. Umberto Eco, *Semiotics and the Philosophy of Language* (Bloomington, Ind., 1984), pp. 171–72: "Language is a code because it is, in the first instance, a correlational device"; Thomas Sebeok, "Zoosemiotic Components of Human Behavior," in *Semiotics: An Introductory Anthology*, ed. Robert Innis (Bloomington, Ind., 1985), p. 295: "Semiotics is concerned, successively, with the generation and encoding of messages, their propagation in any sensorially appropriate form of physical energy, their decoding and interpretation"; Colin Cherry, *On Human Communication* (Cambridge, Mass., 1957), p. 32: "Communication essentially involves a language, a symbolism, whether this be a spoken dialect, a stone inscription, a Morse code signal, or a chain of binary number pulses in a modern computing machine"; Claude Lévi-Strauss, *The Savage Mind* (Chicago, 1966), p. 149: "The social group can code the message without any alteration in its content by means of different lexical elements."

12. Whorf, *Language, Thought, and Reality*, p. 85.

13. Jerrold Katz, "Common Sense in Semantics," in *New Directions in Semantics*, ed. LePore, pp. 157–233, reduces this attitude almost to the point of absurdity when he speaks of "pretheoretically clear cases" (pp. 158–59)—a wonderfully revealing phrase that for all its claim to theoretical sophistication betrays bedrock theoretical naïveté: *nothing* is pretheoretical.

14. See the excellent discussion by Gallie in *Peirce and Pragmatism*, pp. 59–83.

15. This idea was first formulated by Goethe: "Das Höchste wäre zu begreifen, da alles Faktische schon Theorie ist" ("The most important thing is to understand that everything that is factual is already theory"). *Werke*, Hamburger Ausgabe, 10th ed. (Munich, 1982), 12:432. Gallie, *Peirce and Pragmatism*, p. 35, reports that Peirce's philosophical reading began, "oddly enough, with Schiller's *Aesthetic Letters.*" Gallie might not have judged this to be an odd fact had he known that Weimar classicism was the source of one of Peirce's most important ideas.

16. The realization that it was a delusion only reached humanists when Peirce's (and Goethe's) insight was finally popularized by Thomas Kuhn in *The Structure of Scientific Revolutions* (Chicago, 1962); from that point on, they suffered from a different delusion, namely, that the insight was recent, and Kuhn's.

17. John Lyons, *Chomsky* (London, 1970), p. 45: "Chomsky points out in *Syntactic Structures* that it is a commonplace of the philosophy of science that, if a theory is formulated in such a way that it covers the clear cases, the theory itself can be used to decide the unclear cases." Lyons's book is typical of the wishful thinking and uncritical acceptance of Chomskyan positions that are even now still common among generativists.

18. E.g., Emmon Bach, *An Introduction to Transformational Grammars* (New York, 1964), p. 3: "The major emphasis of this book lies on the terms and devices that can be used for constructing grammars."

19. Ayer, *Language, Truth and Logic*, pp. 102–3.

20. Much recent thought both in linguistics and in philosophy has either implicitly or explicitly assumed that natural languages are not fundamentally different from formal languages, a consequence of which has been a growing prominence in linguistic theory of writers and ideas whose orientation and origin is mathematical logic. This too is recognizably part and parcel of the same basic error discussed here. For more on this point, see chap. 7.

CHAPTER 3

1. This supposition is in any case incoherent in another way. If a situation were simply recalled *without anything else being involved*, it would not be clear just what it was that was being recalled. As Wittgenstein saw, when we simply point to something, it is not clear what we are pointing at unless we accompany the pointing *with language*. When pointing down, for example, we could be pointing at the color of the floor, its texture, its being dirty or clean, its being full of bugs or free of them, or even at the fact that something is not there that was there a moment ago. See *Philosophical Investigations*, par. 28: "The person one gives the definition to doesn't know what one wants to call 'two'; he will suppose that 'two' is the name given to *this* group of nuts….he might equally well take the name of a person, of whom I have given an ostensive definition, as that of a color, of a race, or even of a point of the compass."

2. C. S. Peirce saw that to know something is not to have a direct intuition of it but to classify it and relate it to other things; these are processes that are not simply available by means of language—they are its very essence. See again the useful discussion by Gallie, *Peirce and Pragmatism*, p. 67.

3. This use of "equivalence" has nothing to do with that of Roman Jakobson in his well-known dictum: "The poetic function projects the principle of equivalence from the axis of selection into the axis of combination." "Closing Statement: Linguistics and Poetics," in *Style in Language*, ed. Thomas Sebeok (Cambridge, Mass., 1960), p. 358. Here Jakobson is talking not about categorizing but rather about selection from (roughly) equivalent words. See also n. 15, below.

4. Quine used this example in his well-known exposition of "radical translation" in *Word and Object* (Cambridge, Mass., 1960), pp. 26 ff.; but although this is a much cited passage, it seems to me that Quine achieves very little in it. Even when speaking of translation into English from a language that is absolutely foreign to the linguist (this is what he means by the word "radical"), Quine never really faces squarely the major issue this should raise, i.e., the possibility that the concept *rabbit* does not correspond to one of equivalent scope in the other language—a possibility that would have led him to a more radical scrutiny of the basis of our own concepts. And this gap in his thinking occurs because he never doubts that similarity is the only basis of classification. Moreover, the project of radical translation is defined in a rough-and-ready, practical kind of way: the target language is simply one that is unknown to the translator. This is not a theoretical distinction of any importance.

5. I have not even touched here on the practical squabbles among scientists about when to recognize a group of animals as a new species or instead as a subspecies of another species. It is fair to say that some scientists in these disputes think they are dealing quite strictly with reality (is this *really* a new species?) and others think of the matter as one of the convenience of scientists and of the most reasonable use of the classificatory system. Only the second of these two attitudes can make sense of an operation that has reached the grey area of scientific language, and the proof of this is that arguments of this kind still go on *after all the facts concerned are agreed upon*. Once that point is reached, the argument can only be about the system, not the animals.

6. W. Haas, "The Theory of Translation," *Philosophy* 37 (1962): 222–23.

7. An interesting case is reported by Derek Freeman, in his "Paradigms in Collision: The Far-Reaching Controversy over the Samoan Researches of Margaret Mead and Its Significance for the Human Sciences," *Academic Questions* 5 (1991): 29. Freeman reports that chiff-chaffs and willow warblers (birds assigned to the same genus) differ by 2.6 percent of their DNA, while chimpanzees and human beings (most definitely not assigned to the same genus!) differ by only 1.6 percent of DNA. It is important to see, however, that the problem of a certain arbitrariness in classification would not be removed simply by rearranging the particular choices that have been made to date.

8. The extreme case of words like *good* is dealt with below, in chap. 6.

9. See the promising beginning spoiled in Rose R. Olver and Joan Rigney Hornsby, "On Equivalence," in *Studies in Cognitive Growth*, ed. Jerome S. Bruner et al. (New York, 1966), pp. 68–85. Olver and Hornsby begin by saying that equivalence making is a necessary defense against the diversity of the environment (p. 68), but soon talk of the child working his way toward "true conceptual grouping, based on the rule of the superordinate class" (i.e., common features) (p. 85). Barwise and Perry, *Situations and Attitudes*, also begin with "a theory of situations and of meanings as relations between situations" (p. 7), but are soon back to classification by "uniformities," and even to "semantic universals" (p. 20); that is, they are back to everyone else's business as usual, and whatever differences their situational approach might have made are in effect abandoned. It is as if having successfully found exactly the point in the road where everyone has taken the wrong turn, they then quite deliberately take that same wrong turn themselves.

10. Sampson, *Schools of Linguistics*, p. 133: "It is significant that in exemplifying the notion 'ill-defined class,' I resorted to beauty, which is an aspect of humans' conscious reactions to things rather than a property that inheres in things independently of human-kind (as does the property of circularity). It seems to be exclusively Man, with his creative, unpredictable intelligence, who gives rise to ill-defined classes." Significantly, Sampson chooses a geometric figure as his example—an artificial human construct. He thus misses the arbitrariness of even "well-defined" categories.

11. Chafe, *Meaning and the Structure of Language*, p. 17: "In its broadest outline, language involves the following process. A configuration of concepts arises within the nervous system of a human being, who, for some reason, often but not necessarily associated with purposeful communication, is led to convert these concepts into sound. The sound travels to whatever other person or persons are within hearing distance, and is normally reconverted within their nervous systems into some facsimile of the original concepts"; Janet Fodor, "Situations and Representations," *Linguistics and Philosophy* 8 (1985): 13–22, e.g.: "The task is hampered by an appalling lack of clear data about the properties of mentalese.... Suppose that at some happy future time we will have achieved this goal of establishing the vocabulary and syntax of mentalese....People have negative thoughts, and it has seemed more or less unavoidable to suppose that mentalese contains some sort of negation operator....natural languages have indexical expressions such as 'I' and 'now' and 'yesterday,' and it is pretty clear that mentalese must too" (pp. 14–15). As the humorist Dave Barry is wont to say: I am not making this up. "Mentalese" as a language sounds suspiciously like Fodor's native language; as a concept, it is the result of a most radical and disabling confusion about the nature of language. All of this harks back to the earlier book of the "other" Fodor: *The Language of Thought*, by Jerry A. Fodor (New York, 1975), the mentalism of which is criticized by Hilary Putnam in his *Representation and Reality* (Cambridge, Mass., 1988). But Putnam, to maintain his theory of direct reference (which takes *cat* to be the label of a natural kind, rather than a concept), uses the term *mentalism* somewhat indiscriminately and consequently fails to make a radical distinction between the mentalism of "mentalese" and the wholly different case of a linguistic theory that takes concepts to be the specific mental constructs of particular languages. (Saussure is the most celebrated example, but Saussure is a name never mentioned by Putnam.) Worse, Putnam calls Fodor's mentalism "sophisticated mentalism of the MIT variety," a bad misjudgment of the relative value of these two in any case fundamentally different kinds of thought.

12. The assumption of a "mentalese" also ignores the whole body of thought (in which Wittgenstein is only one among many others) that has set out the powerful case against treating meaning as a mental state; once again, the self-imposed isolation of MIT linguistics is in part the source of the trouble, but much the same fruitless obsession with mental states perseveres in other strands of recent thought on semantics, e.g., Gilbert Harman's "(Nonsolipsistic) Conceptual Role Semantics," in *New Directions in Semantics*, ed. LePore, p. 55: "The meanings of linguistic expressions are determined by the contents of the concepts and thoughts they can be used to express." Though Sydney Lamb is one of few linguists to have maintained an independence of the MIT tradition in recent years, his "basic sememes" are of the same logical type. *Outline of Stratificational Grammar* (Washington, D.C., 1966), p. 32.

13. Everyday terms have to be made artificial by the device of stipulated definitions if they are to share the tightly organized qualities of mathematical terms; e.g., a "loud" noise is strictly defined in decibels only for the purpose of a local ordinance regulating noise as a public nuisance, and "repetition" is strictly defined as a second occurrence only within a very specific period of time for purposes such as those of a scientific experiment. But the need for such stipulations shows that these are artificial uses of language and therefore that "well-defined classes" in the sense that Sampson (*Schools of Linguistics*, p. 131) invokes give us a poor sense of the way in which language works.

14. To the general principle that taking "clear" cases in order to interpret unclear cases is bad scientific logic, we must add the further problem that, in the case of scientific terminology, the claimed "clear" cases are barely cases at all: they are simply artificial.

15. E.g., John Lyons, *Introduction to Theoretical Linguistics* (Cambridge, 1968), who on the one hand is committed to the simplest version of the realist theory of meaning ("words *refer to*...things," p. 404) but on the other hand praises Saussure as "the founder of modern linguistics...the great Swiss scholar, Ferdinand de Saussure" (p. 38). It is also puzzling to see Lyons calling "reference" a modern term, as if the idea involved were new.

16. It should be noted that the common term *functionalism* is one that is very loosely and inconsistently used and that it has no necessary connection with my use of "functional" here. See, e.g., the judgment of František Daneš that "the attribute *functional*" is sometimes "treated in a somewhat vague manner or appears rather as a mere terminological convention." "On Prague School Functionalism in Linguistics," in *Functionalism in Linguistics*, ed. René Dirven and Vilém

Fried (Amsterdam, 1987), p. 3. Specifically, it is quite commonly used in connection with linguistic theories that take a realist view of categories. Putnam, *Representation and Reality*, p. xi, even used the name "functionalism" for the "thesis that the computer is the right model for the mind." André Martinet is commonly thought of as a functionalist but in fact happily used the "code and message" terminology, which is inconsistent with true functionalism, and while he maintained that some categories were language specific, he also thought that "living creatures" formed natural kinds. *Elements of General Linguistics*, trans. Elisabeth Palmer (Chicago, 1964), pp. 20, 33. Roman Jakobson, also in this loose sense a "functionalist," similarly saw language in "code and message" terms; see, e.g., Roman Jakobson and Morris Halle, *Fundamentals of Language* (The Hague, 1956), pp. 5, 61.

17. An analogous case here is that of George Lakoff's *Women, Fire, and Dangerous Things: What Categories Reveal about the Mind* (Chicago, 1987), which makes a promising beginning by stressing the importance of categories and criticizing the "objectivist" notion of categories, but then returns to what are also essentially objectivist notions of the basis of categories with the notion of "prototypes," basic-level effects, and idealized cognitive models (pp. 58, 68) that even gradually lead to traces of an almost Fodor-like mentalese (e.g., p. 271).

18. A case in point is that of Olver and Hornsby, "On Equivalence," p. 318: "The loose-knit complex, as Wittgenstein and others have noted, is a vehicle for searching out possibilities of kinship. It is also the vehicle of poetry and fantasy. What it lacks in tidiness, it recovers in richness." The *logical* basis of Wittgenstein's idea of family resemblances is completely misunderstood if it is thought of simply as "poetic."

19. E.g., Renford Bambrough, "Universals and Family Resemblances," in *Wittgenstein: The Philosophical Investigations: A Collection of Critical Essays*, ed. George Pitcher (Princeton, N.J., 1966), p. 186: "I believe that Wittgenstein solved what is known as 'the problem of universals.'" But Wittgenstein had not *solved* the problem: he had shown that one particular solution was not possible, and beyond that he had shown only one limited feature of a possible solution.

20. Humphrey Palmer, "Words and Terms," *Philosophy* 61 (1986): 71–82. Palmer sees the whole issue as one of the vagueness and untidiness of ordinary language, and speaks as if the concepts for which the notion of family resemblance is needed are those which are simply not very well defined.

21. It must be remembered here that my assessment of the gaps in Saussure's exposition deals of necessity only with the account published by his students after his death. Perhaps Saussure was much clearer about the full ramifications of his ideas than he seems in their text; such would be my assumption.

22. A prime source of this misinterpretation is Emile Benveniste's

essay "Nature du signe linguistique," in *Problèmes de linguistique générale* (Paris, 1966), a thoroughly confused account of Saussure, the conclusions of which are repeated by too many; a random example is Robert Scholes, *Textual Power* (New Haven, Conn., 1985), p. 92: "The Saussurean formulation, like many 'linguistic' views of language, eliminates the third term and with this gesture erases the world." One must have read Saussure very carelessly to reach this conclusion.

23. Other oddities abound in current accounts of Saussure. Lyons barely mentions Saussure's contributions to linguistic theory and completely omits his important ideas when discussing semantics, yet he pronounces Saussure "the founder of modern linguistics" (*Introduction to Theoretical Linguistics*, p. 38). Sampson, on the other hand, devotes a whole chapter of his *Schools of Linguistics* to Saussure, but one so muddled as to be nearly valueless; symptomatic is the absence of any serious exposition of the theory of the sign.

24. This confusion has proved to be very tempting for deconstructionist literary critics; see John M. Ellis, *Against Deconstruction* (Princeton, N.J., 1989).

25. Jaako Hintikka goes so far as to assimilate this idea to mathematical logic, and even to a kind of verification-and-falsification game of truth claims (a line of thought it was clearly designed to avoid), in his "Game-Theoretical Semantics as a Synthesis of Verificationist and Truth-Conditional Meaning Theories," in *New Directions in Semantics*, ed. LePore: "Game-theoretical semantics (GTS) is...closely related to Wittgenstein's notion of a language-game, if Wittgenstein's true intentions are appreciated....I have taken Wittgenstein more literally than Ludwig did himself" (p. 235). The clash between "true intentions" and "more literally" is evident, the one claiming faithfulness, the other admitting a lack of it. Some literary critics have become fond of the game analogy for the opposite reason, finding in it a license for playfulness and thus for uncontrolled speculation about meaning. Neither of these extremes has anything to do with Wittgenstein's argument.

26. See John M. Ellis, "Wittgensteinian Thinking in Theory of Criticism," *New Literary History* 12 (1981): 437–52, for further argument on how an awareness of Wittgenstein's major contemporary philosophical purpose in the *Philosophical Investigations* (that is, demolition of the basis of logical positivist and logical atomist arguments) makes it much easier to see what he is doing. Most of the time Wittgenstein is writing a series of notes that attack the weak links in an argument that was so well known that he assumed that there was no need to expound it.

27. This kind of attitude continues today: e.g., James Higginbotham, "On Semantics," in *New Directions in Semantics*, ed. LePore, p. 1: "Semantic theory, as a chapter of linguistics, will be concerned with those aspects of meaning that [are]...determined by the design features of human language, and not by the way language is put to use." The distinction proposed here seems harmless enough, but it is far more deceptive than Higginbotham sees. The problem is that those who make and use this distinction have usually (as is the case here) formulated their "design features" prematurely, ignoring aspects of language which they think of as mere "use" and so arriving at far too narrow a view of the "design" of a language. Jerrold Katz, *The Philosophy of Language* (New York, 1966), pp. 88–89, expresses well the essence of this attitude when he says that Wittgenstein (and ordinary language philosophy in general) is "antitheoretical," an extraordinary judgment on so influential a theorist, and one that can only arise because of a radical failure to grasp the purpose and shape of a *different kind of theory*.

28. Wittgenstein, *Philosophical Investigations*, par. 11: "Think of the tools in a tool-box: there is a hammer, pliers, a saw, a screw-driver, a rule, a glue-pot, glue, nails and screws.—The functions of words are as diverse as the functions of these objects."

29. The beginning of this development is J. L. Austin's *How to Do Things with Words* (Oxford, 1962). See also John R. Searle, *Speech Acts* (London, 1969).

30. What later became known as ordinary language philosophy reduced the content of philosophy of language even further, at its worst constituting no more than a call for more than usual patience in looking at normal usage, a position that was very slight in theoretical content. It was not surprising that respect for philosophy as a discipline declined during this period of its history.

31. Again, Goethe had seen the point and made it explicit in the preface to his *Farbenlehre* (*Werke* 13:317): "...und so kann man sagen, daß wir schon bei jedem aufmerksamen Blick in die Welt theoretisieren" ("and so it can be said that every time we look attentively at the world we are already theorizing").

32. This notion is of course by no means new: the common charge that relating metaphysics to the structure of our language is a mystical notion would make Kant and a host of other philosophers mystics.

33. See below, chap. 8, for the details of this development.

34. Putnam, *Language, Mind and Reality*, pp. 272–73, greatly overestimates the distance between his own position and that of positivism because of his exclusive focus on the notion of "verification." But verification of the truth of a sentence must presuppose matching up a state of affairs on the one hand and a set of words referring to that state on the other; and that means that a verification theory is only a particular emphasis within the group of denotative and referential theories. David Wiggins, however, sees this kind of continuity in his essay "Meaning, Truth-Conditions, Proposition: Frege's Doctrine of Sense

Retrieved, Resumed and Redeployed in the Light of Certain Recent Criticisms," *Dialectica* 46 (1992): 61–90.

35. To be sure, there is some equivocation on the question how generally the term *natural kind* can be used; but Stephen Schwartz is not making an unreasonable judgment when he says that "Putnam holds that virtually every term in the common language is rigid" (*Naming, Necessity, and Natural Kinds*, p. 39).

36. Kripke, *Naming and Necessity*, p. 134.

37. David Kaplan, "Afterthoughts," in *Themes from Kaplan*, ed. Almog, Perry, and Wettstein, p. 572.

38. To be sure, there is often something very odd about the praise it receives; a good example is Schwartz, *Naming, Necessity, and Natural Kinds*, p. 9: "This new theory of reference is the most serious challenge ever to traditional theories of meaning." Seen in the broader context of linguistic theory as developed over time in many disciplines, this is an extraordinarily ill-informed judgment; the reality is that this theory is a blunter and more extreme version of traditional theories. Here we see another example of the effects of the fragmentation of linguistic theory, for the devotees of "direct reference" are disproportionately philosophers with an orientation to mathematical logic.

39. Avrum Stroll, "What Water Is, or, Back to Thales," *Midwest Studies in Philosophy* 14 (1989): 258–74, on p. 261; see also his "Observation and the Hidden," *Dialectica* 45 (1991): 165–79.

40. See n. 1. It is an odd fact (odd, that is, in light of his addiction to "direct reference") that Kripke wrote a short book on Wittgenstein: *Wittgenstein on Rules and Private Language* (Oxford, 1982). But G. E. M. Anscombe, in a review of this work in the *Canadian Journal of Philosophy* 15 (1985): 103–9, shows convincingly that Kripke's argument here can only be understood as Kripke's *thoughts provoked by* his reading of Wittgenstein ("It is Kripke's argument"—not Wittgenstein's). She shows that in fact Kripke has completely misunderstood the fundamental thrust of Wittgenstein on rules, for what Kripke takes as a skeptical argument is actually the reverse: "Wittgenstein was opposing skepticism." He was expressing, not doubts, but instead doubts about certain kinds of doubts. Putnam's few remarks about Wittgenstein seem to me also to display a similar remoteness from what that thinker said, whether he is expressing approval (e.g., when claiming that "meaning as use" is compatible with his own view; *Representation and Reality*, p. 113) or disapproval (e.g., summarily dismissing Wittgenstein's expression "form of life" as "preposterous"; *Mind, Language and Reality*, p. 149).

41. Leonard Linsky, "Reference and Referents," in *Semantics*, ed. Steinberg and Jakobovits, p. 76.

42. E.g., Schwartz, *Naming, Necessity, and Natural Kinds*, p. 39; and Paul M. Churchland, "Conceptual Progress and Word/World Relations: In Search of the Essence of Natural Kinds," *Canadian Journal of Philosophy* 15 (1985): 1–17.

Churchland concludes that "genuine natural kinds form a very small, aristocratic elite among kinds in general" (p. 16).

43. Kripke, *Naming and Necessity*, p. 134. Putnam's examples are very similar to Kripke's.

44. An interesting demonstration of the language-specific and arbitrary range of temperature of the word *hot* can be had by looking at the cognate German words and comparing them to what has become of them in our own low German dialect. *Hot, warm,* and *cold* still parallel the cognate forms *"heiß," "warm,"* and *"kalt,"* but an English-speaking traveler in Germany who uses the cognate form to ask for a hot bath will get a shock: *"heiß"* will be much too hot. In German, the transition from *warm* to *heiß* occurs much further up the scale. Meanwhile, a German traveler who incautiously uses the cognate form to try to get a warm bath will find it much too cold.

CHAPTER 4

1. Chomsky, *Syntactic Structures*, p. 17. I draw attention to Chomsky here not because this view is unusual (it is not) but because he made it the explicit basis of the most influential linguistic theory of our time. Many other versions could be cited, e.g., Frank Palmer, *Grammar* (Harmondsworth, 1971), p. 34: "In linguistics, however, we draw a distinction between grammar and semantics."

2. E.g., Gazdar et al., *Generalized Phrase Structure Grammar*, p. 8: "In fact, we believe that no semantic rules whatever have to be given directly by the grammar"; and p. 10: "What cannot happen is that the matter of assigning a meaning determines grammaticality." How closely *Generalized Phrase Structure Grammar* hews to Chomsky's most fundamental and most flawed assumptions can also be seen in its agreement with a notorious Chomsky claim, one that I examine below: "We would claim, for example, that *Colorless green ideas sleep furiously* is grammatical" (p. 10).

3. Langacker, *Language and Its Structure*, p. 41.

4. Charles Fries, *The Structure of English* (New York, 1952). Quoted with a degree of approval by Sampson, *Schools of Linguistics*, p. 65: "This is not as pedantic as it might seem."

5. Note that "red and green apples" does not violate the rule, because it is felt to be an amalgam of different colored apples, that is, equivalent to "red apples" plus "green apples." It is therefore a kind of shorthand for two different phrases.

6. Joan Bybee in her very interesting book *Morphology: A Study of the Relation between Meaning and Form* (Amsterdam, 1985) also uses the notion of a continuum between lexicon and grammar, but only for linguistic form: "These expression types form a continuum that ranges from the most highly fused means of expression, lexical expression, to the most loosely joined means of expression, syntactic or periphrastic expression" (p. 12). This restriction seems to me not to allow the full force of the idea of a continuum to be seen; its real point emerges in the related idea of a hierarchy of semantic issues in a given language. Bybee's general view of the linguist's task is at issue here: "The study of language is the study of the relation of meaning to form" (p. 207). I discuss this matter further below, chap. 8.

7. There is in fact far more to this distinction than familiarity, and I simplify here only because the many other subtleties of the distinction are not relevant to my argument.

8. It has done so by gradually losing the *thou* form, the historical equivalent of *"du."*

9. Herbert Kufner, in his *The Grammatical Structures of English and German* (Chicago, 1962), called certain grammatical features "compulsory semantic categories." This was a useful idea though not strictly applicable to very much of grammar: only the most central part of a grammar is concerned with categories that are completely obligatory, while the rest shows varying degrees of obtrusiveness of particular semantic issues.

10. A more plausible attempt to distinguish grammar and lexicon is that deriving from J. R. Firth, between closed systems and open sets. For example, the choice among personal pronouns is limited to *I, you, he*, etc., while the choice of adjectives that may occur in the phrase "the [adjective] house" is unlimited. The pronouns are therefore said to form a closed system, the adjectives an open set. But interesting as it is, this distinction also easily disintegrates into a continuum. First, not all that is "grammar" involves choices from entirely closed systems; take the case of color adjectives, where new candidates arise from time to time. Second, the lexicon also provides many relatively closed systems of contrasts, e.g., good/bad or black/white. See J. R. Firth, *Papers in Linguistics, 1934–51* (Oxford, 1957), and "Synopsis of Linguistic Theory 1930–55," in *Studies in Linguistic Analysis*, Special Volume of the Philological Society (Oxford, 1957), pp. 1–32; and the important extension of Firth's approach by M. A. K. Halliday, "Categories of the Theory of Grammar," *Word* 17 (1961): 241–92.

11. See here Whorf, *Language, Thought, and Reality*, pp. 240–42:

We cut up and organize the spread and flow of events as we do, largely because, through our mother tongue, we are parties to an agreement to do so, not because nature itself is segmented in exactly that way....The Indo-European languages and many others give great prominence to a type of sentence having two parts, each part built around a class of word—substantives and verbs—which those languages treat differently in grammar....this distinction is not drawn from nature....The English technique of talking depends on two artificial classes, substantives and verbs, and on the bipartitioned ideology of nature, already discussed.

12. Warren Cowgill, s.v. "Indo-European Languages," *Encyclopaedia Britannica*, 15th ed., Macropaedia.

13. Greville G. Corbett, in *Gender* (Cambridge, 1991), notes that "in Indo-European, for example, most Iranian languages have lost gender (Persian, Sarikoli, Beludzhi and Ossete) as have many Indic languages (Assamese, Bengali, Nepali, Oriya)" (p. 318).

14. Corbett's view is that "the major cause of the decline of the gender system is attrition, that is the partial or complete loss of the markers on which the system depends" (*Gender*, p. 315). Properly speaking, however, attrition and the loss of the markers is not a cause but an integral part of the loss itself: losing the markers *is* losing the system. Attrition is the result of a cause, since it occurs in so many different languages. The cause of this development must lie in a slow shift in semantic priorities, a question Corbett does not consider in his otherwise very valuable and informative empirical survey of gender systems in the languages of the world.

CHAPTER 5

1. Edward Sapir, *Culture, Language and Personality: Selected Essays*, ed. David Mandelbaum (Berkeley and Los Angeles, 1961), p. 69.

2. Edward Sapir, "Conceptual Categories in Primitive Languages," *Science* 74 (1931): 578.

3. Sampson, *Schools of Linguistics*, p. 83.

4. Lyons, *Introduction to Theoretical Linguistics*, p. 433.

5. For example, the German grammatical distinction between *"du"* and *"Sie"* (and related distinctions in other European languages) is of obvious cultural relevance, as is the grammatical distinction made in a western Australian language such as Nyangumata between near past, past, and long past.

6. Max Black, *The Labyrinth of Language* (New York, 1969), p. 95.

7. To be sure, Continental philosophy is also discussed in English, but the translation of, say, Hegel into English remains a formidable task that cannot be achieved without significant loss.

8. E. Lenneberg, "Cognition in Ethnolinguistics," *Language* 29 (1953): 467. More puzzling still, Lenneberg tells us that "a basic maxim in linguistics is that anything can be expressed in any language" (ibid.), attributing it vaguely to "Sapir (1949)" without giving us the page number. He has likely simply misunderstood (and very badly) Sapir's attack on the lay prejudice that assumes that the languages of "primitive" peoples have such limited (i.e., primitive) vocabularies that gesture is needed to supplement them. To this Sapir responds, "The truth of the matter is that language is an essentially perfect means of expression and communication among every known people" (*Culture, Language, and Personality,* p. 1). Sapir meant, of course, that each language is appropriate for its community of speakers, not that all can say exactly the same thing, an assertion he would certainly have opposed.

9. Lenneberg, "Biological Perspective of Language," p. 78. So complete is the confusion here that Lenneberg attributes one of his contrasted pair of views to Whorf (i.e., language causes intelligence). It is a remarkable fact that the most quoted of Whorf's critics evidently could not understand the view he criticized, for Whorf would of course have objected to the separation.

10. Sampson, *Schools of Linguistics,* pp. 87–88, is an exception here, but his account is so confused in other ways that his advantage is largely wasted.

11. Black, *Labyrinth of Language,* pp. 92, 95; Crystal, *Linguistics,* p. 232; and Carroll, in his edition of Whorf's *Language, Thought, and Reality,* p. 29.

12. Black seems to have been influential in this, too; e.g., Sampson, though finding Whorf important enough to devote an entire chapter to his ideas, nevertheless feels compelled to remark that those ideas involve merely "flights of fancy" (*Schools of Linguistics,* p. 85).

13. Whorf, *Language, Thought, and Reality,* p. 239.

14. Lakoff, *Women, Fire, and Dangerous Things,* p. 329.

15. Whorf, *Language, Thought, and Reality,* p. 80.

16. To be sure, Whorf did occasionally talk of the behavioral consequences of linguistic form, beginning one of his essays with a section headed "The name of the situation as affecting behavior" (ibid., p. 135). This is atypical, however, and the behavior concerned is a very local and specific case of individuals who call gasoline drums "empty" being made careless about the explosive potential of the gasoline vapor contained in those "empty drums." As soon as he moves on to the real meat of the essay, however, the emphasis returns to the cognitive patterns inherent in languages.

17. Wittgenstein, *Philosophical Investigations,* par. 19; Saussure, *Course,* p. 74.

18. See esp. Pierce's papers "Questions Concerning Certain Faculties Claimed for Man" and "Some Consequences of Four Incapacities," both in *Journal of Speculative Philosophy* 2 (1868): 103–14, 140–57, and the review of *The Works of George Berkeley,* ed. Alexander Fraser, in *North American Review* 113 (1871): 449–72. The first two of these are reprinted in *Collected Papers of Charles Sanders Peirce,* vol. 5, ed. Charles Hartshorne and Paul Weiss (Cambridge, Mass., 1934). Gallie puts Peirce's point in a more forceful way than his own rather ponderous prose does: "A given word means its distinctive object only through expressing or communicating a distinctive method or technique of action, expectation, or adjustment with regard to that object" (*Peirce and Pragmatism*, p. 15).

19. Wittgenstein, *Philosophical Investigations*, par. 693.

20. The word *tyrannical* was also seized upon in the same way by Langacker, *Language and Its Structure*, p. 40, to attack the view that language exercises a powerful influence on thought, even though he mentions neither Sapir nor Whorf; this may give us some measure of how fixed the association of Sapir's word with these ideas has become. One reason for Sapir's unfortunate choice of word was probably his own inconsistency on this matter, for he often spoke as if he himself did not understand the real implications of the position Whorf later set out with much greater clarity.

21. Lyons, *Introduction to Theoretical Linguistics*, p. 433.

22. Whorf, *Language, Thought, and Reality*, quotations on pp. 138, 159, 221, 65.

23. The prevailing carelessness in discussions of Whorf reaches an extreme in the case of the philosopher Donald Davidson, who on p. 190 of his *Inquiries into Truth and Interpretation* (Oxford, 1984) takes as the key text in which he locates Whorf's basic thesis a sentence which he claims to find in Whorf's essay "The Punctual and Segmentative Aspects of Verbs in Hopi" (*Language, Thought, and Reality*, pp. 51–56) but which is in fact from a quite different essay, "Science and Linguistics" (p. 214). Here is Whorf's sentence: "We are thus introduced to a new principle of relativity, which holds that all observers are not led by the same physical evidence to the same picture of the universe, unless their linguistic backgrounds are similar, or can in some way be calibrated." Having taken this sentence out of its context and inserted it into a paragraph from another essay, Davidson understandably misunderstands one of its key terms and then makes that misunderstanding the basis of his criticisms of Whorf: he thinks that the word *calibration* implies "the failure of intertranslatability," even entertaining the possibility that total failure of translatability is meant. Had he read the essay following the one he cites ("An American Indian Model of the Universe"), he would have found Whorf saying that we *can* attempt to make explicit Hopi thought "by means of an approximation expressed in our own language" (p. 58). Since one system of categories is always (by definition) different from another, approximation will always be necessary.

24. It is worth noting that the "extra step" is also built into the notion that language determines worldview, which is parallel to the notion that language determines thought.

25. Langacker, *Language and Its Structure*, p. 42. Langacker has more recently changed direction with his *Foundations of Cognitive Grammar*, 2 vols. (Stanford, Calif., 1987, 1991), now saying, e.g., that "semantic structure is...language-specific to a considerable degree" (1:2). This is a generally unsuccessful work, however; see below, chap. 8. Another strange feature of the controversy surrounding Whorf is the extraordinarily primitive level to which the argument can descend. Sampson tells us that if language influences thought in the way Whorf says it does, that can only be "because many people are mentally very lazy" (*Schools of Linguistics*, p. 89); Max Black, on the other hand, thinks that "philosophically unsophisticated users of the language" could not be influenced by the worldview of a language in the way Whorf suggests (*Labyrinth of Language*, p. 94). That these two opinions contradict each other is a minor matter: neither remark belongs in any thoughtful analysis of these issues. On the same level is Sampson's reduction of Whorf's comments on the treatment of time in Hopi to the assertion that Hopi treats time "in an odd way" (*Schools of Linguistics*, p. 87). Time, evidently, is what we British all know it is, and anything else is, well, just "odd"! A reviewer of Sampson who agrees with him only manages to expose this poverty of thought even more: "Maybe Hopi has the same basic time conceptualization as Standard Average European, as the argument goes, but just expresses it more exotically." Kaye, "Schools of Linguistics," p. 191.

26. Whorf, *Language, Thought, and Reality*, pp. 235, 221.

27. Davidson, *Inquiries into Truth and Interpretation*, p. 194.

28. One last criticism of this kind, made by Langacker, *Language and Its Structure*, p. 400: since we can think of a new idea before we have given it a name, ideas must be available without language. The answer to this is given by Haas, "Theory of Translation," p. 216: "Long before it is named, the new thing has already been placed....It has been so placed and contrasted by the help of expressions which were already dealing with it." Finding a name for a new idea in a language is thus rather like filling in a gap in a map that is already dominated by certain characteristic shapes: it is an activity that is already quite circumscribed.

29. E.g.: most of the essays in the anthology of studies in psychology and linguistics entitled *Language and Thinking*, ed. Parveen Adams (Harmondsworth, 1972), are guilty of the practice I describe here.

30. See Jean Piaget, "Language and Thought from the Genetic Point of View," *Acta Psychologica* 10 (1954): 88–98, for a particularly confused version of this pattern of thought: children, he confidently asserts, know objects physically before they know them conceptually or linguistically. The notion of perception without even the beginnings of conception is an impossible one.

31. In Piaget's case, the susceptibility of the researcher to having his ideas confirmed by what he allows himself to observe was doubtless exacerbated by his surrounding himself with admiring coworkers who actually did the work. Without such an arrangement one can only hope that he would not have been able to persevere in finding and pronouncing the truth of such results.

32. Piaget, "Language and Thought from the Genetic Point of View," pp. 89, 98.

33. L. S. Vygotsky, *Thought and Language*, translation rev. and ed. Alex Kozulin (Cambridge, Mass., 1986), p. 124.

34. Ibid., p. 130. Naturally enough, this view will require the concomitant assumption that all abstraction is simply and only a matter of discerning *real* similarities among things, rather than equivalences of dissimilar things.

35. Ibid., p. 249.

36. See chap. 2.

CHAPTER 6

1. Ayer too, in *Language, Truth and Logic*, chap. 6, set out to give a solution to the problem of value judgments derived strictly from a theory of how language works but did not see that this approach would require very serious prior research into and thought about language and language theory. Largely unacquainted with linguistic theory, Ayer instead relied on popular ideas about language.

2. Of these the most celebrated is David Hume, who remarked that he could never find any justification for the transition from statements of what is the case to statements of what ought to be the case, in *A Treatise of Human Nature, Book* 3: *Of Morals* (London, 1740), part 1, sec. 1, par. 27. A useful collection of essays devoted to Hume's statement is *The Is/Ought Question*, ed. W. D. Hudson (London, 1969).

3. See, e.g., the discussion by Ruth Saw in her *Leibniz* (Harmondsworth, 1954), pp. 170–71.

4. John Stuart Mill, "Utilitarianism," *Fraser's Magazine* 64 (1861): 391–97, 526–30.

5. G. E. Moore, *Principia Ethica* (Cambridge, 1903); Immanuel Kant, *Critik der practischen Vernunft* (Riga, 1788), English translation: *Critique of Practical Reason*, ed. and trans. Lewis Beck (Chicago, 1949).

6. John Rawls, *A Theory of Justice* (Cambridge, Mass., 1971).

7. See J. O. Urmson's interpretation of Mill as a "rule" utilitarian in "The Interpretation of the Moral Philosophy of J. S. Mill," *Philosophical Quarterly* 3 (1953): 33–39. J. D. Mabbott, on other hand, argues that Mill was inconsistent and did not clearly distinguish between the two. "Interpretations of Mill's 'Utilitarianism,'" *Philosophical Quarterly* 6 (1956): 115–20.

8. Ayer, *Language, Truth and Logic*, p. 107.

9. C. L. Stevenson, *Ethics and Language* (New Haven, Conn., 1945); R. M. Hare, *The Language of Morals* (Oxford, 1952); P. H. Nowell-Smith, *Ethics* (Harmondsworth, 1954); Searle, *Speech Acts*.

10. Though the argument of Bernard Williams's recent *Ethics and the Limits of Philosophy* (London, 1985) feels very different, it is still recognizably in the same defeatist mode typical of Ayer's legacy. Williams takes the view that no objective grounding can be found for ethical thinking, and even that philosophy cannot provide ethical theories. The basis of this position is again the seemingly intractable problem of the fact/value split.

11. In the mid-sixties there was a brief flurry of interest in John Searle's "How to Derive 'Ought' from 'Is,'" *Philosophical Review* 73 (1964): 53–58; but most observers, myself included, soon concluded that Searle had only managed to achieve evaluative conclusions through concealed evaluative elements in his premises. In other words, this was once again the inclusion of value on both sides of the equation. See John M. Ellis, *Schiller's Kalliasbriefe* (The Hague, 1969), p. 88.

12. See John M. Ellis, *The Theory of Literary Criticism: A Logical Analysis* (Berkeley and Los Angeles, 1974), pp. 75–82, for a fuller statement of this point.

13. See here Whorf's enigmatic remark on the "persistent notion in Western learned circles...that objective experience is prior to subjective" (*Language, Thought, and Reality*, p. 157).

14. Ellis, *Theory of Literary Criticism*, chap. 4, gives a similar account of value judgments in aesthetics.

15. David Wiggins, "On Sentence-Sense, Word-Sense and Difference of Word-Sense: Towards a Philosophical Theory of Dictionaries," in *Semantics*, ed. Steinberg and Jakobovits, pp. 14–34, makes this readjustment in the wrong way by suggesting in effect that *good* actually means "good for" and is thus localized, with a number of different senses corresponding to the typical local meanings. This is a complete misunderstanding of the function of the word *good*. The point is rather that *good* is *not* localized and that that is its logical limitation, and that it is a primitive, undifferentiated term whose nature is misrepresented if an extra level of differentiation is imputed to it.

16. In *Theory of Literary Criticism*, pp. 39–40, I made the distinction between causes and reasons, the former emerging only after empirical analysis, the latter delineating the function rationale, and thus definition, of the category. That is to say, the reason for the categorization of a plant as a weed is that we do not want it; the causes of the categorization are to do with the plant's (various) physical characteristics.

17. John M. Ellis, "Great Art. A Study in Meaning," *British Journal of Aesthetics* 3 (1963): 165–71.

CHAPTER 7

1. Alfred J. Ayer, *The Problem of Knowledge* (Harmondsworth, 1956), pp. 31ff.

2. Richard A. Aaron, s.v. "Epistemology," *Encyclopaedia Britannica*, 15th ed., Macropaedia 6:604.

3. Ibid., p. 602.

4. Davidson, *Inquiries into Truth and Interpretation*, is a recent and uncompromising example, but also one showing how this mistake leads naturally into another and even more destructive error—the assumption that formal languages will show us how natural languages work:

> I suggest that a theory of truth for a language does, in a minimal but important respect, do what we want, that is, give the meanings of all independently meaningful expressions on the basis of an analysis of their structure. And on the other hand, a semantic theory of a natural language cannot be considered adequate unless it provides an account of the concept of truth for that language along the general lines proposed by Tarski for formalized languages. I think that both linguists and philosophers interested in natural languages have missed the key importance of the theory of truth. (p. 55)

5. Aaron, "Epistemology," p. 605. When at last Aaron mentions the question how "language, as an instrument used in thinking, affects the thinking," he talks oddly enough only of two "natural languages" (French and English) and their conceptual *similarities*; that effectively prevents any consideration of the real issues that should arise here, for those could only emerge from the conceptual *differences* between languages. (One would surely wish in any case to take a language more remote from English than French for any serious comparative purpose.) He then tells us that "the first use of language was for communication," and this too helps to obscure all the really important questions in epistemology. This blindness to fundamental issues must be related once again to the destructive extra step in how the problem is formulated: to speak of how language "affects" thought is to ensure that the issue cannot be dealt with intelligently.

6. Chomsky, *Language and Mind*, p. 76. It should be noted here that the reference of the apparently very general phrase "the theories of philosophical grammar, and the more recent elaborations of these theories" is in reality highly specific: it refers to Chomsky's own standpoint.

7. Richard Rorty, *Consequences of Pragmatism* (Minneapolis, 1982). It should be noted that, to judge from the language he uses to criticize it, Rorty still appears to believe that the standard account of the goals of epistemology is coherent; he objects to its triviality rather than to the unsoundness of its logic when he says that "there is no interesting work to be done in this area. People... might have found something interesting to say about the essence of Truth. But in fact they haven't" (p. xiv). For a good analysis of some of the flaws in Rorty's argument, see the review by Bernard Williams in the *New York Review of Books*, 28 April 1983, pp. 33–36.

8. The error of thinking that the falsity of one of a pair of views requires that the other be embraced is a major liability in the work of Derrida and his many followers; see Ellis, *Against Deconstruction,* chap. 2.

9. A curious but certainly ineffective attempt to avoid either alternative is what Ernest LePore calls "dual aspect semantics," in *New Directions in Semantics,* ed. LePore, pp. 83–112. A theory of this kind splits theory of meaning into "two distinct components. One component is intended to provide an account of the relations between language and the world: truth, reference, satisfaction, etc. The other is supposed to provide an account of understanding and cognitive significance" (p. 84). Here the clumsy notion "component" is out of place and artificially makes separate what could not be: the two aspects cannot be separated since one is needed for the definition of the other.

10. Whorf, *Language, Thought, and Reality,* p. 157; on Peirce, see above, chap. 5. It is an odd fact that Peirce is thought of as the progenitor of the field of "semiotics," and yet for the most part his central insights seem absent from typical contributions to that field, even when he himself is explicitly invoked. Indeed, the most wooden reference theory of meaning seems to predominate there. See, e.g., the contributions to *Semiotics,* ed. Innis, esp. those by well-known "semioticians," such as Sebeok's "Zoosemiotic Components of Human Communication" or Benveniste's "Semiology of Language." Typical is Benveniste, p. 233: "The role of the sign is to represent, to take the place of something else while alluding to it by virtue of a substitute." The general impression that semiotics is currently an incoherent field of inquiry emerges also from the recent *History of Semiotics,* ed. Achim Eschbach and Jürgen Trabant (Amsterdam and Philadelphia, 1983). Thomas Shannon, reviewing this volume in *Language* 62 (1986): 232–33, concludes that "the heterogeneous, often contradictory character of the contributions reflects the varying views of the contributors on how the task is to be approached and what it should include."

11. W. B. Gallie, "Art as an Essentially Contested Concept," *Philosophical Quarterly* 6 (1956): 97–114. The implausibility of Gallie's idea has not impeded its acquiring a devoted following among aestheticians, most notably Morris Weitz, *The Opening Mind* (Chicago, 1967). Weitz bolstered this view with the very serious misinterpretation of Wittgenstein that he had reached earlier, in his "The Role of Theory in Aesthetics," *Journal of Aesthetics and Art Criticism* 15 (1956): 27–35. Instead of seeing in Wittgenstein's discussion of games a demonstration of solid reasons for rejecting traditional definition *per genus et differentiam,* Weitz thought he saw there a demonstration of a special class of concepts— "open concepts"—that were special in being exceptions to the general and *still valid* rules that govern definition according to the traditional account. What Weitz also does not see is that "game" is still a well-defined concept after Wittgenstein has done with it, but one that illustrates the need to approach definition in a different way. See my further discussion of this point in Ellis, *Theory of Literary Criticism*, pp. 24–53.

12. It is as well to remember here Whorf's warning against determinism (see above, chap. 5): there is a "connection" but not a "correlation" between language structure and other kinds of cultural phenomena. There is variability within each set of speakers, and a small minority do cross from the intellectual world of the one to the other. It appears to me that rather more English-speaking philosophers are oriented to the typical philosophical attitudes of the German-speaking world than the reverse, though this relatively much smaller group of German speakers includes the important case of the Vienna Circle (i.e., logical positivism)—a group that is no longer celebrated in Viennese memory, however. During my own studies in Vienna in the fifties I recall a summary rejection of contemporary Anglo-American analytic philosophy being accompanied by a reference to the Vienna Circle: "We used to have something like that, but it died out long ago." Indeed it did. The case of a thinker of Wittgenstein's stature is too idiosyncratic for any generalization—a German speaker who moved to Cambridge and developed his mature thought in an English-speaking environment but who wrote his major work in German, albeit in a language most unlike philosophical German and in fact syntactically and stylistically heavily influenced by English.

13. Whorf, *Language, Thought, and Reality*, pp. 138ff., liked to contrast languages remote from ours with what he called "SAE" (standard average European) to show important differences of conceptual structure. Here he perhaps underestimated the important differences *between* SAE languages.

14. See the example of gender in Indo-European languages discussed above in chap. 4.

15. This interest is visible, e.g., in the theory of direct reference, discussed above.

16. A. J. Ayer, *Bertrand Russell* (New York, 1972), p. 56.

17. Susanne Langer's *Philosophy in a New Key* (Cambridge, Mass., 1942), for example, was the title of a book that announced that its author was breaking exciting new ground, but its logic is plainly (see, e.g., the admission on p. 75) that of atomic facts.

18. E.g., Barwise and Perry, *Situations and Attitudes*, p. 29: "We must have a way of representing the way the world is, one that is independent of the language whose meanings we are trying to study." What is distressing here is not simply that Barwise and Perry take this view, but that they seem to have no idea that there is any possibility that it could be problematic or that it has an unhappy history. Fred Landman's exposition of the essential structure of Barwise and Perry makes clear its simplistic positivist assumptions, but without really understanding the liabilities of those assumptions. "The Realist Theory of Meaning," *Linguistics and Philosophy* 8 (1985): 35.

19. A very similar case in its initial straying from but finally returning to the fold is that of Ray Jackendoff, *Semantics and Cognition* (Cambridge, Mass., 1983). Jackendoff's beginning, too, has promising features; e.g., he looks to the cognitive capacity rather than to reference and objects for conceptual structure. But, alas, he looks at them for a "theory of cognition...to account for nonlinguistic categorization" (p. x), and tells us that he uses "the term *conceptual structure* when talking about nonlinguistic matters" (p. 95). All of which can result only from the most radical misunderstanding of the nature of categorization and from the standard attraction to semantic primitives. For all his initial boldness, then, Jackendoff disappoints us by settling for something rather like Janet Fodor's very naive version of positivism (see above, chap. 3). An interesting review of Jackendoff is that by Greg Carlson in *Linguistics and Philosophy* 8 (1985): 505–10, who argues that Jackendoff raises some substantial issues in his attempt to refute the currently fashionable model-theoretic semantics.

20. See, e.g., Searle, *Speech Acts*, and *The Philosophy of Language*, ed. J. R. Searle (London, 1971), where there is still more life in such ideas as propositional content and reference than is consistent with the spirit of the later Wittgenstein. Searle's according philosophical importance to Chomsky's linguistic theory is also hard to square with anything but continuing acceptance of much of the positivist logic that underlies Chomsky's work. Lyons, *Chomsky*, pp. 104–5, also attempts to set out "the philosophical consequences of Chomsky's notion of universal grammar," but when he does so those results are so commonplace that it becomes obvious that there really are none of any consequence. E.g.: "Human beings are genetically endowed with a highly specific 'language faculty,'" and "All the evidence available suggests that children, regardless of race and parentage, are born with the same ability for learning languages." These are both empirical, not philosophical, claims, and neither has been doubted for some considerable time. A. J. Ayer similarly repeats the well-worn claim that Chomsky "has done most...to supply linguistics with a philosophical foundation" but is unable to mention anything in his short account that could conceivably justify it. *Philosophy in the Twentieth Century* (New York, 1982), p. 239

21. Take, for example, the discussion of whether a broom is simple or complex and the doubt thrown in this discussion on the possibility of "simples." Here it becomes obvious that Wittgenstein intended his game analogy to do more than simply show that there are uses of language that supplement those of Saint Augustine's account. See also the discussion of this point in chap. 3, above.

22. Ian Hacking's *Why Does Language Matter to Philosophy?* (London,

1975) is striking evidence of the way in which the linguistic-theoretical legacy of the *Philosophical Investigations* has been eroded by its transformation into sterile positions after Wittgenstein's death. Hacking devotes a chapter to Wittgenstein's *Tractatus* but includes no discussion at all of his mature work, and he even leaves the reader with the vague impression that this would only have been more of the same. Hacking's full discussions of Ayer, Russell, and the early Wittgenstein leave the impression that the really characteristic developments of postpositivist theory of language never happened. Not surprisingly, Hacking never manages to persuade his reader that language matters to philosophy in any important way.

23. Shifts in grammatical status (i.e., from verb to noun) sometimes result in essentially new usages and new concepts that then require strict definition because they lack any established place in the linguistic system.

24. Wittgenstein, *Philosophical Investigations*, par. 88.

25. A representative example is Davidson, *Inquiries into Truth and Interpretation*, p. xv. Dissenting voices are Fred Sommers, *The Logic of Natural Languages* (Oxford, 1982); and Lakoff, *Women, Fire, and Dangerous Things*, pp. 219ff.

26. See here Wittgenstein, *Philosophical Investigations*, par. 242: "If language is to be a means of communication there must be agreement not only in definitions but also (queer as this may sound) in judgments. This seems to abolish logic, but does not do so."

27. As Hilary Putnam notes (contentedly enough): "The methods used in logical research today are almost exclusively mathematical ones." *Philosophy of Logic* (New York, 1971), p. 3.

CHAPTER 8

1. See esp. n. 28, below, on "cognitive linguistics."

2. Chomsky, *Syntactic Structures*, p. 106. Further citations are in the text.

3. Lyons, *Chomsky*, p. 79. See also Newmeyer's historical survey *Linguistic Theory in America*, 2d ed. (Orlando, Fla., 1986), where new diagrams to reshuffle the components are constantly being introduced, e.g., pp. 58, 74, 93, 118, 140, 163, 172.

4. Langacker, *Language and Its Structure*, pp. 97, 119–20.

5. Janet Fodor's exposition in "Situations and Representations" of how to do "representational semantics" is still the same kind of struggle with the unnecessary extra step that Chomsky introduced: "We make up rules which will associate with each sentence of the object language (say English) an expression of some metalanguage (which might be English, or borrowed from first order logic, or fabricated especially for the purpose)" (p. 13). Here is a reductio ad absurdum of the extra step—relating English to English.

6. Katz and Fodor, "Structure of a Semantic Theory," *Language* 39 (1963): 170–210.

7. Katz and Fodor raised this issue only to drop it again: "We must now consider the basis on which to decide to represent some lexical information by semantic markers and other lexical information by distinguishers. In the last analysis, the decision can only be justified by showing that it leads to correct interpretation of sentences" (ibid., p. 189). The brief discussion that follows ends only with an appeal to "systematic economy." Here once more we see the curious mix of aggressively precise theoretical language and vague, unformed underlying thought so characteristic of the MIT tradition.

8. Putnam aptly remarks, in *Mind, Reality, and Language*, p. 146: "You may dress up traditional mistakes in modern dress by talking of 'recursive rules' and 'linguistic universals,' but they remain the traditional mistakes."

9. Noam Chomsky, *Aspects of the Theory of Syntax* (Cambridge, Mass., 1965), p. 226.

10. Noam Chomsky, "The Logical Basis of Linguistic Theory," *Proceedings of the Ninth International Congress of Linguists*, ed. H. Lunt (The Hague, 1964), p. 936, and *Aspects of the Theory of Syntax*, p. 16.

11. Newmeyer, *Linguistic Theory in America*, p. 90.

12. See Dwight Bolinger's brilliant paper "Meaning and Form," *Transactions of the New York Academy of Sciences*, 2d ser., 36 (1974): 218–33.

13. Ironically, Chomsky himself had shown in 1957 that the active sentence "everyone in the room knows at least two languages" is not the same assertion as its passive "at least two languages are known by everyone in the room" (*Syntactic Structures*, pp. 100–101). In the first, but not the second, the two languages can be different for each speaker. And yet, incredibly, he had used this example to argue that the relation between active and passive is a grammatical not a semantic one, and thus to support his point about the independence of grammar from meaning. What the example proved was of course something quite different: that the close semantic relation of passive and active is *never one of identity*.

14. In his later *Reflections on Language* (New York, 1975), Chomsky complained that he had been misunderstood: "The term 'deep structure' has, unfortunately, proved to be very misleading." He goes on say that it has been understood in a nontechnical, as opposed to its technical, sense and proposes, therefore, to "simply drop the term, speaking only of 'initial phrase markers' and 'surface structures'" (p. 82). The trouble with this attempt to put the blame on his readers is that in his earlier *Topics in the Theory of Generative Grammar* (The

Hague, 1966), Chomsky had been insistent that the concept was so self-evident that it was obvious to anyone who looked at language: "The distinction between deep and surface structure emerges from even the most superficial examination of real linguistic material" (pp. 18–19). The earlier account, especially when taken together with the scorn poured by generativists on anyone who objected to the distinction, leaves little doubt that Chomsky's forced retreat here is again one of substance, not simply of terminology. Once more, Chomsky's adamant refusal to concede error prevented him from seeing that his thought had been not just superficially misleading, and thus only trivially questionable, but instead incoherent in very important ways. David Hirsch was surely right to say that this whole notion had been a "metaphor out of control" in generative grammar. "Deep Metaphors and Shallow Structures," *Sewanee Review* 85 (1977): 154.

15. Sampson's misreading of Saussure on the distinction between *langue* and *parole* is disastrous: he thinks that Saussure assigns syntax to *parole*, thus making it "not part of the proper subject-matter of linguistics" (*Schools of Linguistics*, p. 54). Newmeyer makes the same mistake: "For Saussure, most syntagmatic relations were consigned to *parole*" (*Linguistic Theory in America*, p. 19). But Saussure's text makes it clear that this is incorrect: "La *langue* est l'ensemble des habitudes linguistiques qui permettent à un sujet de comprendre et de se faire comprendre" (*Cours*, p. 112; "Language…is the whole set of linguistic habits which allow an individual to understand and to be understood," *Course*, p. 77). Both Sampson and Newmeyer probably take out of context Saussure's "The sentence…belongs to speaking, not to language." But this is immediately followed by "Does it follow that the syntagm belongs to speaking? I do not think so" (*Course*, p. 124). Saussure goes on to explain that sentences are formed by two forces, the one being "freedom of combinations," the other "syntagmatic types that are built upon regular forms" (p. 125). Both Sampson and Newmeyer pronounce Chomsky's view of syntax a superior one (in Newmeyer's case, as we shall see, "a revolutionary event"). But in spite of all that has been said about Chomsky's theoretical innovation, here it is clear that he merely copied what had already been said by Saussure: Chomsky's much-vaunted claim of a "creativity" that can produce infinitely many actual sentences is a repetition of Saussure's "freedom of combinations," while syntax is as much a feature of the linguistic system for the one as it is for the other. Again, an unrealistic view of Chomsky's uniqueness is based upon deficient knowledge of earlier theory.

16. Newmeyer, *Linguistic Theory in America*, pp. 27, 125.

17. See, e.g., the statement by Katz and Fodor that "it would be theoretically most satisfying if we could take the position that transformations never change meaning" ("Structure of a Semantic Theory," p. 206). But there is nothing inherently appealing about this impossible notion unless (as seems necessary here) we understand "theoretically satisfying" to mean only "consistent with the beliefs and commitments that we wish to preserve and do not wish to have to reevaluate."

18. See Newmeyer, *Linguistic Theory in America,* p. 42, for an account—an accurate one, as far as I remember—of the missionary zeal of the attacks on nonbelievers, and of the dogmatic assumption that whatever problems might turn up in the theory of transformational grammar, the "other guys" were just wrong. Newmeyer still thinks that "overall the effect was positive" of this lamentable closed-mindedness.

19. Ibid., p. 92.

20. George Lakoff, "The Arbitrary Basis of Transformational Grammar," *Language* 48 (1972): 77.

21. Jerrold Katz and Thomas Bever, "The Fall and Rise of Empiricism," in *An Integrated Theory of Linguistic Ability,* ed. Jerrold Katz, Thomas Bever, and Terence Langendoen (New York, 1976), p. 58.

22. Joan Bresnan, "A Realistic Transformational Grammar," in *Linguistic Theory and Psychological Reality,* ed. Morris Halle, Joan Bresnan, and George Miller (Cambridge, Mass., 1978), p. 2. Newmeyer calls this "one of the most important papers of the decade" (*Linguistic Theory in America,* p. 190).

23. As Dwight Bolinger aptly observed in his "Atomization of Meaning," *Language* 41 (1965): 556: "It is hard to make alterations in a house whose frame has to be torn out."

24. See Palmer, *Grammar,* p. 186: "The deep structure semantics approach may seem attractive, but it faces most of the criticisms of traditional notional grammar." Linking conceptual structure to linguistic structure is indeed not very much different from the older and simpler terminology of linking words to things or ideas.

25. For the beginnings of this newer flow chart of boxes, see Newmeyer, *Linguistic Theory in America,* p. 140.

26. W. Haas, "Linguistics 1930–80," *Journal of Linguistics* 14 (1978): 293–308.

27. Ibid., p. 306; Janet Sternberg, "Crisis in Linguistic Inquiry," *Forum Linguisticum* 3 (1979): 204; Robert A. Hall, "Some Critiques of Chomskyan Theory," *Neuphilologische Mitteilungen* 78 (1977): 92.

28. A partial exception to this generalization is "cognitive linguistics," e.g., Lakoff, *Women, Fire, and Dangerous Things;* and Langacker, *Foundations of Cognitive Grammar.* On some important points—chiefly the decision to reject the ban on meaning and the separation of syntax and semantics—this is serious revisionism. Of the two, Lakoff has strayed most from orthodoxy, stressing categorization and even discussing Whorf and the late Wittgenstein with approval. However, he still views "cognitive grammar as an updated version of generative semantics" (p. 582), and his treatment of categories in terms of prototypes (see above, chap. 5) is realist oriented. The corrective that could have been provided by either Saussure or Peirce is absent; neither name occurs in the book. That perspective is even more absent in Langacker—a brief comment on Saussure shows a complete misunderstanding of the notion "arbitrary" (p. 12), and many names that should occur in a discussion of grammar and cognition (most obviously Whorf) do not. Langacker has also retained the style of MIT thought to a much greater degree than Lakoff. While Lakoff ranges far afield in some ways—his book rambles somewhat as a result—Langacker still deals with MIT-created problems from within, implicitly accepting both its world and 1957 as the beginning of linguistic thought.

29. Richard Montague, "English as a Formal Language," in *Formal Philosophy*, ed. Richmond Thomason (New Haven, Conn., 1974), p. 188.

30. See Katz, "Common Sense in Semantics," p. 173. Naturally enough, on this view language is a *poor* version of mathematics. See, e.g., Paul Ziff, "Natural and Formal Languages," in *Language and Philosophy*, ed. Sidney Hook (London, 1969), pp. 238–39: "Formal logics and formal languages are bright shiny conceptual instruments of great beauty and precision....English fares badly on this account. For the requirements of effectiveness are flaunted [sic] by a natural language and in every quarter....when one speaks in a natural language there is always room for conjecture whether one has managed to communicate anything at all." To be sure, Ziff manages to show us one reason why natural languages might fail—insufficient care in their use: he uses the word *flaunt* when he means *flout*. Such is the inherent strength of the English language, however, that it manages to communicate for him even so; the same would *not* be true of formal logic. Once again, the rule holds: when two different things are compared with respect to the job that is the specific task of one of them, and the other is judged poor by comparison, the job of the second will have been misunderstood.

31. When linguists are attracted to formal languages to solve their problems, they are apt to develop a tin ear for natural language. An instructive case is that of Barbara Partee, "Some Transformational Extensions of Montague Grammar," *Journal of Philosophical Logic* 2 (1973): 509–34. She considers the phrase "the boy who lives in the park." Now two possible structures are involved here, one in which the relative clause defines "the boy," and one in which it is informative rather than defining. In actual speech the latter will likely have a slight pause after "boy." But to preserve a principle of Montague grammar that each syntactic rule must have a semantic rule, Partee tells us that this phrase can be interpreted in only one way, that is, as defining (p. 512). She abolishes a crucial distinction in English to satisfy a theory. Whether even given her dubious premises her conclusion is really required is not at all clear: there are really two different syntactic forms here. Doubtless, the labeling theory is also

involved; it will make both usages refer to the same boy in the same position.

32. Gadzar et al., *Generalized Phrase Structure Grammar*, pp. 7–8.

33. *Situations and Attitudes*, by Barwise and Perry, is another example of influence by formal logic which leads (after some initial hesitation, e.g., pp. 21–22) to truth claims, primitive features of situations, and so on.

34. Noam Chomsky, *The Generative Enterprise* (Dordrecht, 1982), p. 101.

35. Chomsky himself, after all, could not do without the notion of logical form, which he uses in a curiously defensive way. His initial use of "LF" in his *Rules and Representations* (p. 143) is followed by the parenthetical comment "(which I will read, 'logical form,' though with a cautionary note)." *Lectures on Government and Binding* (Dordrecht, 1981), p. 4, also has the parenthetical note: "read: 'logical form' but with familiar provisos," and refers us to *Rules and Representations*, where however, we are referred to "reasons already discussed" for the view that the elements of LF are determined empirically and not a priori— though, again, this is the initial use of the term. Chomsky concludes vaguely: "I use the term, I hope not too misleadingly, because this representation does in fact seem to me to express some basic properties of what is taken to be 'logical form' from other points of view." This is scarcely a masterpiece of clear exposition of a key concept, and the reader gets the strong impression of a man tiptoeing through a mine field, fearful of detonating problems that will be impossible to deal with if he comes down too firmly on any point. See also the following note.

36. Typical is the following passage from the 1980 *Rules and Representations*, p. 145:

> Theories have, of course, been successively modified over the years. This inevitable development in a living subject has given rise to various qualms on the part of people who are seriously misguided about the nature of substantive empirical research and who feel that a theoretical framework is discredited if it is constantly being revised....It has also led to some terminological confusions as notions that were, at one time, characterized in terms of certain properties have come to be characterized in terms of others. In the hope of avoiding further confusion, I will introduce some new terms suggestive of earlier ones. Let's say the base generates "D-structures" ("deep structures") and that the transformations convert these to "S-structures," which are converted to surface structures by rules of various sorts.

But no explanation follows of how "D-structure" avoids the problems that had been seen in "deep structure." Though he claims to be "avoiding further confusion,"

Chomsky's multiplication of terms *of course* confuses the issue further, and only that confusion makes it possible for him to cling to the essentials of a theory that is in far deeper crisis than cosmetic change can rectify. As to misguided "qualms" about constant revision of a theory: it is surely wishful thinking to suppose that the kind of unrest and unsuccessful search for solutions to basic problems that has always been part of MIT linguistics is a normal part of empirical research.

37. In a review of Chomsky's *Rules and Representations* Michael Dummett commented aptly:

There are two worthwhile ways to write philosophical polemics....The first is to enter deep into the mind of your opponent, to bring out the full power of the motives prompting him to say what he does, to present his case better than he does himself, and then to explain why it has to be rejected. The second is to ignore what can be said in its favor, and concentrate upon delivering a crushing blow....Chomsky achieves success in neither of these ways. Though always courteous, he manifests little sympathy with the thought of those he is criticizing: his rejoinders often boil down to saying that they have begged the question, or are appealing to prejudice rather than rational grounds, without any recognition that there is a genuine force to their contentions or a genuine problem to be solved. (*London Review of Books*, 3–16 September 1981, p. 5)

38. This is a view which is repeated over and over again, e.g., in the introductory section of Chomsky's *Topics in the Theory of Generative Grammar*, pp. 7–24.

39. The most muddled of all statements of the distinction is Newmeyer's, *Linguistic Theory in America*, p. 229: "Recent discoveries have provided independent corroboration for the generativist view that the form of language exists independently of its content (i.e., competence independently of performance)." No conceivable discovery could possibly provide evidence for a notion so confused that it equates two quite different distinctions.

40. In a related phenomenon, Chomsky routinely attempts to bludgeon his reader into submission by insisting that no one could seriously doubt what he is saying. Take, e.g., this sequence of statements from *Topics in the Theory of Generative Grammar*, pp. 17–23:

So far I have said little that is in any way controversial....let us reassure ourselves about the uncontroversial character of what has preceded. Is there, in fact, anything in this account to which exception can be taken?... The distinction between deep and surface structure emerges from even the

most superficial examination of real linguistic material. Hence the conclusions outlined so far seem inescapable....This point should be obvious
without further discussion....Once again, it is important to recognize that
there is nothing controversial in what has just been said....I hope that
these remarks will show the complete pointlessness of much of the
debate....

And so it goes on. This habit persists in the latest phase of Chomsky's writing.
E.g., in *Lectures in Government and Binding* we are still assured that "the PF- and LF-
representations we have assumed are relatively uncontroversial" (p. 21). The
decades of turmoil in MIT linguistics and the present widespread sense that
important problems seem to resist solution would all be hard to understand if it
were really so obvious that Chomsky is, simply, correct. But a much deeper
cause for concern arises here: it is that theorists do not keep saying that things
are obvious. They cannot afford to. The worst theoretical mistakes and confusions
commonly have a deceptive simplicity—that is why they cause so much trouble.

41. A different use of the same superficial view of science is that
of Sampson, *Schools of Linguistics*, p. 157: "The semantic structure of a language
can be discussed only in the anecdotal, non-predictive fashion proper to arts
subjects, rather than analyzed scientifically—not just because the data are una-
vailable but because, if objective evidence were available, it would immediately
refute *any* analysis that might be proposed." Sampson believes that this follows
from what Wittgenstein and other philosophers have taught us about the semantic
structure of a language being "not fixed," but this is garbled Wittgenstein.

42. Newmeyer, *Linguistic Theory in America*, pp. 18–21.

43. Maclay, "Linguistics: Overview," p. 163.

44. Newmeyer grasps at straws when he claims in his article "Has
There Been a Chomskyan Revolution?" that Chomsky's status as "the most
attacked linguist in history" shows that he is "the dominant figure in WORLD
linguistics" (p. 8). Many fads and fashions have achieved enormous currency
before they collapsed; to accept this argument we should have to conclude that
Salieri must also have been a dominant figure in music. Arguments like this surely
occur only when real arguments cannot be found.

45. Even would-be innovations themselves regularly undergo more
change: e.g., by 1986, when it was only five or six years old, "Generalized Phrase
Structure Grammar" had "undergone a number of important changes." Newmeyer,
Linguistic Theory in America, p. 212.

46. Robert Dixon, *Linguistic Science and Logic* (The Hague, 1963),
p. 78.

47. Wittgenstein threw much doubt on this kind of analysis in
some early paragraphs (e.g., .pars. 19–21) of the *Philosophical Investigations;* this

is just one more way in which generative grammar failed to come to terms with established thought.

48. Chomsky, *Topics in the Theory of Generative Grammar*, p. 9: "It seems to me that it is the modern study of language prior to the explicit study of generative grammar that is seriously defective in its failure to deal with traditional questions and, furthermore, to recognize the essential correctness of many of the traditional answers and the extent to which they provide a fruitful basis for current research."

CONCLUSION

1. Saussure, *Course*, p. 68.

2. E.g., Corbett's book *Gender* examines comparatively the gender system in over two hundred languages.

3. In his anthology *Language and Social Context* (Harmondsworth, 1972) even the sociolinguist Pier Giglioli accepted this narrow and almost dismissive view of the social dimension of language with his remark that the most significant feature of sociolinguistics "is its stress on *parole*" (p. 8), not on the system of the language itself.

Bibliography

Aaron, Richard. S.v. "Epistemology." *Encyclopaedia Britannica*, 15th ed. Macropaedia.

Adams, Parveen, ed. *Language and Thinking*. Harmondsworth, 1972.

Almog, Joseph, John Perry, and Howard Wettstein, eds. *Themes from Kaplan*. Oxford, 1989.

Anscombe, G. E. M. Review of *Wittgenstein on Rules and Private Language*, by Saul Kripke. *Canadian Journal of Philosophy* 15 (1985): 103–9.

Austin, J. L. *How to Do Things with Words*. Oxford, 1962.

Ayer, Alfred J. *Language, Truth and Logic*. London, 1936.

———. *The Problem of Knowledge*. Harmondsworth, 1956.

———. *Bertrand Russell*. New York, 1972.

———. *Philosophy in the Twentieth Century*. New York, 1982.

———. *Ludwig Wittgenstein*. London, 1985.

Bach, Emmon. *An Introduction to Transformational Grammars*. New York, 1964.

———. *Informal Lectures on Formal Semantics*. New York, 1989.

Bambrough, Renford. "Universals and Family Resemblances." In *Wittgenstein: The Philosophical Investigations: A Collection of Critical Essays*, edited by George Pitcher, pp. 186–204. Princeton, N.J., 1966.

Barwise, Jon, and John Perry. *Situations and Attitudes*. Cambridge, Mass., 1983.

Benveniste, Emile. *Problèmes de linguistique générale*. Paris, 1966.

———. "The Semiology of Language." In *Semiotics: An Introductory Anthology*, edited by Robert Innis, pp. 228–46. Bloomington, Ind., 1985.

Black, Max. *Models and Metaphors*. Ithaca, N.Y., 1962.

———. *The Labyrinth of Language*. New York, 1969.

Blackburn, Simon. *Spreading the Word*. Oxford, 1984.

Bloomfield, Leonard. *Language*. New York, 1933.

Bolinger, Dwight. "The Atomization of Meaning," *Language* 41 (1965): 555–73.

———. "Meaning and Form." *Transactions of the New York Academy of Sciences*, 2d ser., 36 (1974): 218–33.

Bresnan, Joan. "A Realistic Transformational Grammar." In *Linguistic Theory and Psychological Reality*, edited by Morris Halle, Joan Bresnan, and George Miller, pp. 1–59. Cambridge, Mass., 1978.

Budd, Malcolm. Review of *Ludwig Wittgenstein*, by A. J. Ayer. *Mind* 95 (1986): 389–92.

Bybee, Joan L. *Morphology: A Study of the Relation between Meaning and Form*. Amsterdam, 1985.

Carlson, Greg. Review of *Semantics and Cognition*, by Ray Jackendoff. *Linguistics and Philosophy* 8 (1985): 505–10.

Caton, Charles. "Philosophy: Overview." In *Semantics*, edited by Danny Steinberg and Leon Jakobovits, pp. 3–13. London, 1971.

Chafe, Wallace. *Meaning and the Structure of Language*. Chicago, 1970.

Cherry, Colin. *On Human Communication*. Cambridge, Mass., 1957.

Chomsky, Noam. *Syntactic Structures*. The Hague, 1957.

———. "The Logical Basis of Linguistic Theory." *Proceedings of the Ninth International Congress of Linguists*, edited by H. Lunt, pp. 914–78. The Hague, 1964.

———. *Aspects of the Theory of Syntax*. Cambridge, Mass., 1965.

———. *Cartesian Linguistics*. New York, 1966.

———. *Topics in the Theory of Generative Grammar*. The Hague, 1966.

———. *Language and Mind*. New York, 1968.

———. *Reflections on Language*. New York, 1975.

———. *Rules and Representations*. New York, 1980.

———. *Lectures on Government and Binding*. Dordrecht, 1981.

———. *The Generative Enterprise*. Dordrecht, 1982.

Churchland, Paul M. "Conceptual Progress and Word/World Relations: In Search of the Essence of Natural Kinds." *Canadian Journal of Philosophy* 15 (1985): 1–17.

Corbett, Greville G. *Gender*. Cambridge, 1991.

Cowgill, Warren. S.v. "Indo-European Languages." *Encyclopaedia Britannica*, 15th ed. Macropaedia.

Crystal, David. *Linguistics*. Harmondsworth, 1971.

Daneš, František. "On Prague School Functionalism in Linguistics." In *Functionalism in Linguistics*, edited by René Dirven and Vilém Fried, pp. 3–38. Amsterdam, 1987.

Davidson, Donald. *Inquiries into Truth and Interpretation*. Oxford, 1984.

Davidson, Donald, and Jaako Hintikka, eds. *Words and Objections: Essays on the Work of W. V. Quine*. Dordrecht, 1969.

Dirven, René, and Vilém Fried, eds. *Functionalism in Linguistics*. Amsterdam, 1987.

Dixon, Robert M. W. *Linguistic Science and Logic*. The Hague, 1963.

Donnellan, Keith S. "Reference and Definite Descriptions." *Philosophical Review* 75 (1966): 281–304.

———. "Speaking of Nothing." In *Naming, Necessity, and Natural Kinds*, edited by Stephen P. Schwartz, pp. 216–44. Ithaca, N.Y., 1977.

———. "Belief and the Identity of Reference." *Midwest Studies in Philosophy* 14 (1989): 275–88.

Dummett, Michael. Review of *Rules and Representations*, by Noam Chomsky. *London Review of Books*, 3–16 September 1981, pp. 5–6.

Eco, Umberto. *Semiotics and the Philosophy of Language*. Bloomington, Ind., 1984.

Ellis, John M. "Great Art: A Study in Meaning." *British Journal of Aesthetics* 3 (1963): 165–71.

————. *Schiller's Kalliasbriefe.* The Hague, 1969.

————. *The Theory of Literary Criticism: A Logical Analysis.* Berkeley and Los Angeles, 1974.

————. "Wittgensteinian Thinking in Theory of Criticism." *New Literary History* 12 (1981): 437–52.

————. *Against Deconstruction.* Princeton, N.J., 1989.

Eschbach, Achim, and Jürgen Trabant, eds. *History of Semiotics.* Amsterdam and Philadelphia, 1983.

Firth, J. R. *Papers in Linguistics, 1934–51.* Oxford, 1957.

————. "Synopsis of Linguistic Theory 1930–55." In *Studies in Linguistic Analysis,* pp. 1–32. Special Volume of the Philological Society. Oxford, 1957.

Fodor, Janet Dean. "Situations and Representations." *Linguistics and Philosophy* 8 (1985): 13–22.

Fodor, Jerry A. *The Language of Thought.* New York, 1975.

Freeman, Derek. "Paradigms in Collision: The Far-Reaching Controversy over the Samoan Researches of Margaret Mead and Its Significance for the Human Sciences." *Academic Questions* 5 (1991): 23–33.

Fries, Charles. *The Structure of English.* New York, 1952.

Gallie, W. B. *Peirce and Pragmatism.* Harmondsworth, 1952.

————. "Art as an Essentially Contested Concept." *Philosophical Quarterly* 6 (1956): 97–114.

Gardner, R. A., and B. T. Gardner. "Teaching Sign Language to a Chimpanzee." *Science* 165 (1969): 664–72.

Gazdar, Gerald, Ewan Klein, Geoffrey Pullum, and Ivan Sag. *Generalized Phrase Structure Grammar.* Cambridge, Mass., 1985.

Giglioli, Pier Paolo, ed. *Language and Social Context.* Harmondsworth, 1972.

Goethe, Johann W. *Werke.* Edited by Erich Trunz. 14 vols. Hamburg, 1948–60.

Greenberg, Joseph. *Language Universals.* The Hague, 1966.

Greenberg, Joseph, Charles Ferguson, and Edith Moravcsik, eds. *Universals of Human Language.* Stanford, Calif., 1978.

Grice, H. P. "Meaning." *Philosophical Review* 66 (1957): 377–88.

———— "Utterer's Meaning and Intentions." *Philosophical Review* 78 (1969): 147–77.

Haas, W. "The Theory of Translation." *Philosophy* 37 (1962): 208–28.

————. "Linguistics 1930–80." *Journal of Linguistics* 14 (1978): 293–308.

Hacking, Ian. *Why Does Language Matter to Philosophy?* London, 1975.

Hall, Robert A. "Some Critiques of Chomskyan Theory." *Neuphilologische Mitteilungen* 78 (1977): 86–95.

Halliday, M. A. K. "Categories of the Theory of Grammar." *Word* 17 (1961): 241–92.

Hare, R. M. *The Language of Morals.* Oxford, 1952.

Harman, Gilbert. "(Nonsolipsistic) Conceptual Role Semantics." In *New Directions in Semantics*, edited by Ernest LePore, pp. 55–81. London, 1987.

Harris, Roy. *Language, Saussure and Wittgenstein*. New York, 1989.

Heal, Jane. "Wittgenstein, Kripke and Meaning." *Philosophical Quarterly* 144 (1986): 412–19.

Higginbotham, James. "On Semantics." In *New Directions in Semantics*, edited by Ernest LePore, pp. 1–54. London, 1987.

Hintikka, Jaako. "Game-Theoretical Semantics as a Synthesis of Verificationist and Truth-Conditional Meaning Theories." In *New Directions in Semantics*, edited by Ernest LePore, pp. 235–58. London, 1987.

Hirsch, David. "Deep Metaphors and Shallow Structures." *Sewanee Review* 85 (1977): 153–66.

Hudson, W. D., ed. *The Is/Ought Question*. London, 1969.

Hume, David. *A Treatise of Human Nature*. 3 vols. London, 1739–40.

Innis, Robert, ed. *Semiotics: An Introductory Anthology*. Bloomington, Ind., 1985.

Jackendoff, Ray. *Semantics and Cognition*. Cambridge, Mass., 1983.

Jakobson, Roman. "Closing Statement: Linguistics and Poetics." In *Style in Language*, edited by Thomas Sebeok, pp. 350–77. Cambridge, Mass., 1960.

Jakobson, Roman, and Morris Halle. *Fundamentals of Language*. The Hague, 1956.

Kant, Immanuel. *Critik der practischen Vernunft*. Riga, 1788. English translation: *Critique of Practical Reason*. Edited and translated by Lewis Beck. Chicago, 1949.

Katz, Jerrold. *The Philosophy of Language*. New York, 1966.

———. "Common Sense in Semantics." In *New Directions in Semantics*, edited by Ernest LePore, pp. 157–233. London, 1987.

Katz, Jerrold, and Thomas Bever. "The Fall and Rise of Empiricism." In *An Integrated Theory of Linguistic Ability*, edited by Jerrold Katz, Thomas Bever, and Terence Langandoen, pp. 11–64. New York, 1976.

Katz, Jerrold, and Jerry Fodor. "The Structure of a Semantic Theory." *Language* 39 (1963): 170–210.

Kaye, Alan. "Schools of Linguistics: Competition and Evolution." *Studies in Language* 10 (1986): 187–99.

Kripke, Saul. *Naming and Necessity*. Cambridge, Mass., 1972.

———. *Wittgenstein on Rules and Private Language*. Oxford, 1982.

Kufner, Herbert. *The Grammatical Structures of English and German*. Chicago, 1962.

Kuhn, Thomas. *The Structure of Scientific Revolutions*. Chicago, 1962.

Lakoff, George. "The Arbitrary Basis of Transformational Grammar." *Language* 48 (1972): 76–87.

———. *Women, Fire, and Dangerous Things: What Categories Reveal about the Mind*. Chicago, 1987.

Lamb, Sydney. *Outline of Stratificational Grammar*. Washington, D.C., 1966.

Landman, Fred. "The Realist Theory of Meaning." *Linguistics and Philosophy* 8 (1985): 35–51.

Langacker, Ronald. *Language and Its Structure.* New York, 1967.

———. *Foundations of Cognitive Grammar.* 2 vols. Stanford, Calif., 1987, 1991.

Langer, Susanne. *Philosophy in a New Key.* Cambridge, Mass., 1942.

Lenneberg, Eric H. "Cognition in Ethnolinguistics." *Language* 29 (1953): 463–71.

———. "A Biological Perspective of Language." In *New Directions in the Study of Language,* edited by Eric H. Lenneberg, pp. 65–88. Cambridge, Mass., 1964.

LePore, Ernest, ed. *New Directions in Semantics.* London, 1987.

———. "Dual Aspect Semantics." In *New Directions in Semantics,* edited by Ernest LePore, pp. 83–112. London, 1987.

Lévi-Strauss, Claude. *Structural Anthropology.* 2 vols. Vol. 1 translated by C. Jacobson and B. G. Schoepf. Vol. 2 translated by Monique Layton. New York, 1963, 1976.

———. *The Savage Mind.* Chicago, 1966.

Linsky, Leonard. "Reference and Referents." In *Semantics,* edited by Danny Steinberg and Leon Jakobovits, pp. 76–85. London, 1971.

Lyons, John. *Introduction to Theoretical Linguistics.* Cambridge, 1968.

———. *Chomsky.* Modern Masters. London, 1970.

Mabbott, J. D. "Interpretations of Mill's 'Utilitarianism.'" *Philosophical Quarterly* 6 (1956): 115–20.

McGinn, Colin. *Wittgenstein on Meaning.* Oxford, 1984.

Maclay, Howard. "Linguistics: Overview." In *Semantics,* edited by Danny Steinberg and Leon Jakobovits, pp. 157–182. London, 1971.

Martinet, André. *Elements of General Linguistics.* Translated by Elisabeth Palmer. Chicago, 1964.

Mill, John Stuart. "Utilitarianism." *Fraser's Magazine* 64 (1861): 391–97, 526–30.

Montague, Richard. "English as a Formal Language." In *Formal Philosophy,* edited by Richmond Thomason, pp. 188–221. New Haven, Conn., 1974.

Moore, G. E. *Principia Ethica.* Cambridge, 1903.

Newmeyer, Frederick J. *Linguistic Theory in America.* 2d ed. Orlando, Fla., 1986.

———. "Has There Been a 'Chomskyan Revolution' in Linguistics?" *Language* 62 (1986): 1–18.

Nowell-Smith, P. H. *Ethics.* Harmondsworth, 1954.

Olver, Rose R., and Joan Rigney Hornsby. "On Equivalence." In *Studies in Cognitive Growth,* edited by Jerome S. Bruner et al., pp. 68–85. New York, 1966.

Palmer, Frank. *Grammar.* Harmondsworth, 1971.

Palmer, Humphrey. "Words and Terms." *Philosophy* 61 (1986): 71–82.

Partee, Barbara. "Some Transformational Extensions of Montague Grammar." *Journal of Philosophical Logic* 2 (1973): 509–34.

Peirce, Charles Sanders. Review of *The Works of George Berkeley*, edited by Alexander Fraser. *North American Review* 113 (1871): 449–72.

———. *Collected Papers*. Edited by Arthur Burks, Charles Hartshorne, and Paul Weiss. 8 vols. Cambridge, Mass., 1931–58.

Piaget, Jean. "Language and Thought from the Genetic Point of View." *Acta Psychologica* 10 (1954): 88–98.

Putnam, Hilary. *Philosophy of Logic*. New York, 1971.

———. *Mind, Language and Reality*. Philosophical Papers, vol. 2. Cambridge, 1975.

———. *How Not to Solve Ethical Problems*. Lawrence, Kans., 1983.

———. "Truth and Convention: On Davidson's Refutation of Conceptual Relativism." *Dialectica* 41 (1987): 69–77.

———. *Representation and Reality*. Cambridge, Mass., 1988.

Quine, Willard van Orman. *Word and Object*. Cambridge, Mass., 1960.

———. "Natural Kinds." In *Naming, Necessity, and Natural Kinds*, edited by Stephen P. Schwartz, pp. 155–75. Ithaca, N.Y., 1977.

Rawls, John. *A Theory of Justice*. Cambridge, Mass., 1971.

Rorty, Richard. *Consequences of Pragmatism*. Minneapolis, 1982.

Salmon, Nathan U. *Reference and Essence*. Princeton, N.J., 1981.

Sampson, Geoffrey. *Schools of Linguistics*. Stanford, Calif., 1980.

Sapir, Edward. "Conceptual Categories in Primitive Languages." *Science* 74 (1931): 578.

———. *Culture, Language and Personality: Selected Essays*. Edited by David Mandelbaum. Berkeley and Los Angeles, 1961.

Saussure, Ferdinand de. *Cours de linguistique générale*. Edited by Charles Bally and Albert Sechehaye, with the collaboration of Albert Riedlinger. Critical edition by Tulio de Mauro. Paris, 1972. English Translation: *Course in General Linguistics*. Translation and introduction by Wade Baskin. New York, 1959.

Saw, Ruth. *Leibniz*. Harmondsworth, 1954.

Scholes, Robert. *Textual Power*. New Haven, Conn., 1985.

Schwartz, Stephen P., ed. *Naming, Necessity, and Natural Kinds*. Ithaca, N.Y., 1977.

Scruton, Roger. Review of *Wittgenstein on Rules and Private Language*, by Saul Kripke. *Mind* 93 (1984): 592–602.

Searle, John R. "How to Derive 'Ought' from 'Is.'" *Philosophical Review* 73 (1964): 53–58.

———. *Speech Acts*. London, 1969.

———, ed. *The Philosophy of Language*. London, 1971.

Sebeok, Thomas. "Zoosemiotic Components of Human Behavior." In *Semiotics: An Introductory Anthology*, edited by Robert Innis, pp. 294–324. Bloomington, Ind., 1985.

Shannon, Thomas. Review of *History of Semiotics*, edited by Achim Eschbach and Jürgen Trabant. *Language* 62 (1986): 232–33.

Soames, Scott. "Direct Reference and Propositional Attitudes." In *Themes from*

Kaplan, edited by Joseph Almog, John Perry, and Howard Wettstein, pp. 393–419. Oxford, 1989.

Sommers, Frederic. *The Logic of Natural Language.* Oxford, 1982.

Steinberg, Danny, and Leon Jakobovits, eds. *Semantics: An Interdisciplinary Reader in Philosophy, Linguistics and Psychology.* Cambridge, 1971.

Sternberg, Janet. "Crisis in Linguistic Inquiry." *Forum Linguisticum* 3 (1979): 189–207.

Stevenson, C. L. *Ethics and Language.* New Haven, Conn., 1945.

Stroll, Avrum. *Surfaces.* Minneapolis, 1988.

———. "What Water Is, or, Back to Thales." *Midwest Studies in Philosophy* 14 (1989): 258–74.

———. "Observation and the Hidden." *Dialectica* 45 (1991): 165–79.

Thurman, Kelly, ed. *Semantics.* Boston, 1960.

Urmson, J. O. "The Interpretation of the Moral Philosophy of J. S. Mill." *Philosophical Quarterly* 3 (1953): 33–39.

Vygotsky, L. S. *Thought and Language.* Translation revised and edited by Alex Kozulin. Cambridge, Mass., 1986.

Weitz, Morris. "The Role of Theory in Aesthetics." *Journal of Aesthetics and Art Criticism* 15 (1956): 27–35.

———. *The Opening Mind.* Chicago, 1967.

Whorf, Benjamin Lee. *Language, Thought, and Reality: Selected Writings of Benjamin Lee Whorf.* Edited by John B. Carroll. Cambridge, Mass., 1956.

Wiggins, David. "On Sentence-sense, Word-sense and Difference of Word-sense: Towards a Philosophical Theory of Dictionaries." In *Semantics,* edited by Danny Steinberg and Leon Jakobovits, pp. 14–34. Cambridge, 1971.

———. "Meaning, Truth-Conditions, Proposition: Frege's Doctrine of Sense Retrieved, Resumed and Redeployed in the Light of Certain Recent Criticisms." *Dialectica* 46 (1992): 61–90.

Williams, Bernard. Review of *Consequences of Pragmatism,* by Richard Rorty. *New York Review of Books,* 28 April 1983, pp. 33–36.

———. *Ethics and the Limits of Philosophy.* London, 1985.

Wittgenstein, Ludwig. *Philosophical Investigations/Philosophische Untersuchungen.* Edited by G. E. M. Anscombe and R. Rhees. Translated by G. E. M. Anscombe. 3d ed. New York, 1968.

———. *Tractatus Logico-Philosophicus.* Edited and translated by D. F. Pears and B. F. McGuiness. 2d ed. London, 1971.

Wright, Crispin. Review of *Spreading the Word,* by Simon Blackburn. *Mind* 94 (1984): 310–19.

Ziff, Paul. "Natural and Formal Languages." In *Language and Philosophy,* edited by Sidney Hook, pp. 223–40. London, 1969.

Zuckerman, Lord. "Apes R Not Us." *New York Review of Books,* 30 May 1991, pp. 43–49.